THE AUDIENCE REFLECTED IN THE MEDIUM OF LAW

THE AUDIENCE REFLECTED IN THE MEDIUM OF LAW:

A CRITIQUE OF THE POLITICAL ECONOMY OF SPEECH RIGHTS IN THE UNITED STATES

Myles Alexander Ruggles

Ablex Publishing Corporation
Norwood, New Jersey

Printed in the United States of America

Library of Congress Cataloging-in-Publication Data

Ruggles, Myles Alexander.
The audience reflected in the medium of law : a critique of the political economy of speech rights in the United States / by Myles Alexander Ruggles.
p. cm.—(Communication and information science)
Includes bibliographical references and index.
ISBN 0-89391-881-4 (cloth).—ISBN 0-89391-993-4 (pbk.)
1. Freedom of speech—United States. 2. Mass media—Law and legislation—United States. 3. Freedom of speech—Economic aspects. I. Series.
KF4772.R84 1994
342.73′0853—dc20
[347.302853] 92-42917

Ablex Publishing Company
355 Chestnut Street
Norwood, New Jersey 07648

Speech is something different from voice, which is possessed by other animals also and used by them to express pain or pleasure; for the natural powers of some animals do indeed enable them both to feel pleasure and pain and to communicate these to each other. Speech on the other hand serves to indicate what is right and what is wrong. For the real difference between humans and other animals is that humans alone have perception of good and evil, right and wrong, just and unjust. And it is the sharing of a common view in these matters that makes a household or a city.

Aristotle: Politics: Book 1, Chapter 2.

Contents

Introduction: The Allocation of Communicative Power

THE PROBLEM

Most people are familiar with the phrase 'free speech rights,' and there are many occasions on which it is quite artlessly invoked. Dismissal of a civil servant for divulging undenied unsavory facts about a government's actions, or news of a teacher disciplined for critical supplements to the curriculum, may lead us to ask "What about their free speech rights?" This usage perhaps expresses surprise that telling the truth as one sees it might be a punishable offense. At the same time it is also possible to be routinely cynical about 'free speech rights.' There is often no great surprise in finding that 'speech rights' have not prevented a court's injunction against a union's secondary picket, a broadcaster's rejection of a controversial advertisement, a newspaper's refusal to publish a letter.

Both the ingenuous and the worldly are common-sense responses. Americans and Canadians certainly exercise by right a remarkable everyday freedom of expression. They generally may speak their minds, unmolested, on street corners and in classrooms, they may at least mail their letters to editors (or their manuscripts to publishers) without expecting a visit from the police, and occasional public opportunities even arise to ask their elected representatives the most embarrassing questions they can devise.

At the same time certain denials of speech rights are broadly accepted in a liberal democracy: the security of the state, the safety of the public, the protection of property and reputation all furnish grounds for limiting the reach of expressive rights. Most legal activity in the area of free speech rights is directed at determining exactly where these limits are to be drawn in controversial instances. Setting the norm for an actionable case of seditious speech, for example, or of obscenity, will divide judicial opinion across a notoriously mobile and imprecise line.

Such variations in judicial opinion are not my central concern here. Rather, this enquiry, in examining the allocation of free speech rights in the contemporary mass media, asks a more general set of questions about the balance of expressive powers achieved among contending political interests by constitutional rule making. Evaluation of this balance of expressive powers inevitably takes us beyond legal opinion and into the realms of political theory, the political economy of mass communication, and the critical analysis of discourse. When court-made law on mass media speech rights is analyzed in these terms, I believe one is led to an unmistakable conclusion: the general citizenry of North America has no rights to express itself in the mass media. In other words, among the many forms of speech rights recognized by Canadian and U.S. courts, there are no enforceable citizen rights to initiate speech or to reply to speech, whether as editorial or paid advertising content, in the public fora of the mass media.

This is not to say that opportunities for such speech do not occur; it is only to say that, appearances to the contrary, expressive rights in the mass media are not incorporated into the package of civil, political, and social rights of citizenship enjoyed in North America.[1] And what is even more interesting than this apparent occlusion in the constitutional vision is that the inaccessibility of the mass media to our communicative purposes *makes sense* to us, goes unremarked, seems an obvious and common-sense feature of the social world we inhabit. For this reason it seems necessary at the outset to elaborate briefly on the problem of speech rights in the media and the approaches I shall take to its analysis in the main body of this study.

Speech rights in direct interaction with others in a public place—for purposes of a meeting or rally, say, or while distributing a leaflet—are typically equated, first of all, with a notion of the legitimate and effective power of individuals to express themselves and to disseminate that expression. That power is indeed substantial. Freedom of expression as the

[1] For a discussion of the development of civil, political and social rights of citizenship in western societies see T.H. Marshall (1949). Marshall's excellent discussion is, however, somewhat flawed by its almost evolutionary line of argument. He downplays the extent to which the expansion of citizenship rights in the West had to be won in various forms of social and political struggle (e.g., the female franchise).

citizen's right to *receive* a leaflet or to *listen* to a public speaker is a secondary inflection, if only because it seems to us to be *wholly* beyond legitimate regulation. The preventive detention of a speaker at a public rally, for example, would be a highly controversial event, but state action against her *audience* to prevent their attending and listening has become nearly unimaginable in our society. While this aspect of communicative freedom was not always so widely assumed or automatically respected, and was in fact won through long political struggle, it is now so seldom challenged in contexts of direct interaction that it forms only a background issue.

On the other hand, in the mass media (surely the dominant arena of public information and opinion in the industrialized parts of the world) the range of expressive powers available to individuals can easily be seen to be much more limited. The communicative use of physical public spaces—such as streets, parks, and shopping malls—public spaces that are *not* organized by their owners as profitable communications media—rests in the public domain, available with relative ease to most kinds of spontaneous civic use. But expressive use of the *mediated* arena of mass communication for public discourse and debate tends to be a discretionary service in capitalist societies. It is usually privately controlled and available only to selected clients, even when it utilizes publicly owned resources such as radio frequencies. Moreover, in the mass media this is a background issue, a secondary inflection of 'free speech,' while the foreground conflicts are centred on questions of citizens' rights to *receive* particular views, programs, formats, and channels. Thus, as C. Wright Mills has observed,[2] the vast expansion of communicative resources in this century may have been accompanied by a *reduction* in opportunities for citizen participation in public debate relative to the available means.

This new 'enclosure of the commons,' like that in 17th-century England, has been legitimated and enforced after the fact by the institutions of the state. As in that earlier enclosure, this one follows upon changes in the scale and organization of trade and production, and the needs of market producers for control of relevant resources. But unlike the earlier privatization of communal agricultural resources, the realization of commercial value from mass public communication opportunities became the *dominant* cultural practice before any extensive tradition of communal use of these resources could be established.[3]

---

[2] Mills (1956, Chap. 13).

[3] Raymond Williams (1975) makes the same observation on other grounds. William Meckling, however, considers that broadcasting frequencies are still managed in "the same manner as the commons were on feudal estates in the Middle Ages" (Meckling, 1968, p. xi).

Given this commercial tradition of controlled access to mediated communication (and in this respect the tradition within liberalism of state participation in control of the media is unexceptional), we might say that the relationships which obtain between speakers and listeners in the mass media are in a sense modes of public interaction 'indigenous' and 'natural' to a developed commercial culture. It is of course upon these relationships that the realization of commercial (or political) advantage depends. Critical media analyses of various aspects of these relationships[4] yield an aggregate picture which might be summarized as follows: they are characterized on the media side by the communicative dominance of aggrandized personalities through a hierarchical structure of professional specialization, private control, and exclusionary access; and on the audience side by the communicative subordination of a statistical field of unseen, separated, serially quantized 'receptors.'

If we examine the relevant American case law, it becomes evident that the allocation of speech rights in the mass media has not been designed to correct—or even acknowledge—this communicative imbalance. I analyze this state of affairs later in the study through a review of the political and social purposes of free speech guarantees as articulated in liberal political philosophy and jurisprudence, a case study of the actual allocation of expressive rights in the conventional mass media (press and broadcasting) in U.S. constitutional discourse, and a critical assessment of the adequacy of these quite typical allocative practices to their stated purposes.

I have not extended this analysis to consider the 'new media'—cable, pay, and pay-per-view television, videotext, electronic messaging and conferencing services, or direct mail database/publishing facilities—because legal doctrine governing these media is still evolving rapidly (especially where it overlaps with public utility regulation and intellectual property law), and because the context of this evolution is to an important extent supranational. Whether—or in whatever way— the pattern of allocation I have identified for the older forms of media turns out to be predictive for the newer forms, at this point it is possible and, I believe, instructive to adopt a historical perspective on the development of press and broadcast speech rights.

In conducting this study I was unable to find any complete or adequate judicial rationale for the anomalous and widespread exclusionary access so characteristic of public mass communication in the paradigm instance of the United States. On the contrary, the *common* doctrinal grounds for the

---

[4] There are a large number of studies relevant to one or another aspect of the relational structure of mass media. Good examples include Altheide (1976), Clarke (1981, p. 70), Dreier (1982, p. 111), Gitlin (1980), Hartley, (1982), and Mattelart (1983, p. 17).

adjudication of First Amendment conflicts in both direct and mediated communication contexts are frequently asserted by the highest courts. As I understand it, the courts imply that citizens' *lack* of expressive rights in the media carries out the same First Amendment purposes for which they are *granted* such rights in face-to-face encounters. The most important First Amendment doctrine is the linkage between authentic self-government and unconstrained freedom of expression in the public arena, and this principle is unfailingly rehearsed in the judicial discourse in decisions in both contexts.

Vestigial arguments do arise in the caselaw which point vaguely at the technical characteristics of mass communications as the explanation of these anomalies. For example, in commenting on the Federal Communications Commission's 'Fairness Doctrine' requirements in a 1969 case, the U.S. Supreme Court noted that "there are substantially more individuals who want to broadcast than there are frequencies to allocate."[5] But arguments based on technological capacity are as frequently contradicted in these decisions. I will indicate areas of contradiction and ambiguity on the topic in these texts.

More frequent, and certainly closer to the mark, are those holdings which find private property rights implicated in the different results in the two contexts. This is the locus of many speech rights conflicts in both mediated and direct interaction. The very first Supreme Court judgment under the First Amendment, the 1897 *Davis* decision,[6] affirmed with unusual clarity the priority of property rights under the Fifth and Fourteenth Amendments over First Amendment rights.

But it would be a clumsy jurisprudence indeed that found in the First Amendment merely an assertion that media owners' property rights have an unqualified and absolute priority over citizens' rights to opportunities for political expression. Instead, as I will demonstrate, jurists generally perform a much more accomplished rhetorical feat: they find that the priority of property rights in the context of mass communication *is itself* the unfettered right of all citizens to freedom of expression. They similarly find that the expressive requirements of democracy *necessitate* these holdings. The private media themselves find the constitutional doctrines to be fairly bursting with moral force, and frequently drape themselves in the provided mantle of expressive freedom, striking the pose of democracy incarnate. To critique this ranking and allocation of rights is therefore to inquire into the manner in which the rights of citizens in the audience are represented in the constitutional discourse.

---

[5] *Red Lion Broadcasting v. Federal Communications Commission*, 395 U.S. 367 [1969]; see Chapter 4.

[6] *Davis v. Commonwealth of Massachussetts*, 167 U.S. 43 [1897]; see Chapter 3.

A NOTE ON THEORY AND METHOD

Free speech rights are understood in democratic theory to be essential to the maintenance of an informed citizenry, and to distinguish tyranny from self-government in a significant manner. These are simultaneously political and legal propositions. But such broad entitlements and fundamental purposes stand in contrast with the detail, precision, and specialization that characterize the practices and products of the institutions of law.

Legal practitioners conceive of law as an institutional mechanism for the control of social relations through an internally logical structure of procedural and preceptive doctrine, impartially applied to verifiable facts. The profound human ramifications of legal procedures and the importance of testable evidence, logic, and impartiality in its established practices require legal practitioners to draw narrow conclusions and to be careful 'not to read beyond the four corners of the page.'

Social theorists analyze law as itself a social phenomenon linked to and capable of revealing much about other social processes and structures. In a social analysis of law it is necessary to read well beyond the page, and to subject the controlled elegance of jurisprudence to the more uncertain—but more inclusive—frameworks of social theorizing. This is not to say that evidence, logic, and impartiality are irrelevant to social enquiry, but simply that they are subject both to more reflexive conditions of enquiry and to more broadly interpretive goals. Effective legal analysis is governed and certified by rules internal to the legal system; the social analysis of law enjoys no such methodological certitude.

This study shares the latter orientation and makes no claim to be a *legal* analysis. Rather, through a review of some relevant approaches in political theory and an examination of textual and historical features of selected case law, it offers a (provisional) view of the functional relations between the institutions of commercial mass communication and the institutions of law and the state. And because it examines the texts which *define* mass communication in the law, it also describes some of the fundamental conditions of political knowledge and action for citizens in a developed market polity.

The questions raised about freedom of expression in the mass media in the following pages derive from two traditions of social analysis. To enquire into the purposes and uses of speech rights—the basis of their social *value*—and to ask how they are produced and how they are distributed, is to raise questions of *political economy*. And to focus on the relation between human utterance and human agency—on the ways in which we use our expressive powers to *structure* the social world and to influence other actors in that world—is to raise questions from the study of *discourse and ideology*. In this study these concerns meet in the problematization of the *audience's speech rights* in the mass media.

I do not intend a facile distinction between these approaches, but propose rather to treat them as adjacent and overlapping 'layers' of interpretation. A 'political economy of speech rights' confers the important virtues of historical specificity and concrete location on the overall analysis. At the same time a pure political economy cannot help but find objective structures and processes correlative to its defined object, and the very concreteness of the structures thus discovered may too easily overwhelm the practical intent to comprehend how they might be transformed. The *critique* of political economy—the study of ideology—reasserts the (partial, dialectical) agency of the human subjects from whose activities these discovered structures are precipitated. Its task is to reveal the hidden conceptual frameworks linking the structures of *particular* institutions and practices to the interests of *particular* actors. The actors whose interests I have chosen to place in the center of my analysis are those I take to be the most general in this context: the interests of the *audiences* of the mass media.

Freedom of expression is a central notion in the regime of rights and freedoms guaranteed in numerous jurisdictions: the Canadian and U.S. constitutions, many state or provincial codes in both these countries, and the European Convention of the Common Market signatories all make prominent mention of such rights. Article 19 of the Universal Declaration of the United Nations likewise guarantees 'free speech' as a universal human right, as do many other of its member nations. In all of these jurisdictions, court cases in which 'free speech rights' are invoked are the source of authoritative judicial enunciation of the political, social, and economic dimensions of communications processes. Political and economic themes in the study of communication are densely interwoven in the body of American legal texts considered in the succeeding chapters of this study. This study's concern with the political economy of speech rights is advanced largely by disaggregating these themes and showing how they are employed in the legal discourse. Part of the burden of the following chapters will be to show how the legal conditions for stability and expansion of communications activities *as a sector of the market economy* exert an apparently determinative force on the Court's deliberations about this most central of civil rights.

My other concern—with questions of ideology—is advanced by tracing the representation of *actors* and *interests* in the judicial discourse. Conflicting claims to speech rights or regulatory powers, consonant with the different interests of the actors involved, are adjudicated in the courts by a process of textual interpretation: the meanings imbedded in testimony, statutes and legislative documents, academic and professional studies, and, most importantly, other case law decisions, must be weighed and evaluated by jurists, and this is their special skill. These texts are frequently contradictory in their representation of actors and interests. The interpretive efforts of jurists, however, have a literary authority that far surpasses that of any other analyst, in that they command enforcement by the police power of the state. To make constitutional law is to both enunciate and to enforce a political philosophy. The representation of different social actors and interests in the courts' discourse is a part of the effective determination of their real social power.

The appellants in the cases I select for discussion include: the owners and editors of publishing and broadcasting firms; their actual and prospective advertiser-clients; government departments and quasijudicial regulators; and readers, listeners, and viewers of the media. Cases involving individual citizen-appellants in direct, unmediated contexts of speech rights dispute are also described for comparative purposes. Both the theoretical and case-study chapters that follow attend primarily to a) the accommodation of these different interests in the judicial discourse, and b) the discursive strategies by which conforming *definitions* of these different interests are produced—as 'justice'—by the courts.

It would be intellectually gratifying, and far easier, if questions of political economy and questions of ideology—of 'base' and 'superstructure'—could be neatly separated and separately addressed here. But mass communication is in fact a prime example of an area of inquiry in which both concerns must be held in mind at the same time. The point of connection between these concerns is *power*, and especially the multiplication of power: in these materials we have an opportunity to look at the 'overdetermination'[7] of social structure resulting from the confluence of economic and discursive power.

[7] Louis Althusser (1977) borrows this notion from Freud for his structural-marxist account of the mechanisms by which apparently intentional subjective action is called forth and determined in economic ("in the last instance") processes. Freud used the term to describe certain features of the mechanism of dreams; the two most important of these, to Freud, were *condensation* and *displacement*. *Condensation* refers to the plurality of latent elements gathered into any manifest dream element; *displacement* refers to the process by which manifest elements come to 'stand in' for latent elements by a chain of associations. Overdetermination accounts for the numinous quality of dream images through the multiplication of meanings: it is both the direct condensation of several latent elements in a single manifest dream image, and the indirect displacement of additional latent elements by their secondary condensation through the elements of their chains of association. See Freud (1953–1974, Vol. 4). While 'overdetermination' is a useful notion in considering structures per se, I do not subscribe fully to the structuralist view, as should be apparent from the balance of the discussion.

Economic power is a fairly well-understood category, but what is meant here by *discursive power?* In speech act theories human utterances are commonly understood, in addition to their representational and expressive functions, as instruments in the negotiation of social power. Steven Lukes's three-level model[8] is apposite for consideration of the relation between speech and power. Lukes proposes that we distinguish between:

1. the power to cause an event to take place (for example, a judge's order to a bailiff to remove an unruly defendant from the courtroom);
2. the power to prevent an action taking place (the same judge's imposition of a ban on media publication of the trial's progress);
3. the power to authoritatively *define* the situation—to produce the definitions which other social actors must employ to understand the situation in which they act (as when the judge rules on whether a particular line of argument or examination will be permitted).

Alone among these levels of power, the third—the most invisible and pervasive—always and necessarily takes the form of a *symbolic* action; this is not true for the first two. Jurists' texts and utterances may mobilize, in symbolic form, all three levels of power at once; but because of their normative function they are *always* examples of the third level of power.

It is in treating together questions of language, property, and power and their relationship that the category of ideology is perhaps most usefully invoked. John Thompson[9] asserts that the analysis and critique of asymmetrical relations of social power, and the attempt to comprehend the manner in which such relations structure human action and contribute to its unintended outcomes, are fundamental (and frequently absent) terms in the study of ideology. He therefore defines *ideology* as "the ways in which meaning serves to sustain relations of domination."[10] This is the definition of ideology I propose to use in this study, with a friendly amendment to "sustain or contest," since the understanding of actors subject to domination is not epistemologically privileged in any obvious way. Concordance of belief, intention, action, and outcome may be the desired product of an altered social order; but better knowledge of the

[8] Lukes (1974).

[9] Thompson (1984).

[10] Thompson (1984, pp. 130ff). Among the dozens of working definitions of *ideology* of which I am aware, I believe Thompson's is the most alive to the necessity of accounting simultaneously for the symbolic agency of human actors and for the historical limit conditions imposed by the social structures they thereby produce. His is therefore a political definition, that is, a definition uniquely suited to the study of social power.

social world is often the promise, rather than the accomplished fact, of struggles against domination.

Thompson articulates the commitments of this *interpretive* (or *hermeneutic*) approach to political discourse when he invokes

> the deep and ineliminable link between theory and practice in that sphere of social inquiry where *subjects* capable of action and reflection are among the *objects* of investigation.[11]

Many studies of the *subjective* dimensions of mass communications analyze the actual activities and attitudes of audience members in their uses of mediated messages.[12] But this present study aims at revealing the interactional structure of mass-mediated communication by analysis of the corresponding legal structure of mass media 'free speech rights.' Its basic claim is that the relations of commodity production and exchange in the private mass media sector of the economy are "relations of expressive domination"; and that they are sustained to an important degree by the positive ethical and political significance attached to these practices and institutions by most citizens. If this claim can be substantiated, then liberal jurisprudence must be seen as an originating site of a much wider, populist discourse that understands these relations of communicative domination in the mass media *as freedom*. The analysis in the following chapters develops the argument that the structure of interaction sanctioned by the courts' discourse misrepresents, 'represses' or effaces significant parts of the *audience's* communicative interests. It is appropriate therefore to characterize this analysis of the liberal ideology of free speech as a study of the image of the audience as it appears in the discourse of law.

ORGANIZATION AND KEY SOURCES

Part One of the following study consists of two chapters comparing liberal and critical approaches to mass communications law. In Chapter 1 the fundamental principles of liberal political philosophy as they relate to 'freedom of expression' are reviewed. These are broadly organized to consider, first, the communicative obligations of the state; and second, the communicative freedoms of the citizen. The *rule of law*—the legality of the state itself, and the maintenance of an accepted structure of political

---

[11] Thompson (1984, p. 145).

[12] For a good example, see Morley (1980).

institutions and rules—is found to be logically premised, within liberal theory, on an interactional 'free speech principle.' An important element of liberal political philosophy is its imbrication of democratic and market processes. These are formally distinguished in the area of communication, using the conceptual apparatus of liberalism. The 'free speech principle' emerges here as a pivotal point of *dis*aggregation of market and polity: a *liberal* critique of the commercialization of mass communication then emerges. I am indebted in the general lines of reasoning pursued in Chapter 1 to the formulations of Frederick Schauer, whose illuminating treatment of J.S. Mill's *On Liberty* and conceptual separation of the principles of speech and liberty I partially recapitulate; and to those of Philip Soper, whose project of reconciling the distinct assumptions of Lockean 'natural' law and legal 'consequentialism' has allowed me to dispense with their separate exegesis.[13]

The liberal critique is unable to account for the liberal state's own actual production of law. In search of a more adequate explanation of the distribution of speech rights in the mass media Chapter 2 reviews critical literatures on law and communication. The first section surveys marxist approaches to the institutions of law in a capitalist state; the second section critically examines the organization of mass communication in the context of market exchange. In the area of critical theories of law, I have benefited from the analyses provided by Gerald Cohen, Hugh Collins, Paul Hirst, and Paul Phillips.[14] In the area of critical analysis of mass communications, I have chosen to focus especially on the "Blindspot Debate" among Dallas Smythe, Graham Murdock, Bill Livant, Sut Jhally, and Michael Lebowitz.[15] The economic role of audiences and the allocation of legal rights in mass communication emerge as key problems in the critical paradigm.

The problems raised by both the liberal and Marxist conceptual frameworks can only be laid to rest by a historically specific case study. The review of legal cases that forms Part Two of the study (Chapters 3, 4, and 5) may be read as a critical history of the development of citizens' speech rights in the paradigm instance of the commercial mass communications system of the United States. The distribution of mass communication rights in the First Amendment tradition is explored in Part Two through the reported decisions and dissents of U.S. judges in selected mass media free speech cases and comparative cases of direct, face-to-face communication. Key secondary sources that I used as an initial guide into

[13] Schauer (1982); Soper (1984).

[14] Cohen (1978); Collins (1984); Hirst, (1979); Phillips (1980).

[15] Smythe (1977); Murdock (1978); Livant (1979); Jhally (1982); Lebowitz (1986).

this discourse are: Donald Gillmour and Jerome Barron's *Mass Communication Law*;[16] David Kairys's fine essay "Freedom of Speech";[17] and Edwin Rome and William Roberts' *Corporate & Commercial Free Speech.*[18]

Chapter 3 summarizes the *pre*-mass media First Amendment case law, reviews some fundamental distinctions in mass media doctrine, and explores cases pivoting on the public or private character of communications resources and practices. Chapter 4 looks specifically at key media *access* cases, in which the *audience's* speech rights become the explicit topic of the juridical discourse. Chapter 5 is a study of the audience's speech rights as further developed in recent 'corporate and commercial speech' case law. This brings the case law history up to the present.

The concluding chapter of the study reviews the description of interests and the allocation of rights in the liberal discourse on mass communication and justice. It is suggested here that no model of social communication employed in communicative rule making can be value free: our very definitions of what *communication* is have unavoidable entailments with respect to the concentration or diffusion of social power.

---

[16] Gillmor and Barron (1984).

[17] Kairys (1982).

[18] Rome and Roberts (1985).

Part I

Liberal and Critical Paradigms in Mass Communications Law

Chapter 1

Speech, Property, and the State in Liberal-Democratic Theory

The connection between law and politics is most explicit in constitutional decisions. Here political values are finally brought to bear as the decisive factors in conflicts which have resisted resolution by any and all of the prior technical and bureaucratic instruments the judicial system has available. No one has any sort of 'right' to have their case heard on its constitutional merits: national supreme courts freely select which cases they will hear, and their decisions are subject to no form of review. In their deliberations on the meaning of a Constitution—the primary political document of a state—constitutional courts may even review and overturn the legislated law of elected governments. The legality of a constitutional state and the enforceability of its statutes rest, in theory, on their conformity with the political principles enunciated in the Constitution and developed in court decisions. To rephrase Clausewitz, law is politics by other means.

This chapter explores a liberal-democratic framework for thinking about the constitutional discourse on communication and justice. It simultaneously introduces some key concepts used by jurists in their decisions in this area. The four sections which follow in this chapter explore two complementary approaches within liberal political philosophy, to the appearance of speech rights in law. The first section considers the relation between speech rights and the *rule of law*. In this approach the basic political interests at play in any instance of communicative rule making in a pluralist society are expressed in the vocabulary of jurisprudence. The third section considers the relation between speech rights and *liberty*. The *libertarian principle* is a central political idea sustaining market exchange. The *free speech principle* emerges here as a fulcrum for the conceptual separation of the spheres of market and polity. Each of these abstract discussions is followed by a separate discussion (the second and fourth sections), in which the preceding approach is compared to the actual structure of speech rights in contemporary commercial mass communication.

The applicability of these two approaches is not necessarily confined to formally *democratic* polities, but they *are* applicable especially to varieties of self-government. The chapter may therefore conveniently be read as referring to speech rights in liberal democracies. The terminology and assumptions of liberal political philosophy have been uncritically adopted in this chapter, because it is the anomalous relationship between liberal political theory and liberal legal practice in the area of speech rights which is under consideration here. By comparing theory and practice in this way a *liberal* critique of the commercialization of mass communication is brought into view.

THE COMMUNICATIVE OBLIGATIONS OF THE STATE

Communication and the 'Rule of Law'

> For a Rotinese [inhabitant of the southernmost island in the Indonesian archipelago] the pleasure of life is talk—not simply an idle chatter that passes time, but the more formal taking of sides in endless dispute, argument, and repartee or the rivalling of one another in eloquent and balanced phrases on ceremonial occasions.
>
> Three hundred years of Dutch records for the island provide an apt chronicle of this attitude towards speaking.... If a young administrator could weather the storms of the litigious Rotinese he was due for promotion. The Rotinese, in turn, obliged the Dutch by reviving all old litigation to welcome each incoming administrator.
>
> I was fortunate to arrive on Roti late at night and therefore did not become involved in dispute until early the next morning.[1]

In any political society we can identify kinds of organized behavior that resemble what we know as *law*. The adjudication of marital conflict

[1] Fox (1973, p. 65).

by village council in Bali; the judicial activity of the Indic kings of Thailand in respect to debt, inheritance, theft, quarrels, or treason; or the complex certification of various ranks of official character witnesses by the 'sarica' courts of Islam are functionally similar institutions, as Geertz has magisterially demonstrated.[2] In all societies the uncountable benefits of agreement and coordinated effort require some forms of normative regulation of conflicts among individuals and groups.

We can provisionally define *law*, then, as a neutral institutional mechanism of disputes resolution and enforcement whose authority is derived from—and used in turn to reinforce—the most widely shared values of a politically organized society.[3] The internal consistency of its various decisions and its willingness to account for their normative basis links a legal apparatus to the social value system which it functions to sustain.[4] Some final source of regulatory authority in resolving social conflict is widely taken as necessary for the ongoing operation of all other organizations in a society, and the institutions of law therefore are accorded legitimacy in the use of coercive force.[5] Where sovereignty is held to reside in the people, the normative authority of the institutions of law give them a claim to a *monopoly* on licensing the use of overt force.

It is the intention of a government to serve the best interests of society as a whole, rather than any particular or partial interests, that constitutes the authority of its law as superior to all other secular authority. It is the claim of legal institutions that they insure the *rule of law*, rather than the rule of particular actors and interests. *Law* then cannot be defined simply as coercive order (the enforcement of arbitrary rules). History certainly provides examples of the monopolization of state force unaccompanied by any defensible public interest rationale (e.g., Haiti under Duvalier, or Caligula's Rome), but precisely because such governments fail to seek the public interest, they fail the test for *legality*.

The members of such a society may even cooperate with arbitrary rules to avoid coercive sanctions, but if they consent to those rules only to avoid sanctions and without any sense of moral obligation to regulate their own behaviour in accordance with them, those rules do not have the legitimacy and authority of law. *Law* stands as a separate concept from *government:* governments can be legal or not legal, but legal government creates moral obligation on its citizens, by means of its pursuit in good faith of the public interest.

---

[2] Geertz (1983). See also Berman (1978); Davies and Fouracre (1986); Nader and Todd (1978).

[3] See, for example, Hart (1961); Ehrlich (1975).

[4] Hart (1961).

[5] This quite modern argument originated in Thomas Hobbes's 1651 *Leviathan*.

It is of course nearly certain that members of any society will disagree frequently about how the *public interest* is to be served. It may even be possible in some circumstances to demonstrate conclusively that the *public interest* requirement has not been met. Neither of these eventualities render government illegitimate: there is always the strong possibility of the state committing errors or oversights in its efforts to define and enforce the common good, but if it can demonstrate sincerity in its pursuit of that end its monopolization of force meets the minimum conditions of legality. It is the good faith of the state's actions that establishes the moral obligation of its citizens to respect its laws.

In this formulation law is the antithesis of naked power, because, by aiming to serve the welfare of society and all its members, it creates an obligation for citizens to regulate their *own* behavior. And it is tautological that, in a society ruled by an accepted legal code, most people do not encounter the institutions of law—the police, the prisons, and the courts—with any great frequency. Most citizens regulate their own behavior with tolerable success, and the legal apparatus is only deployed against the small minority who withhold their consent or deny their obligation to obey the law.

The right of citizens to communicate is a vital element in the foundations of legal authority. Soper suggests that the 'right to discourse' is one of only three 'natural' rights,[6] alongside security of the person, and equality before the law. There are at least three ways in which speech rights function to secure the rule of law.

First, determination of the *public interest* (so notoriously difficult to define) is quite clearly furthered by free and open discussion. Without unhindered public discourse the various private interests (of which the 'public interest' is understood in utilitarian variants of liberal theory to be the vector sum) may be literally unknowable. If, on the other hand, all citizens know that the frank expression of their opinions is permitted and will not expose them to sanctions, at least some among them will take up the task of analyzing, criticizing and crafting alternatives for any policy proposal. We have, as J.S. Mill pointed out, no certainty "that the opinion we are endeavouring to stifle is a false opinion.... All silencing of opinion is an assumption of infallibility."[7] Protection of opportunities for the

---

[6] Soper (1984, p. 140). Soper seems to redefine the notion of *natural rights* to mean 'rights necessary and sufficient to establish legal obligation.' The connection between this formulation, and the Thomist tradition of natural rights which had such a foundational role in liberal political philosophy, is ambiguous. The latter is exemplified in John Locke's anonymous pamphlets of the late 1600s: see for example, Locke (1690/1980). Tully (1980) and Tuck (1979) give excellent historical accounts of the debates and arguments surrounding the natural rights paradigm in the origins of liberal political philosophy.

[7] Mill (1859/1971, p. 24) J.S. Mill was, not a natural rights theorist, but a utilitarian liberal theorist—albeit a distinctly *reformist* utilitarian in comparison with the far more

introduction and debate of conflicting opinion, on the other hand, is the state's greatest available resource for determining the full range of its policy options.

Second, the state's demonstration of good faith requires, not merely its assertion of sincerity, but its respect for the concomitant good faith of, and potentially corrective influence of, dissenting citizens. This in turn requires the state to provide opportunities for normative challenge and a generally successful normative defense in justification of its policies (or, even more convincing, a willingness to alter its position in response to strong arguments). Such opportunities are the best guarantee of the validity— or at the least, the plausibility—of its policy choices.

Third, the all-important obligation on citizens to respect the law is established by the right to discourse, even for those citizens who remain unconvinced of the propriety of the policies subsequently enacted by the state. If no dialogue respecting the public interest and no normative justification by the state of its policies has taken place, dissenting citizens may legitimately conclude that they are not obligated to respect the good faith of government or the legality of its actions. Conversely, if those conditions have been met, the moral autonomy of the citizens's obligation is intact, and her self-respect in conforming to the law's requirements is preserved, even if the outcomes appear erroneous to her, because the *process* of policy determination has demonstrated the government's good faith. In these circumstances the citizen's dissent from the law and her obligation to it are reconciled without loss of autonomy or self-respect: she can obey, in good conscience, a law to which she is substantively opposed.

To sum up, liberal theory makes a global claim that the right (and opportunity) of citizens to speak freely, and to be heard publicly in their discourse about the public interest, and about the state's actions in regard to the public interest, are necessary to establish the good faith of government and the moral obligation of citizens, which together are the hallmark of a legally governed society. The result might well be untidy and cacophonous, as the Dutch administrator found out, but this social cost is arguably good value if it purchases legal government and a law-abiding citizenry.

---

sanguinary variety espoused by Jeremy Bentham, and by his father, James Mill. The transition from 17th-century natural rights and Roman republican traditions in political philosophy to the utilitarian and reform-utilitarian themes central in 19th-century liberal thought cannot be understood outside the context of the intervening century's repudiation of the remnants of Scholastic moral and political philosophy, and the efforts to place legal, political and economic theory on a more sociological footing, found especially in the work of Adam Smith, David Hume, and their contemporaries. A fine introduction to various aspects of the history of classical political-economic thought is Hont and Ignatieff, (1983).

Commercial Mass Communication and Legal Obligation

The analyses in Chapters 3 through 5 will flesh out the details of the situation that must be merely outlined here: that is, the structure of speech rights produced by the courts in the U.S. commercial mass media (and in most liberal market polities) appears inconsistent with the abstract principles of political morality and necessity just described. One is hard-pressed to identify any legally sanctioned right of citizenship to speech opportunities in the print or broadcast media for discussion of public policies. The media are certainly the most significant forum of public opinion in the democratic states, and yet persistent challenges by large and broadly supported organizations (such as the Democratic Party in the U.S.) or branches of government (such as U.S. State Legislatures) have failed to secure even narrowly construed forms of access. Demands for paid access have fared no better than demands for free access.[8]

At the same time the law has explicitly recognized the right of audiences to *receive* what private media organizations choose to offer them, largely free of public regulation, and effectively without regard to the 'balance' of views or interests represented.[9] As it stands in the U.S., governments may neither *prohibit* nor *require* the private provision of mediated speech opportunities. The notion of "hearer-centered speech rights"[10]—the *right*

---

[8] Only one single and ancient U.S. decision (*Uhlman v. Sherman*, 22 Ohio N.P., N.S., 225, 31 Ohio Dec. 54), dating from 1919, affirmed only in a single lower court and rejected since then by numerous higher court decisions, has found a citizen right of access to the press, and even then not on constitutional grounds. This is the net result of literally hundreds of test cases brought forward in the U.S. on this question. See Chapters 3 and 4. The present author is unable to find even this much authority for access—paid or unpaid—to the Canadian press.

In broadcasting the situation is more complex, but the result substantially the same. In the U.S. the FCC's 'Fairness Doctrine' seemed in the early 1970s to promise a new era of broadcast access, but the policy was abdicated by the Commission (under a new chairperson) in the 1980s. The constitutional grounds on which it was originally upheld were not based on an access rationale in any case. See Chapters 3 and 4. In Canada, a recent CRTC policy paper on "Balance in programming on community access media" (CRTC Public Notice 88-161, September 29, 1988) gives the tenor of the situation here when it states that, although licensees in the Canadian broadcast system are "not obliged to provide time to complainants, a licensee may *choose* to satisfy the balance requirement by offering a complainant the opportunity to present a differing viewpoint" (1988, p. 11; emphasis added). The 'balance requirement' is the only policy on which an access claim could be erected in Canadian broadcasting, and 'community access media' are the only licensees explicitly charged with any citizen access role.

[9] This is the rationale for the recent turn towards protection of commercial and corporate speech rights; see Chapter Five.

[10] The formulation of Burt Neubourne in his essay *Free Speech—Free Markets—Free Choice: An Essay on Commercial Speech*, New York: Association of National Advertisers, 1987.

to receive—as the appropriate form of the public's right to discourse in the context of mass communication can be criticized on moral and political grounds from within liberal theory. The *right to receive* privately selected mass media contents without the *right to reply* to them fails to insure the state's interests in protecting political speech rights. The core of these interests of the state are related to the generation of policy consensus and political consent, through opportunities for dissent and dialogue. No legal mechanism exists in these interpretations of constitutional communication rights to ensure that dissenting opinion holders are even representatively sampled, much less given direct access to audiences of other citizens in the mass forum.

This is even more true for the forms of purchased access represented by advertising than it is for the 'free' access sometimes granted in the editorial contents of mass media. Media firms in Canadian and U.S. jurisdictions are not required to grant *any* form of citizen access, paid or unpaid (see note 8). Their exemption from access requirements is generally grounded in an extremely vague judicial recognition of their exercise of "journalistic responsibility" and "editorial integrity." Since journalists and editors have no power to publish or broadcast material rejected by their employers (or to refuse material accepted by their employers), this rationale is subordinate to the media owner's property rights. It does not encode independent 'journalists' rights' superceding, or standing as counterclaims to, the access claims of citizens. But while news reporting and editorial comment do tend to be selected to portray *some* range of views on issues of public concern, no such attempted 'balancing' of *advertised* opinion is visible (although in some disputes broadcasters have preferred to remove existing advertising rather than accept 'counteradvertising' or fight court challenges.

This may be attributable in part to the fact that, while nonadvertising contents are *expenses* to media firms, selected on the basis of their cost-effective appeal to audiences, advertising is the major *revenue* source of commercial media, and revenues are only likely to be declined if their acceptance is going to entail other, unacceptable costs. Acceptance of 'counteradvertising' by a media firm, however, would not likely be well received by large, long-term clients. Absent this set of financial constraints, even pure product advertising—advertising for alcohol or tobacco or children's war toys, for example—*could* be 'balanced' by privately-sponsored advertising *against* those products, if the public interest aspects of their availability were controversial. But a *right to receive* implies neither a right to dissenting 'counterspeech' nor a responsibility for media firms to 'balance' the claims and propositions made in their advertising or other contents. The print media have no legal obligation to balance their nonadvertising content. The balance requirements to which broadcasters are theoretically subject (via administrative law—see note 8, and Chapter 4) may also be unconstitutional under current doctrine, precisely because they are *not* predicated on the citizen's right to speak or reply to speech. In any case the U.S. 'balance' regulations have certainly not been enforced in recent years, and as they now stand may be unenforceable, legally and practically. Speech rights predicated on the audience's singular *right to receive* (but not reply) are therefore inadequate to the state's interest, under the *rule of law*, in protecting speech about matters of public interest.

The fact that these current speech law interpretations are so conveniently correlated to the economic interests of media owners and their advertiser-clients suggests another moral problem with the model of mass media speech rights under discussion. It is clearly in the interests of advertisers that counterclaims about their commercial activities and products be disallowed as far as practicable. But for the liberal state to countenance private determination of the boundaries of public interest debate is to put its own good faith pursuit of the public interest in question. As with the state's own activities, the mere *appearance* of self-interest in matters of public concern addressed by advertisers and private media owners is sufficiently corrosive of any presumption of good faith (for media owners, for advertisers and for the government, as regulator) to require justificatory opportunities for dialogue.

The *right to receive* mass media contents is a suspect construction of the audience's speech rights in a final and encompassing way. We have noted that toleration of dissenting opinion and normative justification of state policy are necessary to establish citizen obligation and consent to the law, in liberal theory. But obligation and consent to *communications* law is a special case in this description of political morality: securing consent to a particular regime of speech rights becomes a fundamental element in the organization of political power, because it simultaneously secures consent to a particular *procedure* for the legitimation of other policies. The justification of communications policies and laws then requires—by the rule of law—an exhaustive and very inclusive heuristic discourse *about* discourse, for which no sufficient opportunity has been provided.

Because the commercial mass media, in the Western liberal democracies, are the primary means of organizing and conducting public debate, and because the question of speech rights allocation is one in which the media themselves have a pecuniary interest, the apparent consent of citizens to the current model of speech rights may have only a spurious legitimacy. I would argue that affirmation of the 'right to receive' (without a 'right to reply') grants the private owners of media firms control of public debate *about* speech rights (and about other policies as well), and leaves them free to *construct* the very norms by which citizen consent and obligation—in any area of policy—are to be justified. This is a good example of Lukes's third category of power.[11] It is a largely invisible, but deeply inequitable allocation of political privilege and power to private interests, and therefore inadequately models good faith pursuit of the public interest.

THE COMMUNICATIVE FREEDOMS OF THE CITIZEN

The Free Speech Principle

It has been noted how, in liberal democratic theory, free speech and the state's obligation to maintain the *rule of law* are connected in a fundamental way. Different provisions in law are derived, however, from different normative rationales for the judgments that uphold them. Liberal democratic theory invokes the *public interest* as a normative principle fundamental to legal government; we could also say that *democratic* government relies on an independent principle of self-government, that equal treatment by courts and police is necessitated by the independent principle of citizen equality, and so on. This section distinguishes the free speech principle from the key principle sustaining commercial activity—the principle of liberty.

The principle of liberty is the idea that all activities not expressly prohibited are permissable. Furthermore, it asserts that no regulation or constraint of individual actions that do not occasion demonstrable harm to other individuals, or to their interests or the exercise of their rights, can legitimately be enacted or permitted by government.[12] The freedom to own and enjoy the use of lawfully acquired private property, or to enter into private contracts for the exchange of property, are justified by appeal to the principle of liberty. The very fact, however, that we distinguish freedom of speech without similarly enumerating all other possible liberties implies that speech liberties have a different rationale from the liberty to own and use private property. The fact that we distinguish speech freedoms from other freedoms means that we think government regulation of speech requires a different method of analysis and/or stronger justification, than government regulation of other activities.

The foremost exponent of the principle of liberty, J.S. Mill, implicitly recognized the distinct character of the free speech principle. His essay *On Liberty*[13] is largely concerned with demonstrating that only the con-

---

[11] See Lukes (1974).

[12] This notion of a private sphere of action that public authority must protect and refrain from encroaching upon is, of course, common to all variants of liberalism.

[13] Mill (1859/1971).

tainment of their effect on others justifies the state's regulation of individual actions. But in Chapter 2 of that work Mill makes a separate argument for speech liberties.

Mill asserts an 'ultimate good' flowing from the exercise of speech liberties, which is found precisely in the effects on one another of individuals' speech acts. The prevention of armed robbery, for example, is a justified constraint on private conduct because of its effects on others. But the suppression of opinion is *not* a justified constraint on private conduct, *despite* its effects on others: The effects on others of freely expressed opinion are always desirable. The ultimate good served by speech freedoms is the discovery of truth. "Were an opinion a personal possession of no value except to the owner," states Mill, "it would make some difference whether the injury [of suppression] was inflicted only on a few persons or on many."

> But the peculiar evil of silencing the expression of an opinion is, that it is robbing the human race; posterity as well as the existing generation; those who dissent from the opinion still more than those who hold it. If the opinion is right they are deprived of the opportunity of exchanging error for truth: if wrong, they lose, what is almost as great a benefit, the clearer perception and livelier impression of truth, produced by its collision with error.[14]

To Mill the potential adverse effects of speech liberties were, because of the ultimate good they serve, always less serious than the adverse effects of their constraint.

Mill's insight can be stated in contemporary terms that are more amenable to our concern with the constitutional court's theory of mass communication. The free speech principle is distinct from the principle of liberty, because speech, as Frederick Schauer usefully points out,[15] is an 'other-regarding' act, which *does* have an effect on others, or at the very least, is intended to. Schauer distinguishes the principle of liberty as applying only to those acts which genuinely do not have demonstrable effects on others—'self-regarding' acts. Acts which can be shown to be 'other-regarding' are not excused by the principle of liberty from government constraint.[16] Because speech acts do have or are intended to have an effect on others, and yet are held to be broadly exempt from government

---

[14] Mill (1959/1972, pp. 23-24).

[15] Schauer (1982). The historian Isaiah Berlin has argued a similar distinction between the conceptual basis of Mill's defense of other liberties, and his defense of freedom of expression. See Berlin (1970).

[16] Here is another legal academic's formulation: "The liberal theory of rights and political justice is premised on the belief that individuals possess a pre-political sphere of pure autonomy and freedom that does not depend for its existence upon the state: individuals are

regulation, the normative principle which justifies this state of affairs is a separate and independent principle from the principle of liberty.

The literature of communication studies endorses this distinction. From the social science perspective communication is by definition an interactive phenomenon requiring the participation of more than one 'communicator'.[17] Communications which have no effect on others cannot really be demonstrated to have taken place: The most we could say about a completely ineffectual communication (a verbal remark addressed to a deaf person whose back was turned, for example) would be that communication was unsuccessfully *attempted.*

Successful communication may also have a *harmful* effect on others without necessarily being proscribed. For example, a new contender for a well-paid electoral office might truthfully communicate with voters in such a manner as to replace the incumbent, and cause her the loss of income and status. The intent of such communication is to effect others' actions (the voters); the communicative action harms the interests of another (the incumbent office holder); and yet the principle of free speech, especially as it is used in a liberal democracy, *requires* the opportunity for such conduct.

While many of the actions that can be justified by the principle of liberty, such as exchanges of private property, involve or require interaction and communication, the part of the activity protected under the principle of liberty is the 'self-regarding' part: The political freedom to exchange property, for example, safeguards the personal acquisition and use of property as unregulated private conduct when it takes place *without* harmful effect on others. If sufficient harm to others by such an activity can be demonstrated, it may become 'other-regarding' and be legitimately constrained (or monopolized) by the state.

Thus where the principle of liberty demands that we protect certain conduct that does *not* effect others, the free speech principle in liberal democratic theory requires us to protect certain activities *despite* their

---

independent and complete entities who interact with others out of a grudging necessity to better satisfy their *self-regarding* wants and preferences. Accordingly, the major function of a liberal charter is to police the boundary that separates the political and the collective from the pre-political and the individual—to contain the state so as to prevent it from intruding, in its utilitarian zeal, upon the "natural" realm of individual liberty" (Hutchinson & Petter, 1986; emphasis added).

[17] This is axiomatic both in traditional social psychology and in newer systems theory approaches. The former approach, now known as *symbolic interactionism*, has its roots in the pragmatic philosophy of William James and John Dewey and was powerfully developed by George Herbert Mead in the first four decades of this century. See Meltzer and Petras (1970, pp. 3–17); Goffman, (1974). For a systems theory approach see Watzlawick, Bavelas, and Jackson (1967).

effect on others. The principle of free speech asserts that communication is *less* subject to regulation than other conduct that affects, or is intended to affect, others' interests. The regulation of speech by government action (and the toleration of speech constraints by government *in* action) therefore require different, or stronger, justifications than the regulation of different kinds of 'other-regarding' conduct.[18]

This is not at all to say that speech freedoms are always of higher priority than other rights and freedoms. Questions of how *much* freedom speech rights confer in particular situations, or of the relationship between free speech and any other values, are separate questions from the independence of the principles on which they rest. The free speech principle may in some cases give rise to very weak rights in comparison to other rights that their exercise may jeopardize.[19] The point here is simply that the free speech principle imposes a distinct restraint on government actions and triggers unique and valid demands for government protection, independent of the limitations arising from other principles, such as the principle of liberty.

Schauer summarizes the distinctions between 'libertarian' arguments and 'free speech' arguments[20] as follows:

1. libertarian arguments do not explain protection of other-regarding conduct.
2. rejection of libertarianism does not entail rejection of the free speech principle.
3. identification of harm caused by speech is not in itself enough to justify regulation.

In weighing the relative claims of free speech and other social values such as liberty, jurists identify four distinct grounds for the protection of speech rights.[21] These are the purposes which must be weighed when speech rights come into conflict with other rights. The first is the 'argument from truth.' Speech rights are held to further the discovery of true propositions through their protection of opportunities for the expression of *all* propositions as potentially useful contributions to debate. As Mill observed in the passage quoted earlier, the public expression of both

---

[18] See, e.g., Emerson (1981, at 802).

[19] See Emerson, (1981, at 808).

[20] Schauer (1982, pp. 11–12). Ronald Dworkin (1977, pp. 190–191) makes the same distinctions.

[21] These grounds are frequently cited by both jurists and legal academics, and derive partly from Mill's argument and partly from caselaw. Schauer analyzes them at length, but see also, for example, Neubourne (1987); Sharpe (1987).

truth and error furthers the *process* of the discovery of truth, as well as its dissemination, acceptance, correction, and periodic re-invigoration. The argument from truth assumes the permanent possibility of fallible judgment, and prescribes open debate as the best available corrective.[22]

The second claim which may be made for protecting speech is the 'argument from democracy.' This is not totally separated from the argument from truth, as *social* 'truths' are usually far from transparent and can at least equally be the product of debate as other desired kinds of knowledge. Thus the often-mentioned linkage between democracy and an informed citizenry—the reliance of effective self-government on a population equipped with relevant knowledge—is only one of the services performed by speech rights for democracy. The *production* of what will count as relevant information in a political conflict is just as much an outcome of the communicative opportunities of a society as is its distribution. In addition, circumstances conducive to development of the fullest range of policy options, opportunities for practical knowledge of *others'* opinions (irrespective of their truth-status), and an obligation to conform to the law created by the citizen's opportunity to participate in policy formation are all generated by the protection of speech rights.[23]

The third claim for speech rights protection is the area of closest overlap between the free speech principle and the principle of liberty: the 'argument from self-expression.' Here it is *not* the other-regarding character of speech acts for which protection is claimed, but the self-regarding interest of speakers in their individual development as creative beings.[24] Where this is extended into a claim for the beneficial effects of public creativity on individual others or on society generally, it becomes a claim for the protection of an other-regarding activity, but it also ceases to be a pure argument from self-expression and partakes of the justificatory claims of the argument from truth. An individual's interest in pure self-expression does not demonstrably require a *public* opportunity to speak, although, perhaps because of the frequent assimilation of speech rights to the principle of liberty, this is the most commonly cited rationale for their protection.

The 'argument from peaceful social change' is the fourth claim for protection of communicative rights. This claim relies on the notion that speech rights give the collectivity of ordinary citizens the potential of

---

[22] A contemporary (critical-hermeneutic) discussion of the 'truth' value as the prime justification for protection of free speech rights is contained in Chevigny (1988).

[23] The foremost exponent of this argument is American political philosopher Alexander Meiklejohn; see Meiklejohn (1948, 1952, 1961); see also Brennan)1965).

[24] Influential legal scholars ranking this value highest for purposes of speech rights protection include Baker (1989); and Emerson (1970, 1981).

exerting a powerful influence on policy choices, and is thus closely related to the argument from democracy.[25] The argument from peaceful social change claims, quite simply, that where the people's desire for change in government policy is sufficiently strong, protected speech, by allowing the strength of these desires to be known and to be effective, may save the polity the experience of otherwise likely or inevitable communal violence.

These four arguments form a very powerful set of potential claims for the protection of speech rights. Considering these arguments, it is perhaps unsurprising that *free speech* is an idea of such widespread rhetorical force, or that the liberal democratic state would wish at all costs not to appear to violate it. It is perfectly possible to imagine circumstances in which libertarian claims to the private enjoyment of property ought to prevail over speech rights claims—but it is also quite easy to see how, in other circumstances, even modest libertarian claims might become justifiably subordinated to these strong and fundamental purposes. The next section explores how these separate claims are advanced and ranked in the context of commercial mass communication.

Commercial Mass Communication and Liberty

To understand the existing regime of mass communication speech rights in liberal democratic societies, it is necessary to analyze the relation between the free speech principle and the principle of liberty, because it is the latter which is rèally being invoked by the advocates (advertisers and media firms) of a 'hearer-centered' model of speech freedoms. Their claim—for the audience member's singular freedom to *receive* mass media contents—is a claim for a self-regarding, libertarian freedom. Invoking the *free speech* principle in the mass media would require a claim for everyone's equal freedom to engage in a protected other-regarding act: the freedom to initiate and reply to mass media contents. But media and advertisers claim that citizens' 'right to receive' (and not to speak) in the media context is protected by the principle of free speech.

It is worth noting that the argument in the preceding section, distinguishing the claims of liberty and of free speech, is separate from arguments which might be (and have been) brought against libertarian claims under the principle of equality. Such arguments usually assert a linkage between justice and substantive equality (as opposed to merely procedural equality), and these arguments can be traced all the way back to

[25] I believe this is the equivalent of, or captured within the scope of, the 'checking' value espoused by Vincent Blasi; see Blasi (1977).

Aristotle's distinction between commutative and distributive justice.[26] The consumption of a meal, for example, quite transparently requires the denial of any other person's consumption of that meal, but the freedom to deny this is precisely what is guaranteed for property owners when only the principle of liberty is applied to the dispute. We can imagine a starving social democrat attempting to apply the principle of equality to this situation in order to justify the seizure of half of the meal—and we can perhaps also surmise that a court would find the claims of liberty overwhelmingly stronger in this situation.

The profitable sale of mass communication opportunities by commercial media firms raises disputes different in kind from those attendant upon the use of other forms of private property. Making advertising sales relies on the constitution of audience members as *receivers*, and not as contributing participants in the communicative event (the contribution of audience members as consumers is addressed below). Control of the topic and format, and exemption from requirements to debate their assertions, are part of the value of such opportunities to advertisers. Strong grounds for exemption from government regulation of the communicative event also enhances its market value. The *value* of advertising services seems, in other words, to depend on the degree of private control exercised over the *audience's* communicative activity.

The propriety of this activity *could* of course be argued purely on libertarian grounds, with the courts deciding whether or not the principle of liberty which sustained media property owners' claims was a weaker or a stronger rationale than the actual or potential free speech claims of audience members. But what media firms argue, and, as I hope to demonstrate later, what the courts find compelling in their arguments, is that this organization of commercial communication is required by the *free speech* principle (and in a subsidiary way, by the principle of democracy). The liberties connected to the use of private property are not absent from this equation: rather, the protections that flow from the principle of liberty, and those that flow from the free speech principle, are quietly added together to produce an extraordinary set of legal privileges for the media firm.

Whatever financial transaction accompanies a communication, some part of the communication is not comprehended by its characterization as property. For example, two parties who communicate both end up with the information they began with *and* the information contributed by their interlocutor—and sometimes with new information neither of them

[26] In the *Nichomachean Ethics*, Book 5.

possessed in the first place!—even if both parties perform this exchange in a market and sell exclusive resale rights. Market exchange entails each party relinquishing one utility in favor of another; but even when one party offers money (and no information) and the other party information, the second party retains the information imparted, and either party could acquire new information in the process of the transaction.

Protection of whatever legitimate self-regarding or self-expressive characteristics communication may display is already given by the principle of liberty. Because it is the (other-regarding) way in which communication differs from (self-regarding) property-oriented activity, which is distinguished by the free speech principle, it is logical to presume that it is the nonproperty or public character of speech which the free speech principle protects. Speech is then 'free' to the extent that its claims for protection—against both government and private constraint—are upheld over claims made under other principles.

The determination of the relative strength of the claims that flow from these different principles in the commercial media context is a subsidiary question. A test of some sort would have to be devised to determine when the libertarian claims, and when the free speech claims, were the stronger. And real situations may call forth justifications based on several independent principles simultaneously. Thus a particular claim (the freedom of individuals to own and operate radio receivers in their private homes, say) may be justified primarily as an instance of the principle of liberty, while still being an exercise in the communicative pursuit of truth. But the convergence of principles in one instance may be succeeded by their opposition in another (e.g., an individual's amplification of his or of her favorite radio frequency to a level unendurable to the rest of the neighborhood). To distinguish the separate claims that flow from independent principles is not to decide in advance which ought to prevail in any given dispute.

The advocates of expanded commercial speech rights in the 'hearer-centered' model of the First Amendment tend more to aggregate these claims than to distinguish them. In fact, they firmly equate three distinct notions: advertising (other-regarding speech), free enterprise (self-regarding activity), and democracy (collective self-determination) are all held to have mutually reinforcing purposes. I have suggested several of the arguments by which liberal democratic theorists hold the free speech principle and the principle of democracy to be fundamentally linked and partially co-extensive. The inclusion of the notion of free enterprise as serving the same purposes requires further analysis.

A characteristic formulation of the view that links all three of these was given by communications lawyer Burt Neubourne in a deposition (on behalf of the Association of National Advertisers) to a U.S. Congressional Committee holding hearings on a bill to regulate tobacco advertising:

> The enjoyment of liberty is the result of... constant respect for the personal autonomy and innate dignity of the individual. The linked experiments in political democracy and consumer sovereignty that characterize free societies are premised on a leap of faith in the capacity of the individual to assimilate information and to make rational, informed choices.[27]

The U.S. Supreme Court echoes Neuborne's view in many of its recent First Amendment texts. Consider which free speech arguments are mobilized in this passage from a 1976 decision[28] protecting pharmaceutical advertising from government regulation:

> The consumer's interest in the free flow of information [the Court said] may be as keen, if not keener by far, than his interest in the day's most urgent political debate. Advertising, however tasteless and excessive it may sometimes seem, is nonetheless dissemination of information as to who is producing and selling what product, for what reason, and at what price. So long as we preserve a predominantly free enterprise economy, the allocation of our resources in large measure will be made through numerous private economic decisions. It is a matter of public interest that those decisions, in the aggregate, be intelligent and well-informed. To this end, the free flow of commercial information is indispensable. And if it is indispensable to the allocation of resources in a free enterprise system, it is also indispensable to the formation of intelligent opinions as to how that system ought to be regulated or altered.

While these three principles of free speech, liberty, and democracy may indeed be linked in some instances, it was suggested above that the principles of liberty and free speech have no *necessary* connection—one may even subscribe firmly to the principle of free speech without any logical entailment regarding the general principle of liberty—and vice versa. Market liberties and political democracy may similarly be linked in some instances, without either being a necessary precondition of the other (the political culture of Chile for the past 18 years, or of the contemporary Persian Gulf monarchies, are sufficient examples of this assertion). The logical relation between the democratic and libertarian principles will not be explored further here, except to cite C.B. MacPher-

---

[27] Neubourne (1987 p. 50).

[28] *Virginia State Board of Pharmacy v. Virginia Citizens Consumer Council, Inc.*, 425 U.S. 748 [1976].

son's historical demonstration[29] that liberalism may lead a robust existence without democracy: according to Macpherson, pluralist values, including both speech freedoms and the franchise, were adopted belatedly and by slow degrees in elite-ruled liberal polities as they became necessary to secure government through the consent of various sectors of the population.

Commercial speech advocates 'discover' the linkage of these three principles by the techniques of analogy and metaphor. Democracy follows from the political choices of citizens, who cast their ballots after receiving political information; and this is analogized to the paradigm instance of liberty, which consists in the market choices of consumers 'voting' their dollars on merchandise after receiving commercial information. Democracy is in this view a species of market exchange, and the sovereignty of the people a special case of consumer sovereignty. Unfortunately, the 'free marketplace of ideas' metaphor which establishes the conceptual link between the decision processes of consumers and of citizens in much of the case law may be disingenuous: the notion of a *struggle for market share* perhaps better describes what has become common to both contexts, partly as a result of these First Amendment decisions. In this more realistic model the function of the media is to service private organizations in the *management of demand* for such political 'merchandise' as candidates and policies.[30]

In this body of law, then, the concept of *democracy* has been assimilated to the rather passive notion of *market choice*, and the dialogical concept of *speech* assimilated to the far more scientistic and message-centered notion of *information.* On simple inspection this model can be seen to rely on a very attenuated version of both democracy and communication: the role of citizens in both activities is conceived in passive, receptive terms, and there is apparently little room for the dissenting question, the civic-minded protest, or the engaged debate. The dimensions of the market process in this model, though, have expanded considerably into the space left by a shrunken public sphere.[31]

The argument that political freedom of speech is an essential element of democracy is a truism in liberal democratic theory. But in determining the proper weight of the claims of liberty and of free speech, in the high-intensity media environment we face, it is necessary to consider whether the current distribution of speech rights in the mass media advances, or harms, the vital social purposes served by the constitutional guarantee of

[29] MacPherson (1977).

[30] See Galbraith (1985); Mauser (1983).

[31] The classic study of the development of the political public sphere into a sector of manufactured publicity remains Habermas (1962/1989).

freedom of expression. I have emphasized that, in Canada and the U.S., citizens have no rights to expression in the mass media, either by way of paid advertising or by way of rights to initiate or reply to nonadvertising contents. This is broadly premised on the claimed deleterious effects such infringements of *media firms'* speech rights would entail. Under the rubric of the audience's *right to receive*, the control of public discourse is even further ceded to private hands. Affirming the audience's *right to receive* media communications without a corresponding *right to reply* to them further augments both the property rights and the speech rights of media corporations and their clients, by granting them nearly total freedom from citizen intervention in or government regulation of their communications. It does *not*, however, extend the effective freedom of expression of the broad mass of citizens. It may be more likely to create an increasingly homogeneous and arbitrarily structured environment of political discourse, and if this is true, it is hardly evidence of an effective application of the free speech principle.

In this century the structure of communications processes in our society has changed dramatically. The rise of mass media in their contemporary forms has radically altered the political, cultural, and economic landscapes of most societies, and especially the liberal democracies. The mass media have created vast new markets, sources of employment, and incentives for technological innovation. They have also taken up a number of new and central roles in the arrangements by which we put democracy into action:

- they are the basic, societywide source of political information;
- they form the major link between citizens and government;
- they share in setting political agenda;
- they make interpretive judgments which have broad authority and persuasive force;
- their judgements are especially influential on political officials, who need the visibility and credibility they can offer.

These political functions of mass communication in a contemporary democracy can be marked off from its function in the market. The audience's interest in the media's commercial functions may accurately be described as its interest *as consumers*; but this is not their *only* interest in mass communication, and in some circumstances their political and commercial interests may be entirely divergent. That which is desirable to consumers in a market may, after all, be injurious to the political rights of citizens in a democratic polity. For example, the offering, for money, of favorable judgements by trial judges would damage the rights of all citizens to equal treatment before the law. The illegality of such actions does not lessen the example's force, for it is precisely the legality of removing a different prerogative from the public realm to a sphere of private determination that is at issue. The fact that much of our system of mass communication is privately owned does not mean that it has no public role or responsibility beyond disseminating its owners' views of events, or that the mass of private citizens' freedom of expression is best guaranteed by placing media firms beyond regulation. It is not legitimate in a democracy to sell utilities such as political influence, and it is a noxious idea that the agenda of democratic institutions and electorates should be governed by nonaccountable private interests.

One theme in the discussion of the relevant caselaw in Chapters 3 through 5 will be this question of how the *separate* claims of speech and of liberty should be weighed in the context of citizen expression. In that discourse one of the few comments on the social consequences of excluding citizens from speaking roles in the mass media was given in U.S. Supreme Court Justice Brennan's eloquent dissent in a 1973 case denying American citizens the right to purchase broadcast advertising (considered in detail in Chapter 4):

> The failure to provide adequate means for groups and individuals to bring new issues or ideas to the attention of the public explains, at least to some extent, the development of new media to convey unorthodox, unpopular, and new ideas. Sit-ins and demonstrations testify to...the inability to secure access to the conventional means of reaching and changing public opinion. [By] the bizarre and unsettling nature of his technique, the demonstrator hopes to arrest and divert attention long enough to compel the public to ponder his message.[32]

This is a variant of the argument from peaceful social change. According to Justice Brennan the inequality of public opportunities for expression in the mass media was part of the explanation for the high levels of political confrontation and civil disobedience the Court was then witnessing. Brennan was prepared (more than any of the other Justices) to enlarge the public function of the privately owned media in order to preserve the continuity of legal authority (the 'Rule of Law') and ensure that the legal conditions for peaceful social change were in place.

Brennan found authority in Mill for his view that the law, since antiquity, has required citizen access to the public forum of expression as a

---

[32] *Columbia Broadcasting System, Inc. v. Democratic National Committee*, 412 U.S. 94 [1973], Brennan dissenting, note 27.

condition of its own legitimacy. Mill, discussing Roman jurisprudence (in *On Liberty*), describes Cicero's forensic methods in this way:

> Nor is it enough that he should hear the arguments of adversaries from his own teachers, presented as they state them, and accompanied by what they offer as refutations. That is not the way to do justice to the arguments, or bring them into real contact with his own mind. *He must be able to hear them from persons who actually believe them; who defend them in earnest and do their very utmost for them.*[33]

[33] Mill (1859/1971, p. 47; emphasis added).

Chapter 2

Critical Perspectives on Law and Communication

Chapter 1 examined the liberal-democratic arguments for state protection of citizen expression. It was argued that, although encoding convincing and even noble value premises, these fundamental principles of liberal political philosophy and jurisprudence didn't seem to account for jurists' actual decisions in mass media cases. The failure of fact and norm to coincide is so systematic in this area that it requires further analysis: why do citizens in capitalist democracies, with their elaborate communicative infrastructures, not have the discursive rights necessary—by *liberal* theory—to effective self-government?

Critical perspectives on liberal-democratic social formations substitute historical analysis of the organizations of civil society and the state for the ahistorical—and thus formally idealist—assumptions of liberal political theory. Such approaches have in common a functional analysis of the role of economic (or allocative) relations and practices in the determination of cultural and political relations and practices. Of course, both the state institutions of law and the civil institutions of communication contain both allocative *and* ideological practices, and the analysis of the structure, function, and interaction of these institutions is consequently replete with complexity and tension.

This chapter is organized into two main sections: first, a summary of several critical perspectives on the jurisprudence of a capitalist social formation, exploring the relation of bourgeois legal institutions to the system of commodity exchange; then a look at the concrete historical forces that, Marxist writers argue, have shaped commercial communications organizations and practices. The second section reviews some critical perspectives on the specific property and exchange relations obtaining in the mass media sector.

In critical theories of law, rights—in the present case, speech rights—are conferred on 'legal persons' by the state and not by 'natural justice.' The common claim of these approaches is that the pattern by which rights are distributed is better explained by reference to innovations in commodity production and concomitant changes in property relations and class power than by considerations of moral claim. A critique of the liberal notion of *rights* is thus initiated here (and revisited in the concluding chapter). In a sense the example of mass media speech rights serves simply as a contemporary and illustrative case in point for this general critique of rights. But this is a signally *important* case, because, as noted in Chapter 1, rule-making about communications processes plays a central role in *producing* the rules and norms by which other policies are decided.

Capitalist legal ideology, following Althusser,[1] is understood in the discussion that follows as arising in conjunction with, and as formally structured by, the allocative practices of the capitalist mode of production. But in distinction from Althusser (and following Plamenatz[2] and Pashukanis[3]), the argument is aired that legal ideology is a discursive structure that is also *prerequisite* to the capitalist mode of economic production, rather than only a post facto form of appearance of it. This is consonant with Marx's account of the development of the capitalist mode of production:

> Bourgeois society is the most developed and the most complex historic organization of production. The categories which express its relations, the comprehension of its structure, thereby also allow insights into the structure and the relations of production of all the social formations out of whose ruins and elements it built itself up, whose partly still unconquered remnants are carried along with it, whose mere nuances have developed explicit significance within it.[4]

Notwithstanding the materialist critique, the normative flavor of liberal legal discourse on 'rights' must be seen as central to its ability to effect obligation on and consent from citizens: the moral pronouncements of jurists resonate with social power because they *unite* tradition and

---

[1] See, especially, Althusser (1977).

[2] Plamenatz (1963, pp. 274–293).

[3] Pashukanis (1978).

[4] Marx (1858/1973, pp. 104–105).

current practice. Dissident individuals confront a system in which ethical norm, economic interest and coercive force are powerfully unified through the mutual accommodations of state and market. In this context individuals have every incentive to question and redefine their *own* values in conformity with it. But full acquiescence to capitalist relations then requires—one could almost say 'legally requires'—that social actors understand their unequal economic relations as just, and therefore the allocative function of liberal law is in permanent tension and contradiction with its ideological function. Its ideological function is to secure consent to (or the recognition of justice in) capitalist property relations; its allocative function is to continually redefine those relations in conformity with the developing requirements of the capitalist economy as a whole. This conflict is expressed in the critical literature on law as a debate between *class instrumentalist* and *economic determinist* positions.

An identical tension between economic and political functions is played out in the institutions of mass communication. The second section of this chapter begins with a brief examination of the historical development of the mass media, addressing the conditions of development of media firms in exchange-oriented markets and focusing on their role in linking production and consumption: their *distributive* function. This is followed by a more extended review of some recent and relevant exchanges between Marxist researchers in the political economy of mass communication. Known as the *Blindspot Debate*, these contributions raise in explicit form in the context of commercial communication the difficult questions of political legitimation, class power, and the allocation of rights already uncovered in the discussion of critical perspectives on the law.

LAW, CIVIL SOCIETY, AND THE RELATIONS OF PRODUCTION

> The aim [of the State] is always that of... adapting the 'civilization' and the morality of the broadest popular masses to the necessities of the continuous development of the economic apparatus of production.... But how will each single individual succeed in incorporating himself into the collective man, and how will educative pressure be applied to single individuals so as to obtain their consent and their collaboration, turning necessity and coercion into 'freedom'?[5]

[5] Gramsci (1971, p. 242).

Marx and Engels: Law as a Reflection of the Relations of Production

For Marx, it was in the destruction of feudal European society with its various 'estates'—each with its own economic and political role and characteristic internal rules of obligation, ownership, succession, and so on—that 'civil society' emerged, with its emphasis on the individual and its radically new conception of individual, privately transferable property. In this atomized social environment the law was thought by Marx to acquire several new and important roles: it provided the major link between the individual and the community, it secured the coherent functioning of the emerging urban market, and it removed and abstracted the institutions of the state ('political society') from responsibility for the conflict and immiseration generated by capitalist relations of production.[6]

Marx and Engels described the institutions of law as fully within the ideological 'superstructure' of a social formation, a 'reflection' of the 'real' relationships between people which obtained and were given their form in economic production. The feudal mode of production, for example, was seen as 'organically' linked to (or 'giving rise to') its characteristically local, informal, and customary rules of tenure, inheritance, and obligation. This was contrasted with the capitalist mode of production, in which the bonds of communal tradition, first at work, later in the family, are broken and replaced by the relations of atomized individuals to impersonal and 'neutral' mechanisms of state and market, and are 'reflected' in law in a vast panoply of legal rules and codes and an elaboration of professional roles and specialized courts and other institutional structures (notably the public prisons and police).

Marx and Engels's writings on law were ambiguous on such questions as whether there could also be reciprocal effects of the 'superstructure' on the 'base'; of how direct and hydraulic the mode of production's determination of the law might be (as against the 'relative autonomy' of legal institutions[7]); or of whether 'uneven development' as between different areas of law and economy was possible, and if so, what its effects might be.[8] But both in their early and their later writings they strongly asserted the primary causal force of productive relations on legal and political practices. This view is clearly stated in a well-known passage from one of Marx's relatively later (1859) works:

---

[6] See Marx and Engels (1975, p. 89). See Marx, (1971).

[7] Althusser (1977).

[8] For an extended study of the Marx-Engels texts on these questions see Phillips (1980). Phillips shows that, in their explicit writings on *law*, Marx and Engels were more forceful in asserting an 'economic determinist' argument than in some of their other writings. This ambiguity is visible, for example, in the quote from Marx (1858/1972) above.

> In the social production of their existence, men inevitably enter into definite relations, which are independent of their will, namely relations of production appropriate to a given stage in the development of their material forces of production. The totality of these relations of production constitutes the economic structure of society, the real foundation, on which arises a legal and political superstructure and to which correspond definite forms of social consciousness. The mode of production of the material life conditions the general process of social, political and intellectual life. It is not the consciousness of men that determines their existence but their social existence that determines their consciousness.... [C]hanges in the economic foundation lead sooner or later to the transformation of the whole immense superstructure. In studying such transformations it is always necessary to distinguish between material transformation of the economic conditions of production, which can be determined with the precision of natural science, and the legal, political, religious, artistic or philosophic—in short, ideological forms in which men become conscious of this conflict and fight it out.[9]

Collins[10] points out four conceptual problems in the original economic determinist position on law:

1. It offers "no analysis of the relation between law and other social institutions—all parts of the superstructure are characterized as a direct reflection of the mode of production."
2. It contains "no explanation of *why* law is needed to express the relations of production."
3. "The role of law in controlling relations *outside* the processes of production is not addressed." There is no "detailed explanation of the mechanisms by which social practices are transformed into legal systems....Crude materialist theories of law aim to demonstrate that there are constraints of functional compatibility or correspondence between legal rules and modes of production. In this task they are moderately successful as long as their account is restricted to laws intimately bound up in the relations of production."[11]
4. A "deeper problem" in 'crude materialist' theories of law, for Collins, is that they contain no explanation of "how conscious action is determined by the material base."

Lenin and Class Instrumentalism

Many members of the following generation of Marxist theorists, most notably Lenin, focused on the *class* character of the state and of the legal

---

[9] Marx (1971, 20–21).

[10] Collins (1984, pp. 23–25).

[11] On this point see also Phillips (1980, 187–199).

apparatus. The function of the law was seen as identical to the function of the state: the suppression of subordinate class interests by the ruling class. Conflicts between the interests in a class-divided society, seen as inevitable by Marxists, raised the problem of explaining the *stability* of the social order and the relative infrequency with which these structural conflicts of class interest were internally resolved by directly coercive measures. The 'class instrumentalist' view understood law as a consciously employed tool for the domination of society by that group—the 'ruling class'—who occupy a privileged place in the relations of production: the ownership of the means of production. 'Class instrumentalism' postulated that, rather than some unexplained, unconscious and 'organic' link between the relations of economic production and the ideational forms produced in other social institutions, the members of the ruling class used—and had to use—the surplus of wealth and power which accrued from their privileged place in the relations of production to secure political control over other social classes. "In short, the economic base determines the legal superstructure, not instantaneously and mechanically, but through a process of class rule in which the participants further their interests through the legal system."[12]

This mode of explanation, sometimes under the rubric of 'conflict theory,' has attracted much support among modern Marxist theorists of law. In its more forceful variants it asserts that law always serves the direct and planned interests of the ruling class, is always therefore a coercive institution whose function is the suppression of other social classes, and is effective because it is backed up by the more overt coercion of military force. This version of Marxist theory on law provided a much more direct route for criticism of liberal theories of law. In these, as I have noted in the last chapter, the authority of law is supposed to derive from its disinterested and neutral adjudication of a system of rules which apply equally and fairly to all, and which proceeds from the recognition of a set of original and ahistorical personal rights vested in every (legally recognized) individual. Class instrumentalism contests this view of law by insisting that the evocation of equal and individual rights simply preserves the existing relations of production, privileges of wealth and power, and class structure of society through a set of ancillary social institutions whose claim to independence from ruling class control is wholly specious. (It also concentrates wonderfully the attention of jurists on the cogency of governments' claimed needs for legal sanctions against revolutionary speech.)

Collins[13] finds that the class instrumentalist view offers solutions to the three problems he found in the economic reductionist model. First, "it

[12] Collins (1984, p. 29).

[13] Collins (1984, p. 30).

supplies a description of the links between different parts of the superstructure...[by] securing the interests of the ruling class [along with] the state and the military forces." "Second, there is a clear view of the functions of law in terms of coercion to back up rules which serve the interests of the dominant class."

> Finally...the mechanism linking the material base with the legal superstructure is pinpointed. The determining force of the relations of production upon the conscious acts of legislation is provided theoretically by the concept of a social class. If it is historically true that the dominant social class, that is a group in a special position in the relations of production, has always pursued its interest by using the legal process instrumentally, then it follows that the material base does indirectly determine the content of law.[14]

Two substantial problems remain. If class instrumentalists assert that the laws which are enacted are those which advance the interests of the dominant class, are they implying that members of the dominant class are all more or less perfectly prescient and in agreement about what measures best serve their long-term interests, *as defined by historical materialism*? If so, how did they acquire this absolute knowledge and collective unity of intention (especially given their traditional hostility to Marxist accounts of the dynamics of class-divided societies)? Or, equally problematic, are they merely asserting that the laws enacted by the dominant class serve their *perceived* self-interest? If so, could accumulated misapprehension of their 'real' interests lead to a system of legal rules which were poorly articulated to their base of privilege in the relations of economic production, and even *undermined* this privileged position?

Secondly, there is the great difficulty of *defining* the relations of production without resort to the notion of law:

> The crucial process of the extraction of surplus value from labour could not occur without a reliable framework of rules similar to the contract of employment....There is the problem of defining the relations of production so that they do not include significant elements of the superstructure....It is impossible to maintain that the material base determines the form and content of the legal superstructure when the material base is itself composed of law.[15]

---

[14] Collins (1984, p. 30).

[15] Collins (1984, pp. 33–34). The same thing can of course be said of *other* 'superstructural' institutions: public educational institutions, for example, prepare the labor force to perform the tasks demanded by employers, and stream individuals into the training their class roles will require. Can the relations of production be defined so as to exclude this practical formation of productive labor?

Both of these caveats about the class instrumentalist view of law raise again the problem of consciousness: in the first case the question 'How does the ruling class know how to rule?'; in the second case, 'How are the relations of economic production to be accounted for without reference to the prior ideological function of law?'

Gramsci and Class Struggle in the Superstructure

Gramsci, often described as the germinal Marxist "theorist of the superstructure," had a lively appreciation of the role of the institutions of law and politics (and of schools, press, party, church, and the other 'superstructural' institutions) in the continuing development of the productive forces in a capitalist system. Gramsci's strategies for revolutionary change (he was an early leader of the Italian CP) focused on ideological struggle in, and working-class domination of the 'superstructural' institutions of civil society. (It is worth noting that his use of the term *civil society* was different from Marx's in inferring not only the 'private' and nonstate sphere of relations, but also the possibility in that sphere of developing nonalienated, self-regulating social and political organizations.[16])

Gramsci described law as having two specific and closely-related roles:

> Through 'law' the State renders the ruling group homogeneous, and tends to create a social conformism which is useful to the ruling group's line of development.[17]
>
> If every State tends to create and maintain a certain type of civilization and of citizen (and hence of collective life and of individual relations), and to eliminate certain customs and attitudes and to disseminate others, then the Law will be its instrument for this purpose.[18]

For Gramsci the role of law was always an *educative* one, though this was always a "negative and repressive" education.[19] It had only two subjects on its curriculum. The first was the 'elimination of certain customs and attitudes and dissemination of others,' that is to say, the suppression of resistance to the expansion of capital into new sectors of commodity exchange, replacing use-value-oriented types of production. The second was the 'creation of social conformism' along lines to which the dominant class can also subscribe, that is, the articulation of a moral

---

[16] Gramsci, (1971, pp. 12–13; 210–276).
[17] (p. 195).
[18] (p. 246).
[19] (p. 258).

justification for the existing relations of production at every stage of development of the capitalist mode of production.

Gramsci's perspective on the 'ruling group's' hold on state power and the law was different from Lenin's. In his view the importance in an *advanced capitalist* polity of winning the *consent* of the subordinate classes to the further development of market relations rendered the direct rule of the capitalist class ambiguous. Gramsci was not directly challenging Lenin's views, for his analysis was focused on the revolutionary conditions in urbanized, industrialized states. Rather than naked class instrumentalism, he hypothesized that, in developed capitalist countries, the ruling class ruled—and enacted its laws—so as to meet *some* of the *real interests* of subordinate classes who had been recruited as allies (e.g., professionals). Retaining overall, long-term control over the direction of a national economy by this method required that the immediate interests of particular dominant class elements must sometimes be sacrificed to the needs (economic or ideological) of the 'hegemonic alliance' or 'bloc.' His revolutionary strategy was to construct and cement a new 'historic bloc' through class struggle within the institutions of the superstructure as a part of, rather than a postscript to, the transformation of capitalist relations of production.

If we refer back to the criticisms that were raised by Collins about Lenin's 'class instrumentalist' view of law, we can discern some responses in Gramsci's arguments. In response to the question 'How does the ruling class know how to rule?' he says that the capitalist ruling class's interest is known by the *direction of development* of market relations. In response to the question of how the relations of production are to be defined, he proposes they *are defined in law* to include the representation of ruling class interests as *moral* relations.

In Gramsci's view the entire capitalist social formation is an "ensemble of relations" with complex reciprocal influences between the institutions of base and superstructure, and with a class character rooted in the capitalist mode of production but stabilized and perpetuated by bourgeois dominance of the superstructure. Denial of obligation and consent by a class alliance led by the workers and peasants, and their development of a superstructure that redefines and legitimates new relations of production that better reflect their interests, are the key to the destabilization and overthrow of capitalism. Gramsci concludes that, if law *did* ever manage to express the real interests of the popular classes (as claimed by liberal legal theory), it would disappear:

> A class claiming to be capable of assimilating the whole of society, and which was at the same time really able to express such a process, would perfect this conception of the State and of law, so as to conceive the end of the State and

of law—rendered useless since they will have exhausted their function and will have been absorbed by civil society.[20]

Cohen's Defense of Determination by the Base

Subsequent Marxist theorizing about law and its institutions has continued to focus on questions of 'base and superstructure': Are laws 'expressions,' ('reflections,' etc.) of the relations of capitalist production? Or do legal institutions and practices exert their own determining forces on economic relations? Are laws in fact superstructural, or do they embody rules and norms prerequisite to capitalist production? One point of debate turns upon the analysis of the appearance and recognition in law of *new* market relations. (This coincides with Gramsci's emphasis on the relation of law to the "line of development" of market relations.) It is apparent that not all types of commodity exchange are initially 'legal' but may in the first instance be extralegal, illegal, or even coercive and illegal. It is also apparent that many new processes and products give rise to extensive litigation over property rights.[21] Does the law's retroactive sanction of new coercive or exploitive economic relations show it to be, after all, a simple 'reflection' of the economic base? (And how does it then come to encode a *moral* consensus?)

Gerald Cohen gives a strong modern account of the base/superstructure model.[22] Cohen examines the Marxist claim that the noneconomic institutions of a social formation constitute a 'superstructure' in that they are explicable in function and form by their relationships to the economic 'base.' While leaving aside the question of whether *ideology* is uniquely part of the superstructure, Cohen makes the institutions of *law* central to his analysis. Cohen studies the treatment of the notion of property rights in Marx's texts. He observes that the particular relations of production of a capitalist mode of production seem, in Marx's account, necessarily to include the *legal* relations of which property rights are composed.

Cohen postulates that the legal concept of a *right* is inadequate to the accurate description of productive relations, explaining Marx's own use of the legal terminology of property rights by suggesting that "there was no

---

[20] Gramsci (1971, p. 260). On this point, see also Plamenatz (1962, pp. 351–387); Marx (1971).

[21] For a telling historical example in the field of communication property rights see Edelman, (1979). The international turmoil in the area of intellectual property rights attending the development of the computer software industry furnishes numerous contemporary examples.

[22] Cohen (1978).

attractive alternative. Ordinary language lacks a developed apparatus for describing production relations in a rechtsfrei manner."[23] Cohen suggests a substitution of the term *power* for the term *right* in describing the relations of production, and further suggests that the coincidence of *legal* rights with *effective* power *stabilizes* productive relations, which are often organized in the first instance by coercion, and not by normative consensus. In (and only in) a law-abiding society, legal rights may appear to precede production relations: an individual's economic power is effective because it is legal. But the *structure* of rights in such a society "obtains because it secures a matching structure of [economic] powers," and is therefore, actually and logically, an ex post facto form of their appearance.[24] Cohen is thus able to defend the base/superstructure model with respect to the institutions of law by his assertion that "bases need superstructures":

> Might without right may be impossible, inefficient, or unstable. Powers over productive forces are a case in point. Their exercise is less secure when it is not legal. So, for efficiency and good order, production relations require the sanction of property relations. Hence men fight, successfully, to change the law so that it will legitimate powers they either have or perceive to be within their grasp, and lawmakers alter the law to relieve actual or potential strain between it and the economy.... If production relations require legal expression for stability, it follows that the foundation requires a superstructure.[25]

Cohen examines the appearance of coercive force along the same lines: just as law "can look more fundamental than the economy,"[26] so too can coercion appear to underlie the structure of the economy. But both law and coercion function, for Cohen, to *sustain* the precedence of market development and expanded exchange over traditional rights in a capitalist mode of production:

> when productive forces 'come into conflict' with property relations it is because the forces conflict with the production relations those property relations formulate and protect. The solution is either a change in production relations in violation of the law, with the law later falling into line, or a change in law which facilitates a change in production relations. History is full of both solutions.[27]

---

[23] Cohen (1978, p. 224).
[24] (p. 232).
[25] (p. 231).
[26] (p. 233).
[27] (p. 234).

Pashukanis and the Commodity-Exchange Theory of Law

The Soviet jurist Pashukanis, writing in the period after the Russian Revolution, was the only Marxist to attempt a positive theory of law,[28] all other Marxist theorists (sampled above) taking as their task its criticism. Pashukanis was convinced of the vital and autonomous role of law in a capitalist social formation. He argued that widespread and automatic respect for rights, most importantly property rights, was so crucial for the operation of a system of commodity exchange, with its built-in centrifugal conflicts of interests, that the legal system acquired central importance and had to be understood in terms of its own specific practices.[29]

The central feature of bourgeois law, in Pashukanis' view, was its recognition (in legal discourse and by the activity of legal institutions) of autonomous individuals defined by their *possessions*. The focus of law on the individual as the possessor of *rights* (possessions acquired from the State), and its enforcement as necessary of mutual recognition of rights produces, in civil society, a strong vindication of the autonomy of the individual. This authoritative description of the individual person as recognized by the state legitimates, reinforces and extends the atomized relations between people in commodity production.

For Pashukanis legal institutions have their own structure, which corresponds, but is not reducible, to the structure of capitalist production. In the same sense in which the *commodity* is the *form* in which the products of capitalist production appear, the *form* of bourgeois law is visible in its production of *rights*. Rights are then produced by the legal system, in response to each development of the productive forces and the relations of production, to secure real and prior relations of *possession*. The rights thus created by courts and legislatures make the relations of production effective because they are themselves *forms of property* bestowed equally on all citizens. In a mode of production in which social identity is constituted by (unequal) possession, the possession of rights *as* property secures the identity and consent of each juridical subject.

Paul Hirst points out that Pashukanis' theory of law is similar in structure to Locke's.[30] For Locke, rights are derived from an a priori law of nature, apprehended by human beings through their use of 'natural reason':

---

[28] Pashukanis (1978). See also Balbus (1977); Cotterell (1976).

[29] See also Althusser (1977).

[30] Hirst (1979, pp.157–163). The relevant text from Locke is the *Second Treatise of Government*. And for another influential derivation of legal right from 'natural' possession, see also Hegel (1820/1967).

> human beings are created by God and are His property; *as such* they are forbidden to injure one another, since to do so is to violate God's right of possession. Law, apparently founded on God's will, is based on property right.[31]

Locke theorizes that God has granted human beings dominion over the earth and the free use of their own attributes and capacities, including their labor and the products of their labor. But government and law, which protect their rights to the products of their labor and enforce their obligations to respect the equivalent rights of others, are derived from the status of human beings as God's property and their origin as the fruits of His labor. In this interpretation God is the original possessive individual: His identity (along with everyone else's) is secured by the ownership of property, and we are His property-agents.

Thus, says Hirst, both Locke and Pashukanis conceive of law as the recognition of a prior state of property ownership: for Locke, the 'state of nature' given by God; and for Pashukanis the relations of production given by capitalism. In both theories these prior conditions of property ownership are the origin of particular subjective identities: the subject is constituted by, respectively, God's labor, or her own labor under determinate social conditions. In both theories law confirms that subjects' identities originate in the possession of property, and produces their minimally necessary possession of themselves—by producing their *rights*.

* * *

In the foregoing critical perspectives on law two modes of explanation predominate: law is understood variously as the regulation of individual property and economic activity, or as the regulation of the struggle between classes, which, in Marxist theory, the private ownership of productive property inaugurates. In some instances these modes of explanation are combined in a single theoretical approach (e.g., Gramsci's) and in other instances they are in competition (as between the *class instrumentalist* and *commodity-exchange* theories of law). These different approaches were reviewed, not so that we might choose between them—for I believe all of them make a distinct contribution to understanding the phenomenon of law—but to underline the complexity of the law's social functions and its linkages to the other institutions of base and superstructure. In fact what emerges most clearly from reviewing them together is perhaps the futility of choosing definitively between the models they offer. For can we say that Gramsci, for example—the 'theorist of the superstructure'—has in any sense displaced the role of property relations

---

[31] Hirst (1979, p. 158). See also Macpherson (1962).

in the organization of class struggle? Or that Cohen, who defends the notion of 'determination by the base,' is able to do so without relying on the notion of class power?

These two modes of explanation are useful in different ways. In the first—the various analyses of the functional relation of civil law to the operation of the economy—the law was theorized to encode the existing conditions under which production takes place, to give expression to particular relations of production and roles *in* production. Here the expression of the relations of production in the *form of rights* is a consequence of its function, as ideology, *within* economic production. In the second mode of explanation the function of law is explicitly related to the function of the *state* as instrument of class rule: criminal law, especially, is the "form in which individual and collective acts of resistance by the subordinate classes are repressed."[32] It is not necessary to collapse ideological and coercive functions together to recognize that civil and criminal law may both have a functional relation to the operation of the capitalist mode of production.

In the area of constitutional law of communication the former function of law—as ideological condition of development of the economy—is salient, in my judgment (at least in the chosen context of contemporary North America). But this is by no means its *exclusive* function. As in the critical literature on law, the critical literature on communication contains much spirited debate over the relative explanatory power of class instrumentalist and commodity-exchange perspectives. The next section concludes our theoretical preparation by exploring some critical views on the economic organization and political function of the mass communications media.

THE POLITICAL ECONOMY OF MEDIA ORGANIZATIONS

Consumer Sovereignty and Demand Management

Free enterprise economists like to speak of the 'utility-maximizing behavior of self-interested individuals' as the appropriate motor of wealth-creation and public policy alike. On the production side, since capitalism is organized explicitly for the maximization of surplus, the efficient capitalist will seek, not the greatest correspondence of production and need, but the stationing of capital where it will expand the fastest. The

[32] Hirst (1979, p. 97).

same force, translated on the consumption side as 'consumer sovereignty,' is said to automatically result in the close correspondence of production and need without public planning or incentive (the 'invisible hand' of the market). Competition among profit-seeking producers to satisfy consumers will drive investment where consumers' purchasing behavior has dictated.

Enterprises in a true laissez-faire market are potentially in competition for everything: for clients and market share, loan capital and shareholders, skilled personnel and cheap labor, favorable locations and regulations, raw materials supplies and technological advantage. Only continual growth guarantees that a firm will be able to compete in all these areas.

They are in competition for all these utilities, because they must seek a surplus, not by increasing prices, but by reducing their factor costs for each product below the costs of competing products. In general, factor costs are most effectively reduced by growth in the rate and scale of production. Failure to achieve a surplus prevents growth, which in turn impedes the ability to reduce factor costs, and so on in an expanding or contracting spiral of exchange. There is no 'steady-state'—there is only growth and survival, or weakened competitive positions leading to assimilation into other firms, or business failure.[33]

Thus, as Gerald Cohen shows,[34] a capitalist economy has an inherent bias towards increased output. The expansion of production so efficiently brought about in a capitalist economy cannot lead to an equilibrium state of output and an equitable reduction in necessary toil as the economy reaches the point of reliably meeting basic needs (however defined). Since cessation of growth would cause a flight of capital, which would bankrupt debt-financed firms, and at least seriously damage equity-financed firms, it would collapse the economy and *halt* production. To prevent such a collapse, output (whether considered from a macro- or a microeconomic perspective) must continually be expanded, and therefore consumption must also continually increase.

Market firms see both natural resources and nonmarket practices as the source of labor and materials (including cultural materials) for the manufacture of commodities. Nonmarket cultures are also important potential commodity sales markets. But nonmarket practices may also form a barrier against the extension of the market. Even in developed

---

[33] Of course, as Theodore Levitt (1960, p. 56) suggests, "mere survival is a so-so aspiration.... The trick is... to feel the surging impulse of commercial mastery... the visceral feel of entrepreneurial greatness. A vigorous leader is driven onward by his own pulsating will to succeed. He has to have a vision of grandeur, a vision that can produce eager followers in vast numbers. In business, the followers are the customers."

[34] Cohen (1978, pp. 297–326).

market cultures law and government policy (e.g., policies to promote agricultural or energy self-sufficiency, cultural subsidies, protection of religious observances, minority language rights) may constitute significant barriers to output expansion and growth. Communications firms are the cutting edge for the penetration of market practices into new cultural contexts, and the expansion of established markets.[35]

The keystone in the architecture of neoclassical economic theory is the notion of the utility-maximizing consumer. The modern consumer was 'invented' during the crisis of overproduction in the capitalist countries in the Great Depression of the late 1800s, and was the new basis of industry thinking by the late 1920s.[36] Although urbanization, advances in transportation and machine processes, and other aspects of 19th-century industrialization had already brought enormous increases in the rate and scale of output of industrially produced commodities, and were accompanied to a degree by lower unit costs, these new conditions only exacerbated the conflict between labor and capital. The new scale of production was not matched by the low-paid industrial workforce's scale of consumption, and the resulting cyclical stagnation in domestic demand led to a severe depression in the 1890s, and a war (1914–1918) over the control of markets.

The industrial countries made use of the cheap labor of their populations in this period, but in a sense finished industrial commodities had not yet fully penetrated their working-class *cultures*. Although industrial techniques had long since been applied to 'carriage-trade' markets, household remanufacturing of basic commodities into finished goods for direct use—lumber and nails into housing, textiles into clothing, flour into bread—was also routine among the masses of rural agricultural and urban industrial laborers and their families. Also, the household economy often dealt with cyclical unemployment in the industrial economy by retaining features of the 'putting-out' system, in which part of the family's collective labor went into independent craft production.[37] The continuing educative and regulatory roles of the church in the early period of industrialization reflected the continuation of early and precapitalist modes of community life and organization existing side by side with the industrial state.[38]

---

[35] See, for example, Schiller (1980, p. 299), Fejes (1981, p. 281), and Boyd-Barrett (1982, p. 174).

[36] See Ewen (1976). The original statement of this industrial strategy is Edward Bernays (1928).

[37] See Brown and Harrison (1978) for an analysis of the European transition; for an excellent treatment of U.S. industrialization, see Braverman (1974).

[38] See Kemp (1969), Mathias (1969).

But in the mass media, industry found the means of extending its rationalization of the production process outside the factory and into the home and the community. The first tool of this generalization of market relations was the existing newspaper publishing industry, and film, radio, and TV were appropriated to these purposes as they appeared. Newspapers in particular were markedly transformed by commercial pressure, evolving from limited-circulation organs of partisan political opinion into mass-appeal vehicles for the distribution of market information and the brand-name messages of the nascent advertising industry.[39] The immediate payoff to all industry from this new use of the media was the prospect of managed, rationalized, controlled demand for a growing range of industrial products.[40] If demand for this vast diversification of goods could be predictably generated at a level which matched the productive capacity of industry, investment risks would be drastically reduced, and virtually limitless new markets created *within* the existing industrial economies.

Through the massive propagation of their new vision of an industrial cornucopia flowing endlessly into the lives and homes of workers-become-consumers (backed up by a huge expansion of the credit mechanism, and underpinned by the massive development of state institutions of education) the leaders of industry effectively transformed *workers* into *consumers*, in terms of their social identity. The replacement of domestic production of household goods and family and community-based forms of recreation with market goods and entertainments provided industry with its needed market growth. The commercial sponsorship of entertainment spectacles, and the recruitment of schools and other public institutions to boosting the new norms of consumption, also inflected consumption itself with patriotic significance. The mass media, then, were the key to forming consumers who not only knew what, where, and for what price new commodities were available, but were also equipped with a vision of the part they could play in living a satisfying social and personal life.

In its very origins the popular culture of the marketplace drew workers and their families into the market process, not only in their working hours, but also in their consumption and recreation activities. This now well-tested process continues apace in the ongoing extension of market practices in the less developed nations, and also in the continuing intensification of the media environment in the developed world.[41]

---

[39] Ewen (1976), Hartley (1982); Dyer (1982).

[40] "Commercial propaganda is part and parcel of the mass-production process.... Business could no more operate without advertising than it could without the automatic machine or the assembly line." (McGarry, 1958, p. 139). For an extended treatment of demand management see Galbraith (1985).

[41] See references supra, note 35.

Through their role in the distribution of commodities, the mass media themselves have become leading sectors of profit and growth in the civilian economy, and this has triggered further intensification of the media environment as media capitalists' own market competition heats up.

The media sector has become one of the most profitable because of its unique function as a factor in production. Media firms are not the direct producers of the physical goods they help distribute through advertising: they are part of the apparatus of distribution, or circulation of goods, in this way somewhat like railways or shipping lines. But "in so far as circulation itself creates costs... it appears as itself included within the production process."[42] As the number of consumers (and the geographic scale of the market) for a given product rises, its unit cost of factory production drops, and therefore the relative proportion of the total costs of the delivered product taken up by its distribution, including media costs, rises. Moreover, increasing geographic scale dampens the *velocity* of circulation, and the concomitant inventory costs and risks of stranded investment are best offset by *predictable* demand, again secured by media and information-gathering (and other marketing and distribution) expenditures.

But *unlike* the distributive economics of railways and shipping lines, the saturation of a market with similar products also increases the media costs of distribution in absolute terms, as producers struggle *in the media* to maintain their low factory costs (or other advantages) by maintaining or increasing consumer allegiance and market share. Marx clearly perceived the *distributive* function of the communications sector, but was silent (understandably, given the period in which he worked) concerning the relation of this function to the struggle for attitudinal and behavioral influence in the marketplace:

> The creation of the physical conditions of exchange—of the means of communication and transport—the annihilation of space by time—becomes an extraordinary necessity.... Only in so far as the direct product can be realized in distant markets in mass quantities in proportion to reductions in the transport costs, and only in so far as the means of communication and transport themselves can yield spheres of realization for labour, driven by capital; only in so far as commercial traffic takes place in massive volume—in which more than necessary labour is replaced—only to that extent is production of cheap means of communication and transport a condition of production based on capital, and promoted by it *for that reason.*[43]

---

[42] Marx (1858/1972, p. 524).

[43] Pp. 524–525; emphasis in original.

Instrument of Expanded Circulation, or Ideological Apparatus of Class Rule?

The communications sector has in part a *distributive* economic function, and this function can readily be perceived as achieving proportionately greater importance in capitalist markets at each new stage of their geographic growth and regional and international integration. This is the central role of communications firms at the *extensive* margin of the market. The development of mass communication is also the key to the continuation of market growth at the *intensive* margin of the market: each *intensification* of the market—each further commoditization of experience—must overcome barriers that are in essence not so much geographic as they are cultural and communicational. Here the distinction between *production* and *distribution* becomes more ambiguous. If one of the classes of *products* distributed by the media consists of persuasive messages directed at altering the attitudes and behavior of audience members, then it is perhaps itself a sector of production, albeit production of a unique kind.

This question of the media's possible function as a direct instrument of opinion management has been addressed by Herbert Schiller in a manner that takes into account the analysis in the last section. Schiller argues that the continuing development of communications technologies, which furnish "the most up-to-date means, in a long historical process of mechanization, to achieving an edge in world-wide competition"[44] may decisively change the relation between the private power of corporations and the public power of the state. Schiller's analysis suggests that through the expansion of the communication and information sectors a global transformation is taking place in the relation between the economic sphere of the production and circulation of goods, and the traditionally nonvalorized areas of politics, law, and cultural expression. In his more recent work[45] he develops this line of inquiry to take account of crisis indicators—investment, employment, interest rates, trade balances, and capacity utilization rates—explaining government and corporate policy in the communications sector within the frame of large-scale economic crisis management and planning. The media do function, in Schiller's analysis, as agents of political legitimation. But, although this function has been considered in a large number of other studies, it is significant in Schiller's treatment that he models the media as *profitable* agents of legitimation.

It is widely argued in the critical literature of communications that legitimation—the consent of the plurality of working, enfranchised cit-

---

[44] Schiller (1981, p. 140).

[45] Schiller (1986).

izens to elite agenda—is a *product* directly manufactured in the mass media. For example, Chomsky and Herman[46] present voluminous evidence of corporate and state intervention in the agenda of the media. By a combination of misinformation and missing information citizens are manipulated, in this view, towards electoral support for the dominant order. Deviating points of view are held to be actively suppressed. But despite the evidence that such manipulations do take place during specific crises, this robustly class-instrumentalist model significantly fails to address, first, the real "normal" day-to-day activities of journalists and editors, and second, the divergent interests and competitive environment of the various 'capitals' who are supposed to have organized this intervention. (It is one of the strengths of Schiller's model that it does account for these objections.)

Tuchman[47] and Gans[48] also offer exemplary analyses relating to the first of these objections. They examine the institutional environment in which political information is produced, and suggest that news is more or less unconsciously encoded by journalists in a manner which reproduces the dominant ideology among their sources. A complementary approach to the study of the media production process is offered by Altheide,[49] who finds that the news gathering and selection routines of most commercial media firms imitate the news reporting practices of *other* media firms. While this is efficient both in terms of costs and in terms of competition for mass audiences, it of course tends to emphasize the apparent importance of whatever is reported. No malevolent intention on the part of journalists, editors or media owners is required, in this model, to end up with the kind of political discourse we have: just the 'invisible hand' of the market. The particular images and texts that reach us as news are then the rational expression of the institutional structure of media enterprises, which in turn conform to the broader requirements of capitalist production: growth and profitability. Elite interpretations of events are the most *cost-effective* ones for media firms.

The second objection to class instrumentalism—the divergent interests of competing capitalists—is partly addressed in Altheide's model, and also by work such as Murdock and Golding's,[50] who focus on the relation of economic power to political power as represented in the composition of national elites. Through their analysis of the structure of ownership and control in the media sector of the economy Murdock and Golding, like

---

[46] See, for example, Chomsky and Herman (1979).

[47] Tuchman (1978).

[48] Gans (1980).

[49] Altheide (1976).

[50] Murdock and Golding (1977, pp. 1243), Murdock (1982, pp. 118–150).

Schiller, are able to make a strong case that media enterprises function quite effectively, *within* the structural constraints of the market, as mouthpieces for the policy initiatives of their owners and executive managers—who tend to be full members of the elites. As such, their competition for profits in no way precludes cooperation in the reproduction of the ideological conditions necessary to the expanded circulation of capital. Murdock approvingly quotes Ralph Miliband to this effect:

> Making money is not at all incompatible with indoctrination... the purpose of the 'entertainment industry', in its various forms, may be profit; but the content of its output is not by any means free from ideological connotations of a more or less definite kind.[51]

The Role of the Audience

Dallas Smythe has offered another way of analyzing the mass media[52] that focuses directly on the *property exchange relations* obtaining within mass communication, rather than on the content, professional routines, or ownership of the media. His project foregrounds the role of the audience in a manner which has attracted controversy; this debate is known as the 'Blindspot' debate, after the title of Smythe's inaugural paper on the subject.[53]

The point of departure for Smythe's theory is the fact that the great bulk of mass communication is supported by revenues from the advertising industry. When radio listeners or TV watchers turn on their sets, they in general are able to receive a variety of program offerings at no charge. Similarly the cost to a reader of a newspaper is less than its cost to the publisher in ink and paper alone: even if the publisher is thought to have sold the *materials* at a loss to the reader, the *contents* of the newspaper are supplied free. Most other media—magazines, cable TV, much public broadcasting, opera, ballet, symphonies, theatre, and film —derive at least part of their revenues from advertising of one sort or another, so that the user receives these texts and programs at less than their delivered cost. Two questions arise: (a) What is the *advertiser* buying? (b) What kind of transaction is taking place between the media firm and its audience members?

Consider the case of free commercial broadcast television. There is no sense in which the audience member can be said to have bought anything but a television set. The media firm itself sells nothing to its audience

---

[51] Murdock and Golding, (1982, p. 144), quoting Miliband (1973, p. 202).

[52] Smythe (1981).

[53] Smythe (1977).

members, receives no revenue from them. There is absolutely no economic transaction between the media firm and the watcher, and there is likewise no contract between them, implied or otherwise. It cannot then be said to be in the business of selling information, or programs, or messages, or even opinions or points of view to audiences: although its programs are very expensive to produce, *it receives absolutely no revenue from their sale* (unless to another broadcaster). The relationship between broadcaster and watcher is, apparently, simply a communicative relationship, not an economic one.

From its advertisers, on the other hand, it receives virtually *all* of its operating revenue. There is an economic transaction, and a contractual relation, between broadcaster and advertiser—something is sold and something is bought. That something, says Smythe, is *audiences*.

Or, more precisely, he says it is *audience power*. The broadcaster's revenue is derived from advertising, and profits are found in the difference between that advertising revenue and the costs of producing (or buying) programming. When, therefore, a commercial TV station produces or buys programming—a movie, for example, or the evening news—and broadcasts it, complete with 10 or 12 minutes of advertising, what product has it brought to the market? What has it produced and sold for more than its cost? Smythe's answer is: It has produced and sold *audience power* to advertisers.

Smythe argues that advanced capitalist economies provide markets for organizations which produce *audience power* as a factor of production in the same way that they provide markets for suppliers of raw materials, machinery, and wage labor power. Mass audiences are the key to the management of consumer (and political) demand, and the commercial mass media are the industry that produces this audience power for sale to other enterprises, mass manufacturing it to customer specification. The audience is itself the commodity produced by commercial media for exchange in the market.

It is easy to show that it is specifically audience power, and not broadcast airtime, that broadcasters sell to advertisers: If you are an ad agency executive placing TV commercials for a soft-drink-manufacturing client, it is not x seconds of airtime that you will be offered, but a choice of audiences of different descriptions (matching your consumer target groups) at x dollars per thousand per second. Because you will pay for the entire metered audience of the commercial, you will choose a time which contains the highest proportion of your targeted audience.

Because the bottom line for the commercial media organization is the revenue it earns from advertisers for access to the audience, it must be able to guarantee the number of audience members in order to compete. And because the advertiser is interested in particular *kinds* of audiences, ones that have the income level and 'lifestyle' characteristics of their expected customer groups (for whom they have carefully constructed their advertising messages), the media firm must also be able to show what kinds of people are in the audience. Audience survey firms, such as Nielson or the Bureau of Broadcast Measurement, provide the reliable and independent means of gathering this vital information from the audience.

The (purely statistical) opportunity for freedom of expression provided by a Nielson survey is admittedly a narrow one, consisting most importantly of the binary message that one is, or is not, attending the medium. But this is precisely the message the media firm, and the advertiser, need in order to proceed with their end of the interaction. The information that targeted groups are continuing to pay attention is sufficient to elicit more reports and programs, and more advertising; and the message that they have ceased to listen, watch or read is sufficient to stimulate a remarkable flurry of program cancellations, secondary research, new programming, and so on. The corollary to the 'right to receive'—precisely capturing the audience's role in commercial mass communication—is the common-sense exhortation: 'If you don't like it, you can always turn it off!'

Without this monitoring of the audience's response (however vegetative), media and advertisers (including political advertisers) would be at a complete loss, not only as to how to price their transaction, but as to whether anything was even being exchanged, economically *or* communicatively. There is a good deal of sophistication in the monitoring, as well. In the case of soap operas, for example, producers may combine ratings and demographic information with the direct responses available from letters and phone calls to aid in the shaping of sequential episodes of a program series. Advertisers also employ open-ended forms of direct interaction with audience members, such as the *focus group*, to assess more creatively the targeted consumer's response to their messages. But if all of this careful 'listening' by media organizations indicates that an insufficiently affluent audience is on the other end of the transmission, the result is to try to evict them from their chairs. Jhally[54] gives an example of this: CBS cancelled a number of prime-time, *high*-ratings programs in the late 1960s, such as "Andy Griffith" and "Ed Sullivan" —because their very large audiences were found to be mostly elderly, rural, and low income.

The debate which followed Smythe's analysis of the *audience commodity* focused on his very provocative notion of *audience work* or *audience power*. Smythe himself has more recently qualified the notion,[55]

---

[54] Jhally (1982, p. 205).
[55] Smythe (1982, pp. 192–200).

emphasizing that the price mechanism between media firms and advertisers—the real site of economic exchange—is the more significant feature of his theory. But some of his interlocutors in the Blindspot Debate, notably Jhally and Livant, have continued to develop the notion of an actual property or activity of the audience that is altered by its valorization in economic exchange. In this view labor's exploitation by capital is, in the media context, capital's appropriation of some of the value to itself of the audience's activity in attending to and acting upon media messages.[56] The economically most important and communicatively most effective messages, according to Smythe's analysis, are those of advertisers, and he adduced data to show that this was so. Jhally's use of Smythe's argument[57] extends an axiology of the work of the audience in a form analogous to Marx's labor theory of value.

The recent tendency of media holding firms to diversify into publishing *and* broadcasting, and into *both* subscriber *and* ad-based media (with likelihood of cross-subsidization at various points), and to hybridize the two, should be noted. The mix of advertising and subscriber revenues is an effective hedge against fluctuations in volatile consumer markets. This strategy of diversification also helps media firms stay current in an environment of rapid and unpredictable technological change (as is emerging, for example, in the convergence of digital image processing, telecommunications, and broadcasting technologies and infrastructures). Cross-ownership has also been explained more straightforwardly[58] as a result of the better rationalization of plant and personnel and vastly easier cost recovery possible for all *chain* media firms (and the fact that, as a consequence of this, there really is nothing more profitable in which media firms could legally invest their often huge profits). Whatever growth strategy mass communication firms pursue, as Smythe points out, audiences make a further contribution to their economies. In the case of broadcasting he shows that, by purchasing and maintaining all of the receiving apparata, audiences contribute by far the largest part to financing the broadcast plant. This contribution is an important factor under present conditions of rapid technical innovation, with its very high capitalization requirements.

In the Blindspot Debate Jhally's and Livant's contributions were speculative elaborations on Smythe's thesis. The sharpest attack, and thus the other side of the debate proper, came from the British doyen of studies in the political-economy of communications, Graham Murdock.[59] Mur-

---

[56] Jhally (1982, 1984); Livant (1979, 1982); Jhally and Livant (1986).

[57] Jhally (1984, pp. 158–198).

[58] Canada, House of Commons (1981).

[59] Murdock (1978).

dock engaged Smythe on the implications of his proposal for theorization of the contemporary relations between base and superstructure within and among the developed capitalist nations.

In his original *Blindspot* article[60] Smythe criticized the Western tradition of marxist analysis for its primary emphasis on the function of the mass media as part of the ideological superstructure and its inattention to the media's integration into the economic base. "The first question that historical materialists should ask about mass communications systems," he says, "is *what economic function for capital do they serve?*"[61] In response Murdock, while crediting the insight and power of Smythe's economic analysis, discerns three "important omissions" from it:

1. "He drastically underestimates the importance and centrality of the state in contemporary capitalism."[62] Murdock suggests that at the same time as falling profitability fuels concentration of ownership in many sectors, including communications, it also causes structural crisis requiring the intervention of the state in economic policy. "The result is an indissoluble but contradictory relationship between the centralized capitalist state on the one hand and concentrated monopoly capital on the other."[63]
2. Murdock asserts that Smythe's attention on the exchange relations between media firms and advertisers leads him to underestimate the *independent* part played by commercial forms of culture in the relay of dominant ideology. He points to the existence of media such as the film, recording, and popular fiction industries, which do *not* rely directly on advertising revenues, as evidence that the media are also "in the business of selling social order and structured inequality and packaging hope and aspiration into legitimate bundles."[64] (He does not, however, give much time to Smythe's argument that these are best understood as elements of a larger system of 'cross-marketing' organized primarily to realize the circulation and expansion of capital.)
3. Murdock also criticizes Smythe on the grounds that he fails to show how class conflicts are played out in the realm of mass communication. Murdock lists demands for national ownership, public interest accountability, and regional and community production objectives for media systems, and struggles between media owners and production

---

[60] Smythe (1977).
[61] (p. 1; emphasis in original).
[62] Murdock (1978, p. 111).
[63] (p. 112).
[64] (p. 113).

personnel, between intellectual and technical workers in the media, and between media firms and citizens' organizations, as some of the indicators of class struggle in communication.

By raising these concerns—the relation of state and economy, the mechanisms of ideological reproduction, and the appearance of class struggle—Murdock takes a class instrumentalist position against what he sees as Smythe's extreme economic determinism. It should be said, however, that Murdock is offering this critique as a corrective, rather than as the embodiment of a full and self-sufficient materialist theory of communication. Here, as in his other work,[65] he has tried to bring the two positions together:

> mass communications systems... play a double role in reproducing capitalist relations of production. They complete the economic circuit on which these relations rest and they relay the ideologies which legitimate them.... Therefore it is not a question of choosing between theories of ideology and theories of political economy, but of finding ways of integrating the two into a more adequate and complete account.[66]

A different point raised by Jhally[67] perhaps goes furthest towards untying this theoretical knot. He asks: who *owns* the audience commodity? This question planted the seed for this study, because the audience's status as commodity is equally a question of law as of economics, in the sense that the commodity *forms* in communications industries must be consonant with the legal *forms* of property rights in communications law to be legitimate and enforceable in civil society.

Jhally's question about ownership was accompanied by an example. In 1971 the CRTC gave cable companies permission to substitute Canadian commercials for the advertisements carried on their U.S. feeders, and in 1973 Rogers Cable Co. began to delete ads from Buffalo station broadcasts.

> Three Buffalo stations immediately threatened legal action.... The Buffalo stations were threatened with the loss of their Canadian audience, meaning that this audience could not be sold to advertisers, thus resulting in a loss of advertising revenue. While the programmes of the American stations would be used to *produce* the audience commodity, the *selling* would be done by Canadian cable operators. As one broadcasting consultant put it: "substitution is plain stealing."[68]

---

[65] Murdock (1982).
[66] Murdock (1978, pp. 113–114).
[67] Jhally (1982).
[68] Jhally (1982, p. 206).

Livant analyzed Jhally's example, noting that, if the situation had been reversed by deleting and substituting for U.S. programs, but keeping the U.S. advertisements, "there would be no theft at all." About the question of ownership he asks

> Why is it most vital...? Because to sell a thing you have to own it. And why most ambiguous and problematic? Because it is unclear what the commodity *is.*[69]

Michael Lebowitz[70] is in a state of disbelief regarding Smythe's, Jhally's, and Livant's positions. "How much credibility," he asks, "can be assigned to a paradigm which starts from the assumption that the media sells what it can never have property rights over: the audience?"

> Ultimately the blindspot paradigm collapses on the point that if media-capitalists sell an audience to industrial capitalists it must first of all be theirs to sell. The begged question then becomes: how did this commodity become the property of the media capitalists in the first place? What is the transaction in which the property rights over the disposition of "watching-power" were transferred from the original owners, the audience, to the media-capitalists? How is the contract specified—and how is it *enforced?* [71]

Are audiences composed of individuals possessing themselves and their own property (and communication) *rights*, or are audiences *commodities* produced by media firms? The importance in liberal political theory of unfettered communication as the guarantor of an informed citizenry and democracy's main bulwark against tyranny is incommensurable with a view of the audience as itself a commodity. And yet Smythe's persuasive account of the political economy of the commercial media insists that audiences are produced by media firms for profitable exchange with advertiser clients, and that this is the main economic activity of such firms. Does the relevant jurisprudence—the regime of rights and freedoms obtaining for mass media audiences—confirm or repudiate this theory?

Technology and Policy

Before concluding this discussion it is appropriate to address directly the question of *technological determinism.* To what extent is the organization

---

69 Livant (1982, p. 212).

70 Lebowitz (1986).

71 (p. 171).

of mass media systems a result of private or public policy choices, and to what extent is it prefigured in the character of the technology itself?

The mass media systems we have seem 'natural' to us—it is difficult to imagine them taking any other form than that of a (seemingly) one-way conduit for a narrow range of socially and institutionally approved opinion (even though most people also readily criticize them for 'bias,' or triviality, or philistinism). But the media systems we have were developed in a particular historical matrix of market forces, institutional pressures, and policy goals. I would argue that the forms of media we have, and the uses to which we put them, do not simply reflect the intrinsic capabilities or limitations of the technologies involved: They are also the product of our choices in policy and law.

The introduction of radio broadcasting provides a good example, as Smythe[72] and Jhally[73] explain. The original application of radio, beginning at the turn of the century, was to coded transmission for merchant shipping and military naval operations. During World War I, governments invested heavily in research and development of radio technology, especially voice transmission; and the military subcontractors who undertook this work (such as General Electric, Westinghouse, and AT&T) began developing a civilian market for their radio products after the war. At first the main commercial objective was the manufacturers' sale of the hardware:

> The first radio stations were established by RCA to provide programmes that would stimulate the *sale of sets*.... There was no advertising on these stations, programming being viewed as a 'public service'... Between 1922–25 RCA sold over $83,000,000 worth of sets to the public.[74]

Many small North American entrepreneurs who started early radio stations simply sold blocks of transmission time to whoever wanted to buy them. The broadcasting (as opposed to radio hardware manufacturing) industry became more organized when some stations began to sell local advertising, and therefore to seek higher quality programming that would attract local audiences and advertisers. Many of these stations eventually affiliated to the NBC network, set up by RCA to sell them this higher quality programming. RCA thus found a way to profit both from the sale of sets, and from the sale of programming.

But radio broadcasting did not become a major commercial concern until the emergence of the CBS radio network. Unlike its rival NBC, CBS

---

[72] Smythe (1981).

[73] Jhally (1984).

[74] Jhally (1984, p. 167).

had no affiliation with a manufacturer, and so it evolved a revolutionary business strategy: instead of being an adjunct to the sale of radio *sets*, it began to sell radio *audiences*. CBS arranged to give away *free*, unsponsored, high-quality, network-produced programming to affiliates at a time when NBC was augmenting its revenues by *selling* programming. In return for its guaranteed free programming, CBS received an option on part of its affiliates' schedules for *sponsored* network shows, which permitted it to guarantee coast-to-coast audiences to *national* advertisers. With adjustments, such as the replacement of sponsored programmes with spot advertising, the sale of audiences has remained the revenue basis of commercial radio (and TV) ever since.

In the same period after World War I there were serious attempts made in most of the industrial nations to have radio broadcasting brought wholly or partially under public control, as a noncommercial medium of communications. In the U.S., after the wartime operation of the radio system by the Navy, it was returned (after a good deal of Congressional conflict) wholly to the private sector. In the U.K. the publicly owned BBC was given a monopoly on radio services, supported by user license fees rather than by advertising. Canada eventually adopted a hybrid of these two models, setting up the publicly owned, license-fee-financed CBC network in 1932 alongside the rapidly growing private commercial radio system (including, by that point, four U.S. network affiliates in Montreal and Toronto).

This brief sketch of the rise of commercial radio illustrates the kind of historical circumstances in which mass communication has become equated with the audience's *right to receive* commercial programming and advertising. It was not the technology of radio which determined whether the market for sets, programs, or audiences would become the dominant commodity market in broadcasting, or whether airtime would be available equally to all interested purchasers, or whether, indeed, it would be a public or private service: These were policy choices. It is predictable that, from the point of view of a business that sells audiences to advertisers, 'communication' would become pragmatically understood as the transmission of messages from speaker to hearer, and that media firms would support a regulatory regime in which the commodity—the audience—would acquire the right to hear, but not the right to speak.

But this commercial preference is not determined by the technology itself. Nor, as the preceeding chapter argued, is it an outcome that fully satisfies the constitutional purposes. Investigation of the historical conditions of possibility of the specific forms of rights developed in the communications sector must consider carefully the specific property and exchange relations obtaining in that sector.

CONCLUDING NOTE: THE RELATION OF MEDIA AND MEDIA LAW TO BASE AND SUPERSTRUCTURE

We have now assembled the elements of a critical standpoint from which to read and evaluate the discourse of communications law on the subject of the audience and its rights and legitimate interests. The failure of liberal political theory to account for liberal judicial practice in this area (problematized in Chapter 1) has been theorized in *two* different ways in marxist theories of law and marxist theories of communication:

1. The 'class instrumentalist' position, which emphasizes the ideological and coercive agency of capitalists as a class, and their conscious use of legal institutions and media organizations to advance their class interests; and
2. The 'commodity exchange' position, which emphasizes the structural determination of the activities, products, and institutions of law and communication by the exigencies of commodity exchange, expanded circulation, and market growth.

These were not in all cases competing theories—some sources, such as Gramsci (for law) or Murdoch (for communication) tried to integrate them as potentially complementary approaches. But terminological entanglements around these very abstract concepts—particularly *base* and *superstructure*, and *political economy* and *ideology*—persisted. Murdoch, for example,[75] characterized the debate in communication studies as polarized between "theories of ideology" and "theories of political economy", thus revealing, through his attempt to understand the institutions of communication as simultaneously part of the base and part of the superstructure, a possible assumption that *superstructure* and *ideology* are uniquely correlated. Cohen was more careful (in his analysis of law and property) to eschew judgment on whether ideology is only part of the superstructure, even while arguing that "bases need superstructures" to stabilize their economic arrangements. Pashukanis, Plamenatz, and Hirst suggested in different ways that, while one of the products of the legal superstructure is the ideology of property rights, this ideology is a *requirement* of capitalist relations of production and might therefore be conceived as also part of the base. Hirst summarizes this view by remarking that:

> Possession and commodity relations in large part take their form from and are differentiated by legal institutions, rules and rights. Possession and exchange have both economic *and* legal conditions of existence.[76]

---

[75] See text at note 66.

[76] Hirst (1979, pp. 155–156).

Mapping this account of legal function onto Smythe's analysis of the media, it's possible to see that the operation of the ideology of property rights *within* the economic organization of communication systems—as a *condition of operation* of their highly evanescent transactions—accounts in a powerful manner for the structure of the relationship between media organizations, their clients, and their audiences. The audience commodity is perhaps an archetypal commodity form of a particular stage of development of the capitalist mode of production: the *information economy*. Like the labor commodity, the audience commodity has a fantastical and illusory existence, defying common sense, and yet it exists, not as 'pure' ideology (based only on the power of belief) but also as the practical and visible expression of a real and existing set of material economic relations. If we wish to examine the *interaction* of the institutions of law and communication, and to account for the legal *forms* in which property rights in communication make their (ideological) appearance as *real and legitimate* social relations, formulations like Smythe's will be, I believe, highly predictive.

I do not mean here simply to pretend to decide the question unequivocally for the commodity-exchange mode of explanation, and against class instrumentalism in all its variants. I *do* mean to propose, as an interpretive framework for the case law analyses that follow, that contemporary communications law encodes the conditions under which *profitable* communication may take place, and that it gives expression to particular 'relations of communication' and roles *in* communication. The expression of these relations of production in the *form of rights* is a consequence of the function of law, as ideology, *within* economic production.

Historically, the function of communications law as the expression of class power was more salient before the modern emergence of highly profitable communications industries, as will be apparent in Chapter 3 opening discussion.[77] It is therefore convenient to distinguish between the *criminal* law of communications (e.g., sedition), which is clearly related to the function of the *state* as instrument of class rule, and the *civil* communications law regulating and legitimating commercial relations. While both may reach constitutional adjudication, only the latter is considered in the case law analysis below. The discourse of commercial communications law, however, easily mobilizes the authoritarian inflections of state power in difficult and ambiguous cases,[78] and this instrumental presence behind the curtains of civil law could usefully be understood as 'overdetermining' the ideological force of property relations.

---

[77] But see, for an unambiguous post-World War II example, *Dennis v. United States*, 341 U.S. 494 [1951].

[78] See for example the discussion of the *Mandel* case near the end of Chapter Five.

In summary, then, the institutions of law and media are in a state of complex interaction in which both directly contribute to the enforcement of established regimes of commodity exchange and expanded circulation *and* both have a general function in stabilizing and legitimating further development of the capitalist mode of production by sanctioning new configurations of those regimes. The opening remarks to this chapter adverted to the potential for contradiction and tension between these two roles within the institutions of law, in that the moral force of the State's claims to a mere disinterested application of the established rule of law is undermined by its apparent departures from its own established rules to enable new, more productive economic configurations. Thus, when a *profitable* systematic pattern of social and economic injustice cannot be shown to be necessary by the strict application of narrow legal principles and precedents, it is generally refused hearing, or even declared as a political and social question beyond the competence of the Court.

The institutional interaction between law and communications offers a useful viewpoint on the outcomes of these contradictions because of the rapidity of social changes engendered by the efflorescence of new communications and information technologies within mature capitalist economies. As institutions of the superstructure, the media do of course relay and amplify ruling-class ideology as articulated in the institutions of the state and the law; but within that they also relay that part of ruling class ideology that is most vital to their *own* relations of production—the comprehension of speech rights *as* property rights. Thus, by reproducing in popular understanding the legal superstructure's legitimation of their own productive requirements, the media help produce *as superstructure* the ideological conditions of their own economic activity *as base*. Furthermore, communication as legal property thereby becomes, over time, a prerequisite of capitalist production-in-general. This reciprocal influence of base and superstructure between the institutions of law and media may serve several other purposes as well: reinforcement of the legitimacy and common-sense obviousness of 'law-in-general'; education of citizens for their changing economic roles; and a model for the exchange-valorization of other superstructural activities through the example of 'ideology-for-profit' in the media. But it is a reasonable question whether too rapid an alternation between infrastructural and superstructural roles for legal institutions, or too sharp an adjustment of social relations in the law (as are perhaps implicated in the requirements of the contemporary communications sector) might not pose the danger of a general devaluation in the power of legal institutions effectively to *legitimate anything at all.*[79]

---

[79] David Trubek discusses legal 'delegitimation' in "Max Weber on Law and the Rise of Capitalism", 1972 *Wisconsin Law Review* 720.

In the last analysis *base/superstructure* is of course only a metaphor, and not necessarily a very illuminating one: Can we really learn much from equating a complex and rapidly changing global historical process to a building with an elevator that goes up but not down and an attic stuffed with antiques? The great danger of the base/superstructure metaphor is that it predisposes us to ignore the possibility of more complex reciprocal effects among 'levels' and 'instances' of the social formation, and to explain everything by reference to an institutional structure rather than the dialectical interaction of structure and (individual or collective) agency.

This brings us to the other side of our concern with the audience and its representation in the discourse of law. I was careful in the Introduction to identify ideology, not as the determination of subjects by a (linguistic) structure, but as a correspondence of particular kinds of discursive and political *practices* of social actors. In the context of mass media the communicative relations between representatives of the dominant groups (as privileged speakers) and subaltern groups (as their audiences) are clearly structured to legitimate and reproduce capitalist relations of production. But these are not only structural relations: they are also real and existing conditions of social conflict and political action. The purpose of a political economy of communications law, then, is not only to show how the audience's interests and rights are determined by its economic function and structure: the more important purpose is to render the other side of the dialectic—the resistance of citizens to these relations—more visible and more effective.[80]

[80] This concern informs a large and separate tradition of study examining the relation between media and popular movements. Probably the most voluminous areas of this literature are those on the labor and women's movements. Both have a history of affiliated press, broadcasting and film initiatives, and these inflect to some degree the critical interpretation of *mainstream* media content and structure, as well as furnishing a separate set of materials and practises for analysis. These remarks apply equally to the study of relations between media and other popular movements. Similarly oriented practical initiatives, theoretical assumptions, and secondary literatures exist for religious and ethnic minority, antiwar, environmental, and other popular movements.

On popular movements and the media generally see Curran, Ecclestone, Oakley and Richardson (1986); Downing, (1984); Hackett, (1986); Raboy, (1984); Mattlelart and Siegelaub (1983); Rowbotham, (1989).

Part II

The Audience and the First Amendment

Chapter 3

The Structure of the 'Free Marketplace of Ideas'

EARLY FIRST AMENDMENT CONFLICTS

Although the First Amendment to the Constitution was adopted in 1791, the first US Supreme Court decision addressing citizens' rights of free speech was not heard until more than 100 years later, in the 1897 *Davis* case.[1] Reverend Davis, a black minister, was convicted by the Massachusetts Supreme Court of breaking municipal bylaws for preaching his antiracist Gospel in a Boston public park. That Court's 1895 decision[2] was unanimously upheld on appeal to the US Supreme Court. The Massachussetts Court's opinion, written by Justice Oliver Wendell Holmes, dismissed Davis' First Amendment argument, affirming the greater constitutional priority (under the Fifth and Fourteenth Amendments) of the city's property rights as owner of the park. Holmes drew this analogy:

> to forbid public speaking in a highway or public park is no more an infringement of the rights of the public than for the owner of a private house to forbid it in his house.[3]

In 1919 Holmes, now a Federal Supreme Court justice, began with Justice Louis Brandeis to articulate a new theory of the First Amendment

[1] *Davis v. Massachussetts*, 167 U.S. 43.

[2] *Commonwealth of Massachussetts v. Davis*, 162 Mass. 10.

[3] Quoted in Kairys (1982, Introduction, Note 17).

by co-authoring the first of their famous series of free speech rights dissents. These dissents included the controversial *Abrams*,[4] *Gitlow*,[5] and *Whitney*[6] cases, all concerning the speech rights of radical minorities. Their eloquent defense of a normative, 'natural-law' right of free speech in the Constitution achieved its first majority on the bench with the 1931 *Stromberg* case,[7] in which the Supreme Court reversed a state conviction against the operators of a Young Communist League summer camp for expressing themselves by flying a red flag. In the same year the Court made its first ruling against state censorship of the press.[8]

The *Hague* case, in the late 1960s, gives the tenor of Holmes's and Brandeis's reasoning.[9] *Hague* arose from the CIO's (Congress of Industrial Organizations) organizing drive following the passage of the National Labor Relations Act in 1935. The CIO brought suit against a New Jersey mayor for preventing, rather forcibly, their public meetings and pamphleting. In *Hague* a majority concurred with Brandeis and Holmes that

> Wherever the title of streets and parks may rest, they have immemorially been held in trust for the use of the public and, time out of mind, have been used for purposes of assembly, communicating thoughts between citizens, and discussing public questions. Such use of the streets and public places has, from ancient times, been a part of the privileges, immunities, rights, and liberties of citizens.[10]

What happened between 1895 and 1939 to cause, not only a reversal of the doctrines of the Supreme Court and its main speech-rights spokesperson, but also their representation as legal rights from "time out of mind"? Briefly, the development and increasing level of organization among the antiracist and civil rights movement, the 'first wave' of the women's movement, the anarchists, the IWW and the CIO, together account for this shift. During this period all of these movements organized large-scale struggles focused explicitly on the related issues of free speech and free association, including persistent challenges and appeals through the courts. The cases that established popular rights to free public expression of political views in the US were brought forward and fought in the courts (and on the streets) by coalitions of liberal and left organizations in the first decades of this century, notwithstanding the Supreme Court's rhetoric of 'ancient liberties.' As David Kairys writes:

---

[4] 250 U.S. 616 [1919].
[5] 268 U.S. 652 [1925].
[6] 274 U.S. 357 [1927].
[7] 283 U.S. 359.
[8] *Near v. Minnesota*, 283 U.S. 697 [1931].
[9] *Hague v. CIO*, 307 U.S.496 [1939].
[10] Quoted in Kairys (1982).

> No right of free speech, either in law or practice, existed until a basic transformation of the law governing speech in the period from about 1919 to 1940. Before that time, one spoke publicly only at the discretion of local, and sometimes federal, authorities, who often prohibited what they, the local business establishment, or other powerful segments of the community did not want to hear.... The primary periods of stringent enforcement and enlargement of speech rights by the courts, the 1930's and the 1960's, correspond to the periods in which popular movements demanded such rights.[11]

In the early speech rights struggles the new *judicial* champions of the rights of popular movements to express a range of reformist, anarchist, and socialist views defended this position by the metaphorical equation of free speech with laissez-faire capitalism. In this formulation the superiority to other political systems of a social order founded on individualist values, especially those of market exchange, was evident especially in its tolerance of criticism. This oft-repeated metaphor first appeared in Holmes's dissent in the 1919 *Abrams* case.[12] In that case a number of immigrant Jewish anarchists were convicted under the Espionage Act for distributing a leaflet condemning U.S. counterrevolutionary intervention in the Soviet Union. The Government successfully argued that their actions could adversely affect U.S. war efforts. Holmes' brilliant (and ironic) attempt to defend the leafleters read, in part:

> when men have realized that time has upset many fighting faiths, they may come to believe even more than they believe the very foundations of their own conduct that the ultimate good desired is better reached by free trade in ideas—that the best test of truth is the power of thought to get itself accepted in the competition of the market.[13]

THE DEFINITION OF MASS COMMUNICATION

The long-standing practice of U.S. lawyers and jurists is to use *freedom of speech* precedents in *freedom of the press* cases, and vice versa: the distinction depends largely on the circumstances of the case (and the actor invoking the freedom). Similarly, the legal meaning of *speech* and *press*, taken together, really extends to all forms of communication. Cases concerning such disparate media as sound trucks, lawn signs, rallies, performances, bus ads, pickets, and the insides of billing envelopes mailed

[11] Kairys (1982, p. 141). See also Rabban (1981).

[12] *Abrams v. United States*, 250 U.S. 616 [1919].

[13] *Abrams v. United States*, 250 U.S. 616 [1919], Holmes dissenting.

by public utilities, as well as the more conventional print, broadcast, and film media, have all been adjudicated under the First Amendment. Justice William O. Douglas made clear the common constitutional status of mass media in a 1973 case:

> TV and radio, as well as the more conventional methods for disseminating news, are all included in the concept of 'press' as used in the First Amendment.[14]

Consider, further, this statement by one of the architects of First Amendment theory, Justice Frankfurter, in 1946:

> Freedom of the press... is not an end in itself but a means to the end of a free society.... The purpose of the Constitution was not to erect the press into a privileged institution but to protect all persons in their right to print what they will as well as to utter it.... The liberty of the press is no greater and no less... than the liberty of every citizen of the Republic.[15]

In summary, then, *freedom of the press* is, in most First Amendment theory, a special case of *freedom of speech*; and *speech* means 'communication.' In the cases considered in the following sections and chapters, these conventions may be taken as implicit, unless otherwise noted.

While these are fairly widespread conventions throughout First Amendment case law, the doctrines that develop out of actual cases in different media can be startlingly various and contradictory. In a 1952 motion-picture industry case, Justice Tom Clark remarked on this, stating that "Each method [of expression] tends to present its own peculiar problems."[16] This echoed Justice Robert Jackson's assertion 3 years earlier that each medium "is a law unto itself,"[17] and prefigures the fuller analysis in *Red Lion* in 1969, articulating a requirement that First Amendment standards in various cases accord with the "differences in the characteristics of new media."[18] Several justices have, for example, developed 'separate function' theories specifically for the newspaper industry, suggesting that the press clause in the First Amendment should be interpreted as distinguishing the purpose of press freedoms from—rather than including them in—the rationales for free speech. In other cases 'public function' theories have emerged that posit public entitlements inherent in the operations of the private media. Yet other cases justify a variation of the regime of rights in the broadcasting industry away from that in the

---

[14] *Columbia Broadcasting System v. Democratic National Committee*, 412 U.S. 94 [1973].

[15] *Pennekamp v. Florida*, 328 U.S. 331 [1946], Frankfurter, J., concurring.

[16] *Joseph Burstyn Inc. v. Wilson*, 343 U.S. 495 [1952].

[17] *Kovacs v. Cooper*, 336 U.S. 77 [1949].

[18] *Red Lion Broadcasting Co. v. FCC*, 395 U.S. 367 at 386.

publishing industry. These doctrines are outlined in the following sections of this chapter.

A 'SPECIAL FUNCTION' FOR THE PRESS?

Supreme Court Justice Potter Stewart advanced a 'separate function' thesis, in 1975, by suggesting that the free press clause gives—and should give—unique constitutional protection to the press:

> The publishing business is...the only organized private business that is given explicit constitutional protection....The primary purpose of the constitutional guarantee of a free press was...to create a fourth institution outside the Government as an additional check on the three official branches.[19]

Stewart's thesis was considered, and rejected, by a Supreme Court majority in its reversals of *Herbert v. Lando*[20] and *First National Bank of Boston v. Bellotti.*[21] In Lando the lower court had attempted to fashion an extension of editorial and journalistic privilege from Stewart's theory on the press clause, but the Supreme Court explicitly rejected this argument.

First National Bank of Boston v. Bellotti

Bellotti[22] raised some different inflections of the issue: whereas *Lando* (and *Sullivan*) considered special First Amendment protection for media professionals in the exercise of their special role (which was the basis on which Stewart invoked the 'separate function' thesis), *Bellotti*'s reasoning turned on a comparison of the First Amendment rights of private media corporations and private *nonmedia* corporations.[23]

---

[19] Stewart (1975). See also Blasi (1977). A distinct, highly sophisticated rationale for distinguishing between print and broadcast media is offered by Bollinger (1976). And compare these to another model which advances a separate theory of press rights as an emanation of the property rights of copyright holders Nadel (1983).

[20] 441 U.S. 153 [1979].

[21] 435 U.S. 765 [1978]. Although, without subscribing to Stewart's separation of 'speech' and 'press' clauses, the courts *had* already accorded a special constitutional role to the press within their view of the purposes of speech rights—see, e.g., *New York Times v. Sullivan*, 376 U.S. 254 [1964]; *Miami Herald Publishing Co. v. Tornillo*, 418 U.S. 241 [1974].

[22] 435 U.S. 765 [1978].

[23] See also Wright (1976, 1982); Carter (1984). And see Tushnet, (1982, p. 253). According to Tushnet the market fundamentalists have misappropriated the First Amendment much as they did the Fourteenth. In the aftermath of the Civil War the Fourteenth Amendment was enacted to give special legal force to the defeat of slavery. Blacks were meant to acquire civil

In this case the Supreme Court struck down a Massachussetts statute *preventing* nonmedia business corporations from using the mass media for political advertising to influence the outcome of state referenda. A group of large corporations with business interests in Massachussetts had repeatedly frustrated the state government's attempts to win a tax referendum by undertaking major advertising campaigns against it. In response the legislature attempted to make such advertising illegal (unless the vote directly affected their "business, property or assets").

Justice Powell's opinion for the court located the constitutional role of the *press* in *speech* rights terms:

> The press cases recognize the special and constitutionally recognized role of that institution in informing and educating the public, offering criticism, and providing a forum for discussion and debate.[24]

Powell's opinion also rejected Stewart's implicit claim for a hierarchy of corporate speech rights, affirming the equal First Amendment rights of nonmedia corporations:

> If the speakers here were not corporations, no one would suggest that the state could validate silence of their proposed speech. It is the type of speech indispensable to decision-making in a democracy, and this is no less true because the speech comes from a corporation rather than an individual. The inherent worth of the speech in terms of its capacity for informing the public does not depend upon the identity of its source, whether corporation, association, union or individual.[25]

Chief Justice Burger wrote a separate concurrence in *Bellotti* in which he extended Powell's formulation of the role of the press. Burger repudiated Stewart's complaint that, without a separate interpretation of the press clause, the First Amendment was redundant:

> The speech clause standing alone may be viewed as a protection of the liberty to express ideas and beliefs, while the press clause focuses specifically on the liberty to disseminate expression broadly.... Yet there is no fundamental distinction between expression and dissemination. The liberty encompassed by the press clause, although complementary to and a natural extension of speech clause liberty, merited special attention [by Madison's

---

personhood by its guarantees of Federal civil rights (for example, due process) jurisdiction over the States. But a perhaps unplanned outcome was that *corporations* have very successfully used its provisions to assert their own legal personhood, and their civil rights.

[24] See note 22.

[25] See note 22.

committee in the Continental Congress] simply because it had been more often the object of official restraints.[26]

Burger raised another objection to special status for the press. By articulating a unified theory of the First Amendment (speech and press rights as serving the same democratic purposes), he simultaneously buttressed the court's findings in Lando, and Powell's argument for recognition of the speech rights of ordinary business corporations. Note that, in this argument, the court's ability to rule on who was and who was not a journalist becomes ambiguous:

> The... difficulty with interpreting the press clause as conferring special status on a limited group is one of definition. The very task of including some entities within the "institutional press" while excluding others, whether undertaken by legislature, court or administrative agency, is reminiscent of the abhorred licensing system of Tudor and Stuart England—a system the First Amendment was intended to ban from this country. Further, the officials undertaking that task would be required to distinguish the protected from the unprotected on the basis of such variables as content of expression, frequency or fervor of expression, or ownership of the technological means of dissemination.... The evolution of traditional newspapers into modern corporate conglomerates in which the daily dissemination of news by print is no longer the major part of the whole enterprise suggests the need for caution in limiting the First Amendment rights of corporations as such... In short, the First Amendment does not 'belong' to any definable category of persons or entities: it belongs to all who exercise its freedoms.[27]

Chicago Joint Board

Stewart's 'special function' theory of the press is *supported* by a 1969 Illinois Court of Appeals decision in which a union attempted, unsuccessfully, to sue a newspaper for access to its advertising columns.[28] The Amalgamated Clothing Workers wished to advertise in the Chicago Tribune its objections to the sale of imported clothing by a large Chicago department store, but publication of the ad was refused. In finding for the newspaper, the court interpreted the First Amendment free press clause as establishing permanent protection for the newspaper industry, including protection from any compulsion to publish. The speech rights of the union

---

[26] *First National Bank of Boston v. Belloti*, Burger concurring.

[27] See note 26.

[28] *Chicago Joint Board, Amalgamated Clothing Workers of America, AFL-CIO v. Chicago Tribune*, 435 F.2d [17th Cir. 1970].

and the press freedoms of the publisher were separate matters; the union's freedom to speak required no access to the private property of the newspaper.

Chicago Joint Board aired another issue: the question of whether the press has a *public* function, exposing it to First Amendment litigation when its actions (or inactions) can be construed as quasipublic *state* actions. The court found that the press has a *separate* function, but not (at least not in its advertising activities) a *public* one—that, despite the public interest rationale of Stewart's theory, the press had no obligation to function in its advertising pages as a public forum of debate:

> We glean nothing from the constitutional guarantees, or from the decisions expository thereof, which suggest that the advertising pages of a privately published newspaper may so be pressed into service against the publisher's will either in the contest of a labour dispute to which the publisher is not a party or otherwise.[29]

The Court in *Chicago Joint Board* was correct, even if the First Amendment grounds on which they chose to evaluate freedom of expression were discredited along with Stewart's thesis. The owners of newspapers have virtually absolute control over the selection and rejection of content, including paid advertising.[30] This is fairly consistently expressed in the case law as an emanation of Fifth and Fourteenth Amendment *property* rights. While in theory the media firm has the same *speech* rights as any citizen, its greater accumulation of communicatively significant *property* gives it an actual *power* of speech which is amplified in at least the same proportion. The speech rights of journalists and editors are not merely their own ordinary speech rights, but the greater effective rights they wield as the agents of media property owners.

A Florida appeals court, in another landmark decision on the press's right to reject paid ads, put the situation in plain language in 1965, and succeeding cases have only affirmed its judgment:

> The law seems to be uniformly settled by the great weight of authority throughout the United States that the newspaper publishing business is a private enterprise and is neither a public utility nor affected with the public interest. The decisions appear to hold that even though a particular newspaper may enjoy a virtual monopoly in the area of its publication, this fact is neither unusual nor of important significance.[31]

---

[29] See note 28.

[30] See, e.g., *Shuck v. Carroll Daily Herald*, 247 N.W. 813 [Iowa 1933]; *J.J.Gordon Inc. v. Worcester Telegram Publishing Co.*, 177 N.E.2d 586 [Mass. 1961]; *Poughkeepsie Buying Service Inc. v. Poughkeepsie Newspapers, Inc.*, 131 N.Y.S.2d 515 [1954]; *Wisconsin Association of Nursing Homes, Inc. v. The Journal Co.*, 285 N.W. 2d 891 [WISC 1979].

[31] *Approved Personnel Inc. v. Tribune Co.*, 177 So. 2d 704 [Fla. 1965].

COMMUNICATION AND THE PUBLIC FUNCTION OF PRIVATE PROPERTY:

There are only a few newspaper industry precedents which assert affirmative obligations on privately owned media operations. The 1945 *Associated Press* case[32] is among the most far reaching. In finding against Associated Press, and thus enforcing competitor access to its wire services in a Sherman Act (antitrust) case, Justice Black opined that

> It would be strange indeed if the grave concern for freedom of the press which prompted adoption of the First Amendment should be read as a command that the government was without power to protect that freedom.... The First Amendment...rests on the assumption that the widest possible dissemination of information from diverse and antagonistic sources is essential to the welfare of the public.... A command that the government shall not itself impede the free flow of ideas does not afford nongovernmental combinations a refuge if they impose restraints upon that constitutionally guaranteed freedom. Freedom to publish means freedom for all and not for some. Freedom to publish is guaranteed by the Constitution, but freedom to combine to keep others from publishing is not.[33]

Sherman Act cases have perhaps affected the newspaper publishing industry more than pure First Amendment claims. In *Citizen Publishing*,[34] a 1968 antitrust case, the Supreme Court ruled that the public's First Amendment interest in hearing from a variety of newspaper sources was in fact *subordinate* to its interest in preventing monopolistic activities. In that case two separately owned dailies in the same city had formed a pooling arrangement for printing and distribution of their newspapers, and they claimed that this monopolistic arrangement was the only way to prevent the business failure of one or both of them, and that such market failure would be detrimental to the public's First Amendment interest in hearing from a variety of sources of published opinion.[35]

Fitzgerald v. National Rifle Association

One of the few cases to affirm a compulsion on a newspaper to publish was also based partially on competition law (and partly on trusteeship

---

[32] *Associated Press v. United States*, 326 U.S. 1 at 20 [1945]; see also *United States v. Radio Corporation of America*, 358 U.S. 334 [1959]; *United States v. Greater Buffalo Press, Inc.*, 402 U.S. 549 [1971].

[33] *Associated Press.*

[34] *Citizen Publishing Co. v. United States*, 394 U.S. 131 [1968].

[35] Congress responded to the Supreme Court's denial of this argument by enacting the 1970 *Newspaper Preservation Act*, which sanctions such 'Joint Operating Agreements' when approved by the Justice Department.

doctrine). A man named Fitzgerald was a candidate for election to the Board of Directors of the National Rifle Association, and submitted to the official journal of the Association, *The National Rifleman*, an advertisement urging members to vote for him. The NRA, relying on its published statement that it "reserves the right to reject or discontinue any advertisement and to edit all copy," refused to publish the ad.[36] Sticking to his guns, Fitzgerald sued.

The Court found in favor of the plaintiff, Fitzgerald. The antitrust decisions in the newspaper industry[37] were noted as follows: "When balanced against the Congressional policy of preventing monopoly, the right of publishers to refuse advertisements must yield."[38] More to the point, the Court said that in this case a publisher's near-absolute right to decide what advertisements to accept and reject[39] had to be balanced against "the fiduciary duty of corporate directors to ensure fair and open corporate elections."[40] The publication was deemed such a central part of the Association's democratic process that members' opportunities for communicating about its business weighed more heavily in the balance of interests than the First Amendment prerogatives of editors and publishers.

The Court went on to analyze the legal relation between the editors and the member-advertiser in such a way as to reach the question of property rights. First, it found the corporation's executives' duty to publish "of course extends only to the association membership." Then it suggested that the plaintiff, as a member in good standing of the association, and whose dues contributed to the journal's printing costs, was one of its owners. Therefore the judgement was held *not* to be a clear precedent for compelling publication against the publisher's judgement: the Court had perhaps merely adjudicated a conflict among several owners of the *Rifleman*, all of whom had some claim to the traditional First Amendment protection of publishers.

These restraints upon the publishing industry in the antitrust area never reached any implication of a public access obligation for newspapers. At most, they implied that the organization and sale of commercial

---

[36] *Fitzgerald v. National Rifle Association*, 383 F. Supp. 162 [D.N.J. 1974].

[37] See *Associated Press*; *Lorain Journal Co. v. United States*, 342 U.S. 143 [1951]; *Home Placement Service v. Providence Journal*, 682 F. 2d 274 [1st Cir. 1982].

[38] *Fitzgerald.*

[39] "The degree of judgemental discretion which a newspaper has with regard to refusing advertisements is not distinguishable, for purposes of First Amendment analysis, from the degree of discretion it has as to the content of any other editorial materials submitted for publication." *Wisconsin Association of NursingHomes, Inc. v. The Journal Co.*, 285 N.W. 2d 891 [WISC. 1979].

[40] *Fitzgerald.*

publishing services must demonstrably not be undertaken with monopolistic intent (or fiduciary negligence).[41] The *sole* successful U.S. newspaper *access* case was the 1919 *Uhlman* case,[42] and this has been distinguished many times.[43]

Broadcasting was also explicitly deemed *not* to be a common-carrier medium in the contentious post-World War I legislation that moved control of the radio system from the Navy to the private sector. Authority for communications legislation is founded on Congress's power to regulate interstate and foreign commerce. A public interest standard for radio spectrum licensees was codified in the 1934 *Communications Act*, and a regulatory regime enacting this standard was developed and administered by the Federal Communications Commission up to the early 1980s. These regulations (further considered in Chapter 4) derived from the public ownership and technical scarcity of useable radio frequencies, Federal regulatory powers in the broadcast media. All radio spectrum licensees are public trustees, granted use of a frequency *in the public interest.*

FCC v. Sanders Bros.

The public interest in broadcasting was given priority over private interests in the *Sanders Bros.* case on Sherman Act grounds.[44] In this case (not a Fairness Doctrine case but illustrative of the public interest grounds of FCC licensing) an Iowa radio station sought to have a new competitor's license application denied on the grounds that economic injury to its own operations would result. The FCC denied the motion and granted the license. Explicitly recognizing that the absence of common-carrier status for broadcast undertakings under the Communications Act implied that "the field of broadcasting is one of free competition," the Supreme Court accordingly declined to overturn the FCC's (and the Appeal Court's) findings. "An important element of public interest... affecting the issue of a license is the ability of the licensee to render the best practicable service to the community reached by his broadcasts," wrote Justice Roberts.

> The policy of the Act is clear that no person is to have anything in the nature of a property right as a result of the granting of a license. Licenses are limited to a maximum of three years' duration, may be revoked, and need not be renewed... Plainly it is not the purpose of the Act to protect a licensee against competition but to protect the public. Congress intended to

---

[41] See especially *Associated Press*, *Lorain Journal*, and *Home Placement Services*.

[42] Chapter 1, Note 8.

[43] For example, in the *Chicago Joint Board* and *Approved Personnel* cases.

[44] *FCC v. Sanders Bros. Radio Station*, 309 U.S. 470 [1939].

leave competition in the business of broadcasting where it found it, to permit a licensee who was not interfering electrically with other broadcasters to survive or succumb according to his ability to make his programs attractive to the public.[45]

Evans v. Newton

The potential for broader legal protection of a public communicative function of private property emerges clearly in a 1966 Supreme Court case which is not directly concerned with First Amendment rights. In this decision[46] the concept of *trusteeship* again figures importantly.[47]

In 1911, U.S. Senator Augustus O. Bacon bequeathed the use of a parcel of privately owned parkland to the citizens of Macon, Georgia, with the proviso that its use was restricted in perpetuity to white people only. His will stipulated that the park should be managed by a city-appointed Board of Trustees made up of whites.

After some years a dispute arose. The city ceased to enforce the testamentary racial segregation, alleging its statutory impropriety. The then-existing Board of Trustees brought suit asking that the city be removed as trustee and title transferred to a new trust prepared to carry out the will's provisions. Several black citizens (Evans et al.) intervened in the suit, alleging that the original racial limitation was illegal and asking that the court refuse to appoint private trustees. The city resigned as trustee. Finally, some heirs of the Senator intervened, asking for reversion of the trust property to the Bacon estate.

The state court accepted the city's resignation and appointed new white trustees (Newton et al.) to carry out the codicil. The Bacon heirs' claims, and also the black citizens' intervention, were denied. This latter group appealed to the Georgia Supreme Court, which affirmed the lower court's findings. They appealed that decision to the U.S. Supreme Court, which reversed the finding.

A clear majority on the court joined Justice Douglas's opinion, which required reinstatement of the city as trustee, regardless of its wishes, and nonsegregated operation of the park. Despite the fact that title to the

---

[45] *FCC v. Sanders Bros.* See also *FCC v. Allentown Broadcasting Corporation*, 349 U.S. 358 [1954].

[46] *Evans v. Newton*, 382 U.S. 296 [1966].

[47] Broadcast licensees are considered trustees of public property in their use of the radio spectrum. Judicial notice of the activity of newspaper editors and journalists is also often inflected by notions of trusteeship. See discussion of *Fitzgerald*, above; see also Chapter 4 discussion of the *Tornillo* case.

parkland was privately held, said the Supreme Court, "the public character of the park required that it be treated as a public institution" subject to constitutional provisions.

> Where the tradition of municipal control had become firmly established, we cannot take judicial notice that the mere substitution of trustees instantly transferred this park from the public to the private sector.[48]

Justice White, in a separate concurrence, focused on the juridical character of charitable trusts. The general test of what is charitable, he wrote, is whether the "accomplishment of the trust purpose is of such social interest to the community as to justify permitting property to be devoted to it in perpetuity," and concluded that

> there is grave doubt concerning whether a charitable trust for a park could be limited to the use of less than the whole public.[49]

Justice Harlan (joined by Stewart) dissented. Harlan was disturbed by the argument that the privately owned park's "public character" placed it in the "public domain". He noted that the only strong and similar case asserting the public function of a private institution was a 1946 Alabama case, *Marsh v. Alabama*.[50] In *Marsh* the Court found state action to prevent the suppression of free speech on the streets of a company town of 1,500 residents by the town's corporate owner to be permissable and necessary on 'public function' grounds:

> Ownership does not always mean absolute dominion. The more an owner, for his advantage, opens up his property for use by the public in general, the more do his rights become circumscribed by the statutory and constitutional rights of those who use it.[51]

Harlan pointed out that, in subsequent New York state cases involving the suppression of free speech in two privately operated residential apartment complexes, *Marsh* was ignored by a lower court, and that the Supreme Court had refused appeal in both cases.[52]

---

[48] *Evans.*

[49] *Evans,* White concurring.

[50] 326 U.S. 501.

[51] At 506.

[52] *Watchtower Bible and Tract Society v. Metropolitan Life Insurance Co.*, 297 N.Y. 339; certiorari denied, 335 U.S. 886; *Dorsey v. Stuyvesant Town Corp.*, 299 N.Y. 512; certiorari denied, 339 U.S. 981.

The substance of Harlan's concern was the future implications of the decision. He gave as an example the school system, and suggested, rather prophetically, that by the logic of the decision racially and denominationally segregated schools would be impermissible. A great many other private activities might also be subjected to constitutional limitations:

> While this process of analogy might be spun out to reach privately owned orphanages, libraries, garbage collection companies, detective agencies, and a host of other functions commonly regarded as nongovernmental though paralleling fields of governmental activity, the example of schools is, I think, sufficient to indicate the pervasive potentialities of this "public function" theory of state action.[53]

Justice Harlan failed to note the further example of the privately owned media, but Jerome Barron has rectified this oversight. Barron suggests that *Evans* and *Marsh* might provide constitutional grounds for legislation to ensure public access to the mass media. Moreover, he says, "both decisions find that private property may become quasi-public *without* a statute in extreme cases."[54] Supporting legislation "may be justified on a theory that the nature of the communications *process* imposes quasi-public functions on these quasi-public instrumentalities."[55]

Echoing Frankfurter in the *Associated Press* case, Barron suggests that this approach would also entail an affirmative Supreme Court rereading of the First Amendment: "A provision preventing government from silencing or dominating opinion should not be confused with an absence of governmental power to require that opinion be voiced."[56] The state has an interest, according to Barron, in creating opportunities for expression and protecting the necessary conditions for the emergence of expression; and using the 'public function' argument it has the necessary constitutional powers to do so by its Fourteenth Amendment due process and Tenth Amendment police powers.

The allocation of communicative resources furnishes a prime instance of the State's powers of eminent domain. The taking of private property for significant public uses that cannot be readily served by other means is a well-recognized power of the State in Anglo-American jurisprudence, and this power (subject to reasonable compensation) is a fundamental limitation on all private property rights.[57] Since, according to this doc-

---

[53] *Evans*, Harlan dissenting.

[54] Barron (1984, Introduction, Note 16; p. 568, Note 95, emphasis added). On public forum doctrine generally see also Horning(1969); Kalven (1965); Yudof (1979).

[55] Barron, (1984, p. 568; emphasis added).

[56] Barron (1984), quoting *Associated Press*.

[57] Regarding eminent domain as an inherent attribute of sovereignty, see 15 A 2d 647.

trine, enforceable legal rights depend in the first place on the existence of a State willing and able to enforce them, property rights are only contingently enforceable *against* a State's allocation of resources by public interest criteria.[58] Thus the State may, with compensation and due statutory authority, take such resources from private users and devote them to public use.[59]

Pacific Gas and Electric

The 'public function' argument for communicative access to private property did not enjoy broad application. Justice Harlan's dissent in *Evans* finds majority expression in a 1986 decision (about 20 years later) in which the 'public function' argument fails, even in application to *public* property. In *Pacific Gas and Electric v. Public Utilities Commission of California*[60] Justice Powell (for the Court) and Chief Justice Burger (concurring) warn of a "slippery slope" of First Amendment access to corporate property, with "potentially sweeping consequences for various kinds of property interests."[61]

The Pacific Gas & Electric Co. (PGE) publishes a newsletter, *Progress*, which normally contains billing information, feature articles, and political editorials. The newsletter is distributed (and has been for over 60 years) in the "extra space" within its billing envelopes—that is, by using the capacity of the envelopes to contain extra printed matter without incurring additional postage charges. In 1980 a consumer advocacy group petitioned the Public Utility Commission of California (PUCC) to prohibit PGE from distributing its own political views at ratepayers' expense.

The PUCC ruled that the "extra space" in the billing envelopes was the property of the ratepayers, and ordered PGE to share its use with the consumer advocacy group according to a schedule drawn up by the Commission. PGE applied for a rehearing by the PUCC, and was refused; it then appealed to the California Supreme Court on the First Amendment grounds of a violation of its claimed right *not* to speak, and also on the Fifth Amendment grounds of an unwarranted "taking" of its property without just compensation. The California Supreme Court rejected these arguments and upheld the PUCC decision. PGE then appealed to the United States Supreme Court, which granted certiorari only for the question of the purported First Amendment violation.

---

[58] Regarding immateriality of consent, see 29 N.E. 1062.

[59] The State's duty of just compensation is established by 626 S.W. 2d 561, 563.

[60] 106 S. Ct. 903 [1986].

[61] 906–7, n. 4 (quoting PUCC Commissioner Bagley); 914.

Thus, however ambiguously, the Supreme Court accepted that the medium of expression—the "extra space" in the billing envelopes—was the property of the ratepayers, and defined the remaining issue before it as that of the negative First Amendment rights of corporations to refuse to speak or to be associated with speech with which it disagreed. On the basis of that argument, the Supreme Court overturned the PUCC's decision.

In so doing, the Court significantly extended the corporate speech rights which it found in *Bellotti.*[62] Not only did *media* corporations, *nonmedia* corporations, and individuals enjoy the same formal rights to speak out on public issues, but now they also acquired the same rights to remain *silent.* In fact they were explicitly protected, in this decision, from any requirement "to associate with speech with which [they] may disagree," and from circumstances in which they would feel a compulsion "to respond to arguments and allegations" made by citizens.[63]

Now, *Bellotti* protected corporate speech rights on the argument that society had as much interest in hearing the views promulgated by business corporations as in hearing the views of other entities. It did not purport to discover that corporations actually 'thought,' 'felt,' or 'believed' anything at all. But the precedents cited in this extension of *negative* First Amendment rights to corporations depend on a quite different rationale from that in *Bellotti*: both *West Virginia Board of Education v. Barnette*[64] and *Wooley v. Maynard*[65] forcefully assert an *individual's* right to not speak (e.g., the Pledge of Allegiance) on the basis of her "individual freedom of mind."[66] Corporations possess neither minds, nor, therefore, individual freedom thereof, and Justice Rehnquist dissented on this basis.

The decision in *PGE* also relied on the analysis in *Tornillo*,[67] a right-of-reply case in which negative First Amendment rights were affirmed uniquely for newpaper corporations. The rationale for granting negative speech rights in that case was again a social interest: the Court found that the breadth of public debate in the print media would be limited by a compelled right to reply, by creating an incentive for newspapers to avoid raising controversial issues in the first place. Patrick Burke suggests that the First Amendment standard appropriate to utility billing envelopes is either the broadcast or the cable television standard, and *not* the newspaper standard.[68] Broadcast services (like billing envelopes, unlike newspapers) are subject to physical limits, conditions of natural and legal

---

[62] See above Note 21.

[63] 106 S. Ct., op. cit., 911–12.

[64] 319 U.S. 624 [1943].

[65] 430 U.S. 705 [1977].

[66] *Barnette*, 634; *Wooley*, 714.

[67] *Miami Herald v. Tornillo*, 418 U.S. 241 [1974]; see Chapter Four.

[68] Burke (1986–1987); see also text at Notes 16–18, above.

monopoly, and regulatory authority; use public property; and are deemed by the Court to be much less susceptible to the "chilling effect" noted in *Tornillo.* Cable services are likewise subject to conditions of legal monopoly and regulatory authority, and well insulated against the "chilling effect." Both media, for these reasons, face far more stringent access requirements than the privately owned press. Burke suggests that an analysis which had considered the strong similarities between utility billing envelopes and these media would have affirmed the access provisions ordered by the PUCC.[69] The fiduciary obligations of the utility figure importantly in his analysis:

> There is no better example of a private corporation with "public trustee" obligations than a public utility, the rates and activities of which are regulated by state agencies. In exchange for regulation the utilities are granted valuable geographic monopolies and guaranteed profits by the state. Many of the broadcast access interests arise with utility billing envelope insertions.[70]

PGE did more than create a legal fiction that corporations are endowed with the subjective characteristics of natural persons: it also wreaked great damage on a promising consumer movement. Access to billing envelopes had become an important means of organizing membership and financing in a growing network of consumer advocacy groups (the 'consumer utility boards'—CUBs) authorized in a number of states by referenda, statutes, or administrative rulings, and supported by organizations such as the National League of Cities, the National Association of Counties, the International City Management Association, the United States Conference of Mayors, and the National Governors' Association.[71] Before this decision CUBs were beginning to expand their activities into other institutions; after it, their advocacy efforts on behalf of consumers, ratepayers, and citizens have seriously declined.

Burke notes an additional effect in the Court's discovery in this case of negative speech rights for PGE.[72] Ratepayers, he says, must of course pay the full costs of publishing and mailing the utility's newsletter (by paying their bills) or else be deprived of gas and electric services. They therefore must subsidize the use of their own property (the "extra space") to express views with which they may disagree—thus annulling their own right to not speak.

---

[69] ep. 377–385.
[70] P. 380.
[71] P. 396.
[72] P. 375, Note 26.

Chapter 4

Citizen Access and Reply in Three Media Contexts

"Free, robust criticism of government... is the essence of the democratic dialectic," says First Amendment scholar Harry Kalven Jr. "The citizen may criticize the motives and performance of government. The government... may not criticize the performance and motives of its critics."[1] With this assurance of immunity in hand the present study extends in this chapter its critique of the U.S. Supreme Court's recent labors on the First Amendment to the explicit question of the audience member's rights of expressive access and reply to privately owned media.

Justice Burger's remarks in *Bellotti* affirming the First Amendment's protection of citizens' opportunities for both expression and dissemination can be understood to imply that government has, not only a responsibility to refrain from abridgement of speech freedoms, but a more positive responsibility to maintain and enlarge the opportunities for their exercise. Posed in this way, the question of rights of access and reply acquires a 'pure' First Amendment flavor absent from some of the cases considered in the last chapter, in which speech rights often expanded or contracted according to the outcomes of disputes centred more on economic or other grounds of government regulation of private property. (The Sherman antitrust momentum in fact seemed to contribute more tellingly to the expansion of opportunities for expression in the daily press than the First

[1] Quoted by Justice Douglas, concurring, *Columbia Broadcasting System v. Democratic National Committee*, 412 U.S. 94 [1973].

Amendment.) This is not to say that the cases considered in the present chapter are void of property rights implications, only that here these become more subterranean and require closer analysis.

The question of access rights drags several other questions in its wake. For example, the access of others is 'compelled speech' for private owners of media facilities, who therefore claim a corresponding 'right to *not* speak.'[2] There are also various conceivable *kinds* of access, each implying a different right: a straightforward right of access to initiate discussion of an otherwise unreported topic; the 'right to reply' to previous editorial content; the right to reply to advertising content; the right to purchase advertising at all, and so on. Each of these might also have its corresponding negative form of right. Editors and journalists have speech rights which are brought into question by rights of access; so, too, apparently, do those audience-members who do not seek an opportunity to speak, but whose 'right to receive' may be affected.[3] The government's 'right to regulate' (for example, Federal regulatory powers over interstate commerce) arises, along with perhaps the most recondite issue in this area of law, the question of 'state action.' Without the identifiable participation of the government in any putative denial of rights, the Constitution does not apply.

While the First Amendment's requirements command substantial judicial deference, they do not amount to an absolute limitation. Indeed they could not, without rendering punishment for perjury, fraud, threat, slander, conspiracy, or counselling a crime unconstitutional. When First Amendment values are in conflict with other important values, the Court employs a 'balancing test':

> The right to use the streets, parks and open places [for communication] may at times conflict with other uses of these facilities, such as their use for traffic, relaxation, and the like. But the right of expression is not made subordinate to other uses. Rather, the rights coexist, on a roughly equal plane, and the principle for resolving conflicts is not subordination but accommodation of the various interests involved. Time, place and manner controls are valid only within this context.[4]

At the same time, while the values underlying the First Amendment do have a "preferred position" in relation to other values, they are difficult to arrange permanently in any obvious *internal* hierarchical scheme:

---

[2] As in *Pacific Gas & Electric*, (Chapter 3).

[3] See Chapter 5.

[4] Emerson (1981, p. 808); for extensive supporting caselaw citations, see also Nadel (1982, p. 164, Notes 1–2).

> The fundamental principle of constitutional adjudication is that the First Amendment gives expression, as distinct from other conduct, a preferred position. This means that, as a general proposition, individual and societal interests in freedom of expression must be preferred over other individual and societal interests...
>
> When the affirmative side of the First Amendment is involved...the conflicts of interests are mostly within the system, not between First Amendment interests and interests outside the system. In this situation, there is no issue of weighing First Amendment interests against other interests. Rather, the basic principle...is one of improving the performance of the system of freedom of expression.[5]

The following three sections of this chapter analyze the internal ranking of First Amendment values, and the resulting "performance of the system of freedom of expression," through examination of landmark access cases in the three contexts of daily newspaper publishing, broadcasting, and direct, literal public speech in a shopping center. The allocation of rights in these cases—and the *differences* in their disposition—provide a useful entry point for distinguishing the structure of mass media speech rights from that in direct interpersonal communication, for comparing the forms of legal rights in mass communication with the forms of commodities produced by media firms, and for assessing the economic role of the audience.

PUBLISHING

Miami Herald Publishing Co. v. Tornillo

In 1913 the state of Florida enacted a statute compelling newspaper publication of certain kinds of materials. When this statute was overturned in the landmark 1974 *Tornillo* case,[6] the question of access to the privately owned print media was clearly and finally settled, because the narrow form of access and clear legislative intent provided by the statute tested all the outstanding ambiguities in the constitutional doctrines on the subject. The statute provided a *right of reply* only for registered election candidates who were attacked (on the basis of personal character, official record, or charges of malfeasance) in the columns of newspapers. In these circumstances the statute compelled free publication of a reply of equal length.

---

[5] Emerson, (1981, p. 802).

[6] 418 U.S. 241.

Pat Tornillo, a former official of the county teacher's association and the leader of a then-recent teacher's strike, ran in 1972 for a seat in the Florida legislature. During the election campaign the Miami Herald attacked Tornillo in an editorial, calling him a lawbreaker (the strike had continued after the issuance of an injunction) and suggesting that its readers were duty-bound to vote against him. Tornillo's reply to this attack was refused publication, and he brought a suit against the paper under the statute.

The lower court found the statute unconstitutional; the Florida Supreme Court reversed this decision, upholding the statute on First Amendment grounds and granting Tornillo's demand for an order against the Herald compelling publication of his reply. In 1974 the U.S. Supreme Court *unanimously* reversed the Florida Supreme Court and declared the statute unconstitutional. Tornillo was the first clear test of a statutory right of reply to the daily press.

Chief Justice Burger's opinion for the Federal Supreme Court refused this compelled access, despite the fact that (unlike *Chicago Joint Board*) it had the support of a carefully drafted statute which was limited to apply only to candidates' replies during elections. And yet, on the face of it, the situation appears as a clear target for Burger's hostility to the 'separate function' theory of press freedoms, and as an opportunity to enact his declared conviction that *dissemination* must be protected together with expression to fulfill the First Amendment's intent.

The Herald argued that the statute amounted to a form of theft: the publisher is deprived of property without compensation and without due process. The statute was unconstitutional, the publishing firm held, because it violated the Fifth and Fourteenth Amendment rights of a corporation, as a legal person, to the enjoyment of property, and the protection of its property rights by the law. The Herald did not specify the property of which it considered itself deprived by the Florida court's ruling.

Tornillo's lawyers[7] argued that the 'free marketplace of ideas' at the time the Constitution was drafted, in which the press as a whole had communicated the full range and diversity of public opinion, had evolved into a monopoly controlled by the owners of the media. Concentration in the publishing industry, they said, had driven the costs of entry into the 'marketplace of ideas' too high for most citizens to participate. The industry therefore was, because of its recognized and licensed monopoly character[8] and its frequent claims to be "surrogates for the public," in a

---

[7] Among whom were Jerome Barron (1984, 1986; see Chapters 1 and 3), a widely read author on First Amendment issues, member of the Harvard law faculty, and tireless activist for press access.

[8] See Chapter 3, Note 35.

stewardship role. Their brief petitioned the Court to enforce the fiduciary obligations of that role.

The Court took careful note of these arguments in its judgment:

> The same economic factors which have caused the disappearance of vast numbers of metropolitan newspapers have made entry into the marketplace of ideas served by the print media almost impossible. It is urged that the claim of newspapers to be "surrogates for the public" carries with it a concomitant fiduciary obligation to account for that stewardship. From this premise it is reasoned that the only effective way to ensure fairness and accuracy and to provide for some accountability is for government to take affirmative action. The First Amendment interest of the public in being informed is said to be in peril because the marketplace of ideas is today a monopoly controlled by the owners of the market.[9]

Burger summarized this view in the proposition that "Government has an obligation to ensure that a wide variety of views reach the public."[10] He declined, however, to support this proposition, asserting that compelled speech—a "command that the press publish what it prefers to withhold"—was equivalent to and indistinguishable from prior restraint, or censorship. On the substance of Tornillo's arguments, Burger wrote:

> A responsible press is an undoubtedly desirable goal, but press responsibility is not mandated by the Constitution and like many other virtues it cannot be legislated.[11]

Furthermore, according to Burger, statutes like the one in question were most likely to 'chill' free expression, since it gave editors an incentive to avoid controversy. "Government enforced right of access," he said, "inescapably 'dampens the vigour and limits the variety of public debate.'"[12] Burger preferred to rely upon "journalistic integrity" and "editorial control and judgement": journalists, editors and publishers must be left to make the inevitable interpretive decisions, because these are the essence of a free press:

> A newspaper is more than a passive receptacle or conduit for news, comment and advertising. The choice of material to go into a newspaper and decisions made as to...size...and content...and treatment of public issues and public officials—whether fair or unfair—constitutes the exercise of editorial control and judgement.[13]

---

[9] *Tornillo.*
[10] *Tornillo.*
[11] *Tornillo.*
[12] Quoting *Sullivan.*
[13] *Tornillo.*

Nothing in this case or any other First Amendment case law demands that *newspaper* journalists, editors, or publishers keep to any standard of 'objectivity,' 'balance,' 'fairness,' or even 'accuracy.' 'No prior restraint' means that statements in the press can only be sanctioned after the fact, as in a libel suit. Burger's comments (above) that "responsibility *cannot* be legislated," and that all interpretive judgement "—whether fair or unfair—" is the prerogative of the newspaper, can be taken as characteristic. Burger quoted in Tornillo another landmark First Amendment case from the previous year, which suggests that publishers may 'interfere' as much as they wish in the editorial process—if they judge it in their *business* interests:

> The power of a privately owned newspaper to advance its own political, social, and economic views is bounded by only two factors: first, the acceptance of a sufficient number of readers—and hence advertisers—to assure financial success; and second, the journalistic integrity of its editors and publishers.[14]

The last chapter noted a tension between Chief Justice Burger's First Amendment, with its coextensive rights to expression and dissemination of speech which "belong to all who exercise its freedoms," and the private property rights discovered in the First Amendment in *Chicago Joint Board.* In *Tornillo* we find that that 'tension' resides as much *within* the discourse of a particular jurist as *among* the competing interpretations of different jurists. Moving back and forth between the interests represented in the case, Burger eliminates ("responsibility cannot be legislated") all but two interests: that of government in preventing 'chilled' speech, and that of professional journalists and editors in exercising integrity and judgement. Both interests have the same object (undampened "vigor and... variety of public debate"); the latter achieves it more surely. Note that Burger's stirring rhetoric in *Bellotti* to the effect that the First Amendment belonged to all and to no one came 4 years after his opinion in *Tornillo.* The two distinguishing characteristics of that decision were that the statute in question attempted to *prevent* publication of material acceptable to the media owners, and that the rights asserted against this governmental action were the rights of *corporations* to speak in the mass media.

Justice Byron White's concurrence in *Tornillo* is an elegant coda to Burger's first movement. In this text White collapses the same complex

---

[14] *CBS v. DNC*, 412 U.S. 94 [1973] at 117. Cynical readers may decide for themselves how limiting the second factor might be. *DNC* also considered (and rejected) compelled access—in this case, access to paid broadcast advertising that was not a reply to previous content; it is considered in more detail below.

and conflicting array of private interests—publishers, editors, readers, advertisers, voters, and political candidates—into one discursive public valiantly attempting, with the Court's help, to hold its ground *against* the state. This is his quintessentially laissez-faire answer to Pat Tornillo's charges of harmful monopoly:

> Regardless of how beneficient-sounding the purposes of controlling the press might be, we prefer the power of reason as applied through public discussion and remain intensely skeptical about those measures that would allow *government* to insinuate itself into the editorial rooms of this Nation's press.[15]

DIRECT INTERACTION

Pruneyard Shopping Center

Outside of cases involving the daily press—in the broadcast media, for example, or in cases involving face-to-face communication, the precedents are more varied. A powerful rationale for an opposite decision in *Tornillo* is provided in *Pruneyard Shopping Center v. Robbins.*[16] Like *Tornillo*, *Pruneyard* is also about 'compelled speech,' though not set in a context of *mass* communication; it is precisely the different results obtained in mass media and non-mass media settings that are interesting here. The Supreme Court's concern in *Pruneyard*, with the protection of states' rights to expand the opportunities for expression of individual citizens in direct interaction. This case contains some quite narrow distinctions; note especially the changing constitutional status of state law in *Tornillo*, *Bellotti*, *PGE*, and *Pruneyard.*

Pruneyard Shopping Center, in Campbell, California, rents business premises to about 75 retail stores and restaurants and to a movie theatre, and maintains, as part of its services to those tenants and their clientele, five acres of parking lot and a variety of walkways, sidewalks, courtyards, and plazas. One weekend an "orderly and peaceful" group of high school students set up a card table in the central courtyard and began "distributing pamphlets and ask[ing] passersby to sign petitions...to be sent to the President and members of Congress" opposing the U.N. resolution against Zionism.[17]

None of the patrons objected to their activity, but a security guard told them they would have to leave, and suggested moving to the public sidewalk at the perimeter of the complex. He correctly informed them of

---

[15] *Tornillo*; emphasis added.

[16] 447 U.S. 74 [1980].

[17] 447 U.S. 74 [1980].

the shopping center's explicit policy of disallowing "any visitor or tenant to engage in any publicly expressive activity, including the circulation of petitions, that was not directly related to [the shopping center's] commercial purposes." In the words of Justice Renquist in his opinion for the court, "Appellees immediately left the premises and filed this suit" in county court.[18]

In their suit the students sought an injunction against the shopping center's denial of access for the exercise of their First Amendment rights. The lower court denied their injunction; on appeal the California Supreme Court reversed that decision, finding that the California State Constitution protected "speech and petitioning, reasonably exercised, in shopping centers even when the centers are privately owned."[19] The Pruneyard Shopping Center appealed to the Federal Supreme Court, which upheld the California Supreme Court.

Pruneyard's (appellants') arguments resemble those of the Pacific Gas & Electric Co. and the Miami Herald Publishing Co. The right to exclude others, said the shopping center, was implicit in the Fifth and Fourteenth Amendments' guarantees against the taking of property without just compensation and due process of law. Justice Renquist, for the Court, found neither infirmity, dismissing these arguments by observing that tolerance of the students' activity would not "unreasonably impair the value or use of their property as a shopping center."[20] The *Herald*, facing compelled access by the State of Florida, made an argument in *Tornillo* similar to that of the California appellants here, and won, though without the Court directly addressing their argument. (The events leading to *PGE* were just then taking place.) Here again the owner of the medium-as-property argues 'unjust taking,' and the Court again skirts the issue but makes an opposite ruling on the access question. What is the property putatively 'taken' in each of these cases? Would there have been an impairment of property value in *Tornillo* under the Florida Supreme Court's decision?

Justice Marshall's concurrence in *Pruneyard* rejected the due process argument on more general grounds. Marshall referred to a "normative dimension" in constitutional law, derived from or shared with "core common-law rights." By identifying this "core," Marshall suggested, one could also identify permissable degrees of divergence between state and federal constitutional law, and thus ease the necessary process of historical change in the law. The appellants' due process arguments in *Pruneyard*, he felt, imposed an unnecessary rigidity on the Fourteenth Amendment's response to changing circumstances. He did not, however,

[18] 447 U.S. 74 [1980].

[19] 23 Cal. 3d 899, [1979] at 910.

[20] 447 U.S. 74 [1980].

distinguish this from *Tornillo*, where the changing circumstances of press ownership were arguably even more cogent than those of real estate ownership in this case.

The appellants in *Pruneyard* believed that they found support in *Lloyd v. Tanner*,[21] wherein the Federal Supreme Court had denied the State of Oregon the ability to require access to shopping centers for the exercise of *state* constitutional rights of free speech and petition "when adequate alternative avenues of communication are available." In *Lloyd* a group of anti-Vietnam War protesters had sued (and initially won at the level of the Oregon Supreme Court) over their eviction from a Portland shopping center.[22]

Renquist refused the *Lloyd* precedent (without reference to *Logan Valley*), distinguishing it on the basis that there was in the case of *Lloyd*, no *explicit* state constitutional or statutory provision for the "use of private property by strangers," and that there *was* such a provision in California law. He asserted the existence of a "well-established" power of the states to impose restrictions on private property, and to expand on the "individual liberties...conferred by the Federal Constitution"—as long as there was no "taking without just compensation."[23] Thus, where in *Tornillo* the court declined to rule on the 'unjust taking' issue (or to enunciate *what* might or might not have been taken), in *Pruneyard* they ruled that the taking was *not* unjust (but still without saying what had been taken!).

The appellants also advanced First Amendment arguments based on *Tornillo*, and on *Wooley v. Maynard*.[24] In *Wooley*, two Jehovah's Witnesses in New Hampshire had covered up the state motto 'Live Free or Die' on the license plate attached to their automobile because it offended their religious beliefs. Chief Justice Burger, invoking the protection of minority viewpoints by the First Amendment (and offering lexical comfort to this study) held for the Court in *Wooley* that the state's attempt to enforce this display was unconstitutional:

> Where the state's interest is to disseminate an ideology, no matter how acceptable to some, such interest cannot outweigh an individual's First Amendment right to avoid becoming the courier for such message.[25]

---

[21] 407 U.S. 551 [1972].

[22] And *Lloyd* would appear itself to overturn without comment Justice Marshall's opinion for the Court in *Amalgamated Food Employees Union Local 590 v. Logan Valley Plaza*, 391 U.S. 308 [1968], which *affirmed* a union's right to picket a store in a private shopping center on the argument that "property that is privately owned may at least, for First Amendment purposes, be treated as though it were publicly held." First Amendment protection of union picketing in shopping centers was also *denied* in *Hudgens v. NLRB*, 424 U.S. 507 [1976].

[23] 447 U.S. 74 [1980].

[24] 430 U.S. 705 [1977] (Chapter 3).

[25] 430 U.S. 705 [1977].

The court in *Pruneyard* did affirm the negative First Amendment right of individuals, discovered in *Wooley*, to avoid communicating a government-prescribed message. But *Pruneyard* was distinguished by the court on the grounds that no specific message was dictated by the state; that appellants were free to disclaim sponsorship or association with the students' message (e.g., by posting signs); and that the shopping center's standing invitation to the public to visit at will assured that the views of other members of the public would "not likely be identified with those of the owner."[26]

The 'state action' question seems only partly resolved by this justification of its action in *Pruneyard*, though. Because constitutional guarantees only apply to the relation between government and individual, where is the 'state action' that triggered constitutional protection from the California Supreme Court? Is it the County Court's initial affirmation of the shopping center owners' Fifth and Fourteenth Amendment interests? Consensual recognition of an array of private property interests, and the very ability to observe the boundaries between them depend on an accumulation of such interest adjudications. If these qualify as constitutionally regulated *state actions*, then *all* activity in the market must theoretically be subject to constitutional oversight. For a court to find constitutionally significant state action in the mere recognition of a property right is for it to acknowledge property itself as the *product* of state action. Specifically in this case, the relevance of identifying the property in question becomes even greater, since the taking of that property was found to be neither tortious nor unconstitutional: what the state giveth, the state taketh away!

Renquist distinguished *Tornillo* on two grounds. First, the principle in that case, he said, was that a state cannot tell a newspaper what to print. The Florida statute contravened this principle in that it "exacted a penalty on the basis of the content of a newspaper."[27] But many other attempts to enforce press access—on grounds of the *function* of the press rather than its specific *content*—had failed precisely on their generality and overbreadth and their lack of supporting statutory authority,[28] and it was the hope of the respondents in *Tornillo* that the Florida statute would save them from this defect. Jerome Barron's judgement is that access to the press

[26] 447 U.S. 74 [1980].

[27] 447 U.S., 74 [1980], quoting *Tornillo*.

[28] See, e.g. *Mack v. Costello*, 143 N.W. 950 [S.D.1913]; *Friedenberg v. Times Publishing Co.*, 127 So. 345 [La.1930]; *In re Louis Wohl, Inc.*, 50 F2d 254 [E.D.Mich. 1931]; *Wall v. World Publishing Co.*, 263 P. 2d 1010 [Okl.1953]; see also Chapter 3, Notes 30, 31.

has been resisted by relentless invocation of the freedom of contract notion that a newspaper publisher is as free as any merchant to deal with whom he chooses.[29]

In regard to penalties, the Florida statute only provided for court-imposed penalties *if* the newspaper refused equal access to electoral candidates attacked in editorial copy in well-defined ways *during* elections. (Unless the penalty referred to is once again the ghostly property damage entailed in following these conditions, and if so, Renquist has not distinguished this from *Pruneyard*.)

Renquist's second distinction of *Tornillo* is even more suggestive. He identifies Burger's refusal to intrude on "the function of editors" as the key message in that case, and a condition absent from *Pruneyard*. He also reproduces Burger's quote from *Sullivan*[30] to the effect that government enforced right of access would "dampen the vigor and limit the variety of public debate," finding this inapplicable as well. Burger probably didn't realize he was creating a need for shopping malls to have editors!

Certainly it is true that the owners of the shopping center were not functioning as editors: They had not attempted to organize or publicly interpret the presentation of views in their plazas or courtyards as part of their business activities. If they had done so, would this have protected their exclusion of the students' speech? To speculate for a moment: imagine they organized and introduced weekend presentations of consumer product information in the central courtyard, and allowed product advertisers to display, for a fee, promotional material about their wares. Would they then suffer an 'unjust taking' of their property if the California court persisted in allowing the students to use the courtyard as a public forum? What would that property be? And is the communicative function of a public forum public property? If so, can it be transformed into private property merely by organizing the sale of its communicative use?

Pruneyard articulates a concern for protection of states' rights to expand its citizens' access to expressive resources, regardless of the "existence of other appropriate avenues." Its reasoning confronts *Tornillo*'s: Is it really primarily the danger of insult to the editorial profession that stands in the way of realizing, in the *mass* media, the recognized responsibility of government to expand opportunities for public expression?

---

[29] Barron (1984; see Chapter 3).

[30] Barron (1984; see also Chapter 5).

BROADCASTING: THE FAIRNESS DOCTRINE

The U.S. Communications Act of 1934 and subsequent judicial review have affirmed the constitutionality of a narrow degree of government regulation of broadcasting *content* (pursuant to S. 315 of the Act). The constitutional rationale for regulation is known as the *Scarcity Doctrine:* the radio spectrum is *public* property; it is a *finite* resource, inherently not available to all competing uses; its use is allocated by the government by granting limited-term, renewable *licenses* to preferred applicants; successful applicants are *trustees* of public property; and their use of it in the *public interest* is a condition of grant and renewal of licenses.

The content regulations permitted by the Scarcity Doctrine under the Communications Act are administered by, and have been continuously developed and refined by, the Federal Communications Commission (FCC) since the 1930s. The post-World War II content rules of the FCC have articulated (until recently) a rationale known as the *Fairness Doctrine.* The Fairness Doctrine imposes two kinds of obligation on broadcasters: (a) they have an *affirmative obligation*—they must give "fair and adequate coverage to controversial issues of public importance"; and (b) they have a *balancing obligation*—they must provide coverage of *other* sides of controversial issues if *one* side is presented: a *range of views.*[31] The Commission, on the *only* occasion on which it has enforced the *affirmative* obligation, did so by comparing the issues covered by different media outlets in the same region.[32] FCC action with respect to both the *affirmative* obligation, and the *balancing* obligation (which has been the subject of numerous proceedings and studies) is generally triggered by a complaint mechanism.

In practice the Commission has usually considered the affirmative obligation moot if licensees have 'exercised reasonable editorial judgement' or if complainants have had an opportunity to receive coverage on the disputed issue via other media outlets. When licensees do choose to cover an issue the balancing obligation does not require equal time, nor does it require the broadcaster relinquish editorial control: it must simply *represent* a range of views, plausible to the Commission, on issues it chooses to cover. The Fairness Doctrine requires *personal* responses—without editorial control—only to attacks made on individuals during the presentation of 'controversial' issues (as from time to time identified by the Commission). There are also separate regulations (outside the Fairness Doctrine proper) requiring broadcasters to sell advertising spots to candidates for public office during elections, and to political parties for fundraising appeals.

---

[31] Ginsburg (1979).

[32] *Mink*, 59 FCC 2d 987 [1976].

This section's discussion of broadcast access caselaw examines three Fairness Doctrine cases: *Red Lion*, *Retail Store Employees*, and *DNC*.[33] Access rights in the broadcasting sector were bracingly affirmed by the Supreme Court in *Red Lion*, and then ambiguously denied 6 years later in *DNC*. *DNC* has set the subsequent pattern. *Retail Store Employees* is an example of a lower court ruling after *Red Lion* and before *DNC*. In these cases the Court makes explicit reference to the audience's role in mass communication.

Red Lion v. FCC

In *Red Lion* the Supreme Court unanimously upheld, for the first time, the constitutionality of the Fairness Doctrine *against* a broadcaster's claim that

> the First Amendment protects any broadcaster's desire...to broadcast whatever they choose, to exclude whomever they choose...and to refuse to give equal weight to the views of opponents.[34]

These are the events which gave rise to the case: In November 1964, as part of the "Christian Crusade" series carried by Red Lion Broadcasting Co. on its Pennsylvania radio station, the Reverend Billy James Hargis gave a critical review of a recently published book entitled *Goldwater—Extremist on the Right*. Reverend Hargis's review consisted in large part of ad hominem attacks on the book's author, Fred J. Cook, who, he said, had been fired from a New York city daily for slandering a city official, had then worked for a "communist-affiliated newspaper" (*The Nation*), and had in that position defended the satanic Alger Hiss and attacked the saintly names of J. Edgar Hoover and the FBI.

Fred Cook decided that he had been personally attacked and demanded free reply time from the station, which was refused. He complained to the FCC. The Commission concluded that a personal attack had been made, that the station had failed to provide a transcript of the broadcast and an opportunity for reply (as required by the personal attack rules of the Fairness Doctrine), and that the station must provide a free opportunity for reply. Red Lion Broadcasting Co. appealed to the Circuit Court of Appeals, which found against them. They appealed that decision

---

[33] *Red Lion Broadcasting v. FCC*, 395 U.S. 367 [1969]; *Retail Store Employees Union, Local 880, Retail Clerks International Association, AFL-CIO v. FCC*, 43b F. 2d 248 [D.C. Circuit 1970]; and *Columbia Broadcasting System v. Democratic National Committee*, 412 U.S. 94 [1973].

[34] *Red Lion*, plaintiff's brief.

to the Supreme Court, and it also repudiated their claim, firmly upholding the FCC's and the Appeal Court's ruling.

Justice White's opinion for the Court (unanimous, with Justice Douglas absent) began by reviewing in some detail the powers of the FCC, previous Fairness Doctrine case law, and Congressional debate and committee hearings going back to the 1912 Radio Act and the National Radio Conferences of the early 1920s. He found that the FCC's personal attack rules implemented longstanding and well-documented Congressional policy and did not constitute a regulatory "frolic" on the part of the Commission:

> Congress has not just kept its silence by refusing to overturn the administrative construction, but has ratified it with positive legislation. Thirty years of consistent administrative construction... reinforce the natural conclusion that the public interest language of the Act authorized the Commission to require licensees to use their stations for discussion of public issues, and that the FCC is free to implement this requirement by reasonable rules and regulations...
>
> When a broadcaster grants time to a political candidate, Congress itself requires that equal time be offered to his opponents. It would exceed our competence to hold that the Commission is unauthorized by the statute to employ a similar device where personal attacks or political editorials are broadcast by a radio or television station.[35]

White went on to examine the First Amendment rationales underlying this finding. He first drew a parallel from the regulation of sound trucks to the regulation of broadcasting equipment:

> The ability of new technology to produce sounds more raucous than those of the human voice justifies restrictions on the sound level, and on the hours and places of use, of sound trucks so long as the restrictions are reasonable and applied without discrimination.... Just as the Government may limit the use of sound-amplifying equipment so noisy that it drowns out civilized private speech, so may the Government limit the use of broadcast equipment. The right of free speech of a broadcaster, the user of a sound truck, or of any other individual does not embrace a right to snuff out the free speech of others.[36]

White then affirmed the constitutionality of requiring broadcasters to permit individual opinion holders to voice their opinions in opposition to

---

[35] 395 U.S.

[36] 395 U.S. White also adverted in this passage to *Kovacs v. Cooper*, (Chapter 3).

the editorial views of broadcasters, rather than permitting the latter simply to *represent* opposing views within their editorials.[37] Finally, he examined the barriers to equal communication rights posed by broadcast technology in terms which explicitly address the interests of audience members:

> There could be meaningful communications if half the people in the United States were talking and the other half listening.... But only a tiny fraction of those... can hope to communicate by radio at the same time if intelligible communication is to be had, even if the entire radio spectrum is utilized in the present state of commercially acceptable technology.... Where there are substantially more individuals who want to broadcast than there are frequencies to allocate, it is idle to posit an unabridgeable First Amendment right to broadcast comparable to the right of every individual to speak, write, or publish...
>
> As far as the First Amendment is concerned those who are licensed stand no better than those to whom licenses are refused.... There is nothing in the First Amendment which prevents the Government from requiring a licensee to share his frequency with others and to conduct himself as a proxy or fiduciary with obligations to present those views and voices which are representative of his community and which would otherwise, by necessity, be barred from the airwaves...
>
> The people as a whole retain their interest in free speech by radio and their collective right to have the medium function consistently with the ends and purposes of the First Amendment. It is the right of the viewers and listeners, not the right of the broadcasters, which is paramount.[38]

Two related issues with great significance for the later *DNC* case arose in Red Lion. These were the questions of editorial privilege and of the status of the scarcity doctrine. On the first question, White's opinion asserted that without the right of reply license holders would have far too much power to ensure their own views monopolized public discourse. This, he said, was no better than government encroachment on the freedom of the press: "the First Amendment does not sanction repression of that freedom by private interests."

> Congress need not stand idly by and permit those with licenses to ignore the problems which beset the people or to exclude from the airways anything but their own views of fundamental questions.[39]

---

[37] 395 U.S., 392; see also Mill, (1859/1971; Chapter 1, text at Note 26).

[38] 395 U.S.

[39] 395 U.S.

The appellant also argued that the scarcity doctrine no longer reflected prevailing conditions because there were in existence unallocated frequencies, and because new frequencies were being opened to use by technical advances. White, reviewing the FCC's allocation data, did not find an unreasonable gap between available and allocated frequencies. He also pointed out that the mere existence of unutilized parts of the spectrum was not enough to "render unconstitutional the Government's effort to assure that a broadcaster's programming ranges widely enough to serve the public interest," especially in face of the fact that

> Long experience in broadcasting, confirmed habits of listeners and viewers, network affiliation, and other advantages in program procurement give existing broadcasters a substantial advantage over new entrants.[40]

Why did these considerations in the *Red Lion* decision—the narrowing effects of *private* censorship on public discourse, the high entry barriers to the industry, and the legitimate power of legislators to counter both of these problems with right of reply rules—not bleed over into the *Tornillo* decision in the newspaper industry?

Retail Store Employees v. FCC

The 1970 *Retail Store Employees*[41] case is typical of the new view the courts held in broadcast access disputes for a few years after *Red Lion*. Note especially the different outcome from the *Chicago Joint Board* newspaper case[42] in the same year, despite their similar fact patterns.

The union had a labor dispute with a chain department store's Ashtabula, Ohio, operation. A strike was organized, and the union took out a large number of advertising spots on a local radio station to request public support for its picket line. After a few months the union was denied further opportunities to purchase advertising despite the fact that the station continued to air the employer's ads. The union complained to the FCC.

The Commission responded by noting that radio licensees were not common carriers and were not required to sell advertising opportunities on demand, and further noted that, in its opinion, there was no controversial issue of public importance involved in the dispute. The union intervened at the radio station's next license hearing, alleging a violation

---

[40] 395 U.S.

[41] 43 F. 2d 248 [1970].

[42] 435 F. 2d [17th Circ. 1970] (See Chapter 3).

of the Fairness Doctrine, and the FCC again dismissed the complaint. The union appealed, and the court, finding that "controversial issues of substantial public importance" were indeed involved, remanded the decision back to the FCC for rehearing. The court record does not indicate whether the union's expensive moral victory was translated into success on the picket line. In this case the union received, however, an unusually clear affirmation of its broadcast access rights from a court following the *Red Lion* precedent.

CBS v. Democratic National Committee

A more recent precedent in broadcast access is the case of *CBS v Democratic National Committee*, which put an end to the liberal interpretation of the Fairness Doctrine briefly sanctioned by *Red Lion*. *DNC* (the fact pattern is described below) recapitulates the 'opportunities for expression,' 'compelled speech,' 'editorial function,' 'state action,' and private property rights issues in the context of the broadcast media. The access and 'compelled speech' issues are inflected in a new way, not only by the different configuration of the 'state action' question, but also by the fact that this case invoked a structure of access midway between that denied in *Tornillo* and that affirmed in *Pruneyard*. (This new form of access is also denied.) The jurists' concern for editorial prerogatives mirrors that in Tornillo, and all of the egalitarian doctrine so fervently enunciated in *Red Lion* appears to evaporate, except from Brennan's dissent (joined by Marshall).

This case is rendered quite complex in two ways that deserve introductory comment. The first is the court voting pattern and its results: the plurality opinion (written by Burger) denied the 'opportunity for expression' sought by the Democratic National Committee, upholding CBS's appeal and reversing the previous Appeals Court decision in favor of the DNC. But there was *no* majority opinion on the *reasons* for reversing the Court of Appeals: Burger's substantive argument was joined only by Stewart and Renquist, while White and Blackmun, joined by Powell, wrote separate concurrences giving quite incompatible reasons. Douglas concurred on yet other grounds. Furthermore, Stewart wrote a separate concurrence diverging on *some* points from Burger's opinion, joined, on *some* points, by Blackmun and Powell; and Brennan wrote a dissent in which he was joined by Marshall. The Court was *not* unanimous.

Second, the case was one of four considered simultaneously by the Supreme Court, all arising from a broadcaster's exclusionary policy. These cases began with a complaint against CBS to the FCC, in 1970, from an organization called 'Business Executives' Move for Vietnam Peace'

(BEM); but by the time the Federal Supreme Court heard the dispute in 1973, it was faced with a loud rhubarb of texts and voices, including BEM, the FCC, the DNC, CBS, ABC, Post-Newsweek, and the Court of Appeals, as well as an unusually dense welter of legislative, regulatory and case law history and precedents.

The following discussion omits most of these voices, reviewing, as far as possible, only the case of *CBS v. DNC*[43] and the FCC's part in it. Similarly the dialogue between the justices is pared down to Burger's opinion, Brennan's dissent, and some instructive comments from the others. The relevant facts and doctrines are attentively preserved; but for the justices' analyses of, for example, the regulatory issues or the statutory history, the reader should consult the court record.

BEM's complaint to the FCC in January 1970 unsuccessfully asserted its right to buy radio advertising spots from WTOP, a station in Washington, D.C., to air its views on the Vietnam War. The station "followed a policy of refusing to sell time for spot announcements to individuals and groups who wished to expound their views on controversial issues."[44] DNC's case to the FCC 4 months later made a wider claim. It sought a declaratory ruling that broadcasters could not "as a general policy, refuse to sell time to responsible entities...for comment on public issues"[45] DNC did not object to the policies of any particular broadcaster, nor did it specify a particular issue on which it wished to speak. It offered evidence that its efforts to air ads would be frustrated by some broadcasters (e.g., CBS), and asked the Commission to declare such refusal a breach of the FCC's regulations and the limited constitutional right of access to the airwaves established by the Supreme Court in *Red Lion*.

It was really only the personal attack rules of the Fairness Doctrine which were tested and vindicated in *Red Lion*. *DNC* proposed a much broader reading of the FCC's regulatory powers. In effect, if it agreed to find a government-protected right to purchase the broadcast of ads, the FCC would have thereby required broadcasters to carry (paid) messages over which they exercised no editorial control ('personal' messages that did not have to be responses to attacks); would have taken away editorial definition of what constituted a "controversial issue" (by allowing advertisers to raise issues ignored by broadcasters); and would have imposed new conditions for 'balanced' coverage, all at once. If the FCC accepted this interpretation of *Red Lion*, *and* continued to enforce its existing provisions, it would have to require broadcasters to present the *other* sides of issues raised by advertisers like DNC, at their *own* expense.

---

[43] 412 U.S., 94 [1973].
[44] 412 U.S. 94 [1973].
[45] 412 U.S. 94 [1973].

Evidently, the Commission did not want these powers; it rejected both BEM's and DNC's complaint, finding that citizens and citizen groups had no First Amendment right to purchase broadcast advertising to comment on public issues.

The Court of Appeal reversed the Commission on both cases, finding a limited right to present "editorial advertisements" on stations which presented other paid announcements, such as product advertisements. In its view, broadcasters were "instrumentalities of the government" because of the scarcity doctrine—because they were granted a (regulated) use of a part of the public domain. It reasoned that acceptance of one kind of ad, and not the other, was unconstitutional discrimination by the state and counter to the purposes of the First Amendment. The Court of Appeal therefore instructed the Commission to develop appropriate regulations for determining how much editorial advertising must be accepted, and how it was to be selected.

The Supreme Court reversed the Court of Appeal (in the equivocal manner of voting noted above), denying the constitutionality of the DNC's proposed form of access. Burger distinguished the free editorial reply permitted in *Red Lion* from the paid editorial advertising access claimed by the DNC by arguing that the former is, and the latter is not, compatible with conditions of scarcity of available broadcasting frequencies. Therefore, he says (quoting Alexander Meiklejohn):

> What is essential is not that everyone shall speak, but that everything worth saying shall be said.[46]

Burger's opinion for the Court (the position of three of the nine justices—Burger, Stewart, and Renquist) said that this was not a First Amendment case. Broadcasters' editorial policies and judgements were not actions of the state, and were therefore not governed by the First Amendment. DNC's rights were not breached by CBS's refusal to air their ads, or by the FCC's refusal to require them to, because CBS was not acting as the government. Moreover, government action by the FCC would have unconstitutionally infringed on CBS's First Amendment rights. There simply was—and could be—no 'state action' implicated here.

This was consistent with Burger's later majority opinion in *Tornillo*,

---

[46] 412 U.S. 94 [1973]122, quoting Meiklejohn, (1965). The question arises, of course, of whether this standard does not impose a more vague and intrusive form of content review than the standard actually articulated by White in *Red Lion* (requiring access for individual opinion holders), even if the latter were extended to an 'affirmative' Fairness Doctrine claim such as that in *DNC* (see text at Note 37 above).

where the narrow Florida state statute requiring much less of newspapers than the Fairness Doctrine required of broadcasters (only a personal right of reply for candidates attacked during elections) was held to be an unconstitutional infringement on the First Amendment rights of the press. Nor does it contradict his opinion in Bellotti: the Massachussetts statute overturned in that case would have permitted the state to *deny* nonmedia corporations the right to buy political advertising. In *DNC* the government is restrained from either *requiring* media firms to sell such opportunities, or from requiring them *not* to do so: The decisions—and the selections—rest entirely with the owners of the media and their agents.

White and Blackmun, joined by Powell, denied the Democratic National Committee's sought-for access by upholding CBS's policy as consistent with the "substance" of the First Amendment: It *was* a First Amendment case; the broadcaster's policy *was* a government action; the outcome is not affected, because it *is* a constitutionally permissible state action. Douglas's concurrence varied from Burger's opinion only in going further: He found the Fairness Doctrine unconstitutional as well.

Burger gives extensive and deferential acknowledgment to the "delicate balancing" performed by Congress and the FCC:

> Congress and its chosen regulatory agency have established a delicately balanced system of regulation intended to serve the interests of all concerned...the broadcast industry is dynamic in terms of technological change.... Thus, in evaluating the First Amendment claims of respondents, we must afford great weight to the decisions of Congress and the experience of the Commission.... This is not to say...we would hesitate to invoke the Constitution should we determine that the Commission has not fulfilled its task with appropriate sensitivity to the interests in free expression.[47]

Having established the varying jurisdiction and unified intent of the orchestra of government, he waltzes deftly around with his chosen partner, editorial judgement: (a) he affirms the scarcity doctrine, finding in it more evidence of 'balancing'—"between private and public control"; (b) he notes approvingly Congress's rejection of common carrier regulation of broadcasting, in 1934; and (c) he happily discovers, in the Fairness Doctrine, a permissible balancing of the government's, and broadcasters', rights.

> *Broadcasters* are responsible for providing the...public with access to a balanced presentation of information on issues of public importance. Consistent with that philosophy...no private individual or group has a right to command the use of broadcast facilities.[48]

---

[47] 412 U.S. 94 (1973).

[48] 412 U.S. 94 [1973]; emphasis added.

Burger's argument in fact rests a great deal on the Fairness Doctrine. He rejects the Appeal Court's confidence in a number of Supreme Court cases prohibiting states from discriminating in the kinds of speech protected in the press or in public areas,[49] because, he says, the Fairness Doctrine "gives the public some assurance that the broadcaster will be answerable if he fails to meet its legitimate needs." Finally, against the Appeal Court's holding in favour of the DNC, he raises the specter of ruling class control of the media:

> The public interest in providing access to the marketplace of ideas would scarcely be served by a system so heavily weighted in favour of... those with access to wealth.... Moreover, there is the substantial danger that... editorial advertising could be monopolized by those of one political persuasion.[50]

The solution is, again, editors; we must repudiate the view, he writes,

> that every potential speaker is the best judge of what the listening public ought to hear or indeed the best judge of the merits of his or her views... editing is what editors are for; and editing is selection and choice of material.... The question here is not whether there is to be discussion of controversial issues of public importance on the broadcast media, but rather who shall determine what issues are to be discussed by whom, and when.[51]

But this argument is different than *Tornillo's*: the concern there over the 'chilling' of speech in the case of a limited 'right of reply' to the press should be absent in the case of a right to *initiate* debate in the broadcast media. Burger's sanguinary view is that "in a very real sense listeners and viewers constitute a 'captive audience'"; the government, he says, has known this since the Fourth National Radio Conference in 1924, and as the broadcast media have become more "pervasive" since then, "the problem has become more acute." *But*—

> it is no answer to say that because we tolerate pervasive commercial advertisements we can also live with its political counterparts.[52]

Justice Stewart, anticipating the recent fate of the Fairness Doctrine, notes that there are now (due to concentration in the newspaper industry)

---

[49] E.g., *Cox v. Louisiana*, 379 U.S. 536 [1965]; *Fowler v. Rhode Island*, 345 U.S. 67 [1953]; *Niemotko v. Maryland*, 340 U.S. 268 [1951].

[50] 412 U.S. 94 [1973].

[51] 412 U.S. 94 [1973].

[52] 412 U.S. 94 [1973]; note well that this is the same bencher who wrote the Court opinion in *Bellotti* (Chapter 3) upholding corporate rights to advertise on public issues.

"many more broadcasting stations than there are daily newspapers."[53] This he seems to intend as a buttress for the argument that no more regulatory limits on editorial control of public discourse by broadcasters are needed: The broadcast environment is already unusually diverse!

This was a prescient subversion of the scarcity doctrine. Note that the Fairness Doctrine was unanimously abdicated by the FCC in August 1987, on two grounds: (a) that the continuing reduction of the number of daily newspapers made the Scarcity Doctrine—the logical basis of the FCC's regulatory powers to articulate and enforce the Fairness Doctrine—discriminatory towards broadcasters; (b) that the Fairness Doctrine was counter productive in a First Amendment sense, because, by granting a basis for 'counterspeech' claims, it gave editorial staff an incentive to avoid controversy, thus 'chilling' free speech.[54] No explanation was given for the Commission's failure to enforce the 'affirmative obligation' under the Fairness Doctrine, which by itself would cure this perceived defect. The U.S. Congress continued to push for statutory enactment of the Doctrine, but its bills were vetoed by President Reagan. In the face of the Commission's and the Administration's hostility, and in light of the increasingly conservative composition of the Supreme Court, the Fairness Doctrine may now be taken as deceased, or at least comatose, even without the diagnostic aid of litigation. Who would bother? The biggest remaining question is whether this recent FCC action will be followed by abdication of the public trusteeship concept of broadcast licensing.

The 'chilled speech' argument might have had some force in relation to the already existing policies of the FCC under the Fairness Doctrine, since broadcasters were perceived already to have an incentive to avoid, as far as possible, raising issues or making accusations that would trigger its application (though it is hard to understand how such a perception comports with a reliance on 'editorial responsibility'). But the FCC had not applied the provisions of the Fairness Doctrine energetically: at the time of the DNC case, when they had been in place for some 40 years, the provision requiring that controversial issues *be* covered—the 'affirmative obligation'—had never been enforced.[55]

The *DNC* case is another such 'affirmative obligation' case. The form of access sought by the Democratic Party therefore logically precludes the 'chilling' argument on which *Tornillo* was based, and it also suggests how that concern might be addressed in relation to newspaper access. *DNC*

---

[53] 412 U.S., 94 [1973] Stewart concurring.

[54] *New York Times*, August 5, 1987, p. 20.

[55] It has been enforced *once* since then, in *Mink*.

sought a right to purchase editorial advertising on the airwaves *without regard* to whether the issues to be raised had been addressed, or whether their prospective ads completed the coverage of all *sides* of the issue, and as *initiation* of, rather than reply to, specific coverage. If the Democratic Party's case had been upheld by the Supreme Court, new responsibilities would have been *added* to editors' existing responsibilities under the Fairness Doctrine. This could not be described as more 'chilling' than Burger's *preference* for "pervasive commercial advertisements."

In *Tornillo* the question of access also raised the question of the 'costs' associated with it. The Court viewed this issue in terms of whether the newspaper firm would be exposed, by granting Florida's statutory access, to unreasonable increases in the cost of producing the newspaper itself, as a commodity. In *Tornillo* the press medium's provision of 'space' was held to be intrinsically elastic, to some degree, though the disputed access was nonetheless held to be a potentially unreasonable cost burden. In *DNC* this issue was not squarely addressed, though the practice of all justices was to refer to the broadcasters' 'sale of *time*'. In neither case did the Court raise the issue of *what* the media firm's final product was, what the cost components of producing it were, or what the effect of access on revenues *or* expenses might be. No consideration was given in *Tornillo* to the possibility that, since production of editorial content was an *expense*, compelled access could be construed as at least potentially a 'contribution in kind,' replacing other editorial content and thus *reducing* costs; similarly, in *DNC*, no attention was paid to the effects on advertising revenue of *increasing* demand in the ad market and thus, potentially, the rates. What seems to lie unstated beneath these silences is explicit recognition that audiences, prepared in particular ways to receive advertising messages, were the revenue-producing commodities of both media (and not of shopping centers); and the concomitant judgement that the sought-for forms of access would in some way damage the market value of those commodities.

Justice Brennan's dissent in *DNC* (which was joined by Marshall) directly opposed Burger's opinion, focusing on three issues: 'state action,' editorial prerogatives, and the relation between broadcasters and their audiences. Brennan was vehement that state action was indicated more than sufficiently to invoke the First Amendment:

> Given the...public nature of the airwaves, the governmentally created preferred status of broadcasters, the extensive Government regulation of broadcast programming, and the specific governmental approval of the challenged policy...the absolute refusal of broadcast licensees to sell air time to groups or individuals wishing to speak out on controversial issues of

> public importance must be subjected to the restraints of the First Amendment.[56]

Examining the nature of the editorial power granted by the Court's decision in this case he observes that the Fairness Doctrine fails to require broadcasters to allow speakers to present their own views, and that *this* is a constitutional defect:

> Broadcasters may meet their fairness responsibilities through presentation of carefully edited news programs, panel discussions, interviews, and documentaries. As a result, broadcasters retain almost exclusive control over the selection of issues and viewpoints to be covered, the manner of presentation, and, perhaps most important, who shall speak. . . . The Fairness Doctrine, standing alone, is insufficient—in theory as well as in practice—to provide the kind of uninhibited, robust, and wide-open exchange of views to which the public is constitutionally entitled.[57]

Brennan points out that a regime encouraging "uninhibited" debate requires, not only the presentation of issues generally recognized as "newsworthy," but also "exposure of the public to those views and voices that are novel, unorthodox, or unrepresentative of prevailing opinion," and that the Fairness Doctrine goes only far enough to ensure a range of views from among majority currents of opinion. Indeed, in a footnote to this passage[58] he suggests that "sit-ins and demonstrations testify" to the inability of minority viewpoints among the audience to establish access to the mass media by other means.

Putting together the question of whose view is *represented* in the media with the question of who *presents* it, Brennan next recalled the Court to one of the constitutional sourcebooks it relied on in the *Red Lion* case. In *Red Lion* the majority opinion quoted J.S. Mill to support government regulation under the Fairness Doctrine:

> The expression of views opposing those which broadcasters permit to be aired in the first place need not be confined solely to the broadcasters themselves as proxies. "Nor is it enough that he should hear the arguments of his own adversaries from his own teachers, presented as they state them, and accompanied by what they offer as refutations. This is not the way to do justice to the arguments, or bring them into real contact with his own mind.

---

[56] 412 U.S., 94 [1973].

[57] 412 U.S. 94 [1973].

[58] 412 U.S. 94 [1973], Note 27.

> He must be able to hear them from persons who actually believe them; who defend them in earnest, and do their very utmost for them."[59]

Brennan recapitulated this argument to critique the absolute necessity of "journalistic middlemen" implied by sanctioning a ban on editorial advertising:

> The public is compelled to rely *exclusively* on the "journalistic discretion" (Burger) of broadcasters.... This separation of the advocate from the expression of his views can serve only to diminish the effectiveness of that expression.[60]

Brennan locates the underlying dynamic of broadcasters' content selection in the processes of market exchange. He finds, in this case, some First Amendment problems with this:

> In light of the strong interest of broadcasters in maximizing their audience, and therefore their profits, it seems almost naive to expect the majority...to produce the variety and controversiality of material necessary to reflect a full spectrum of viewpoints...it is simply 'bad business' to espouse—or even to allow others to espouse—the heterodox or the controversial.[61]

The case before the Court, however, is not so wide ranging as to require a complete rejection of editorial control; it calls rather for "a balance of competing First Amendment interests." Only the allocation of "advertising time—air time that broadcasters regularly relinquish to others without the retention of significant editorial control" is implicated:

> Thus, we are concerned here, not with the speech of broadcasters themselves, but, rather, with their "right" to decide which *other* individuals will be given an opportunity to speak in a forum that has already been opened to the public.[62]

So for Brennan, the broadcaster policy contested by the Democratic National Committee is discriminatory, in that it refuses access for some speakers and views even during those periods of the broadcast day—the commercial breaks—when it is willing to give over content responsibility

---

[59] *Red Lion*, quoting J.S. Mill (see Notes 37, 46, above).

[60] 412 U.S., 94 [1973], Brennan, dissenting; emphasis in original.

[61] 412 U.S. 94 [1973].

[62] 412 U.S. 94 [1973].

to product advertisers. This is *not* the improvement in "the performance of the system of freedom of expression" required when resolving "conflicts of interest... within the system."[63] According to the Court's ruling,

> any person wishing to market a particular brand of beer, soap, toothpaste or deodorant has direct, personal, and instantaneous access to the electronic media. He can present his own message, in his own words, in any format he selects, and at a time of his own choosing. Yet a similar individual seeking to discuss war, peace, pollution, or the suffering of the poor is denied this right to speak. Instead, he is compelled to rely on the beneficence of a corporate trustee appointed by the Government to argue his case for him.[64]

[63] Note 5 above.

[64] Note 5 above.

Chapter 5

The Right to Receive Corporate and Commercial Speech

When Oliver Wendell Holmes asserted, in his dissent in the *Abrams* case in 1919,[1] that "the ultimate good desired is better reached by free trade in ideas," and that "the best test of truth is the power of thought to get itself accepted in the competition of the market," he was exercising a degree of rhetorical license. Holmes claimed to be paraphrasing J.S. Mill's argument from the second chapter of *On Liberty*, but Mill made no mention there of markets. And real markets, in any case, are only devices for organizing *preferences*, not for certifying the rationality of propositions: The distance between truth and what we might wish were true cannot be eliminated by an auction.

But the 'free marketplace of ideas' metaphor has acquired new rhetorical force in the First Amendment decisions since the mid-1970s. By that point, the drive for citizen access to the mass media had been neutralized by publishers' and broadcasters' success in the courts. The caselaw of the succeeding fifteen years has articulated an innovative and far-reaching doctrine of *corporate and commercial* speech rights, which has stalled any residual momentum towards government regulation to expand media access, and dismantled much of the juridical basis of advertising regulation as well. The Court has affirmed the *audience's right to receive* such

[1] See Chapter 3, text at Note 12.

communication as the most compelling element in these conflicts. The following discussion first maps the general definitional strategies of the Court, and then examines both the key cases in which it articulated its earlier and opposite doctrine, and the decisions in which this new doctrine emerged.

A PROBLEM OF DEFINITION

Since the 1975 *Bigelow* case[2] a long-standing distinction in legal doctrine between the First Amendment protection properly due to 'political' and 'commercial' speech has been progressively erased.[3] Prior to *Bigelow* government had fairly generous discretionary powers in the regulation of advertising. The courts distinguished between the expression of speakers having predominantly financial interests in its distribution, and that of speakers whose motives were explicitly political. They protected political speech from governmental interference far more assiduously, viewing it as the core object of the First Amendment's guarantee. Government regulation of the more tangential category of commercial speech, on the other hand, was widely permitted.

The distinction had obvious definitional problems, and these became salient in the 1960s and early 1970s. As late as 1974 the FCC stated that pure product advertising did not "inform the public on any side of a controversial issue [or make] a meaningful contribution to public debate."[4] But it was by then also a commonplace market positioning strategy for a large firm to attempt to propagate a desirable corporate 'image' as well as advertising the products it produced. 'Image' advertising doesn't concentrate on the attributes of products (or their users), but on the attributes of the company: for example, the patriotic motives guiding its business decisions. Additionally, corporate policy on a wide array of issues with commercial *and* political implications (such as oil pricing, napalm manufacturing, strip mining, effluent dumping, and nuclear power generation) came under broad and vociferous attack in this period. The 'advocacy' advertisement, which presented the firm's view on a public policy issue,

---

[2] *Bigelow v. Virginia*, 421 U.S. 809.

[3] See generally Jackson and Jeffries (1979); Merrill (1976).

[4] *Fairness Report*, 48 FCC 2d 1 [1974]. It should be noted, though, that the FCC made this statement in order to repudiate its own decision in *Banzhaf*, 8 FCC 2d 381 [1967], in which it had extended the Fairness Doctrine to apply to product advertising. *Banzhaf* created, for a few years, an obligation on broadcasters to carry 'counteradvertising' against cigarette commercials when they aired these. The new (1974) policy exempted *product* advertising (but not advocacy advertising) from the Fairness Doctrine.

was one response to this kind of criticism.[5] Were patriotic image advertising and public advocacy advertising instances of commercial or of political speech?

In many rulings the courts have attempted to uphold a definition of commercial speech based primarily on the *content* of the communication, even as they revised their view of the degree of constitutional protection it enjoyed.[6] Eventually they realized how semantically slippery—not to mention unenforceable—this route was. If some kinds of government regulation of advertising are still to be admissible, a content-based definition of commercial speech is inadequate, as the Supreme Court noted in a case contesting state regulation of pharmaceutical advertising:

> Not all commercial messages contain... a very great public interest element [but] there are few to which such an element could not be added. Our pharmacist, for example, could cast himself as a commentator on store-to-store disparities in drug prices, giving his own and those of a competitor as proof. We see little point in requiring him to do so, and little difference if he does not.[7]

The Supreme Court has also used a *combination* of defining variables when distinguishing between commercial and political speech. The content of the communication, the methods of its diffusion, and the motivation of the speaker were considered together to extend First Amendment protection to an advertisement prohibited under state law in the *Bigelow* case.[8] Pecuniary motivation and commercial content were the factors weighed by the court in denying protection to an advertisement in *Chrestensen*,[9] the controlling precedent until *Bigelow*. In *Sullivan*[10] the Court found the fact that a communication took the form of a paid advertisement which solicited money for the civil rights movement did not render it commercial speech because the motive was not profit. An advertised offer of free legal services by the ACLU was protected on the same grounds of exempt motivation.[11]

Other factors were added to the definition. In at least two decisions the

---

[5] See Dreier (1982).

[6] See, for example, *Bates v. State Bar of Arizona*, 433 U.S. 350 [1977] at 363; *Virginia State Board of Pharmacy v. Virginia Citizens' Consumer Council*, 425 U.S. 748 [1976] at 761; *Village of Schaumberg v. Citizens for a Better Environment*, 444 U.S. 620 [1980] at 632; *Ohralik v. Ohio State Bar Association*, 436 U.S. 447 [1978] at 455.

[7] *Virginia Board of Pharmacy*, at 764.

[8] 421 U.S. 809 [1975].

[9] *Chrestensen v. Valentine*, 316 U.S. 52 [1942].

[10] *New York Times v. Sullivan*, 376 U.S. 354 [1964].

[11] *In Re Primus*, 436 U.S. 412 [1978] at 422.

interests of the distributor of the message, that is, of the publisher or other media owner, were considered.[12] The *nature of the product* was also found relevant in several cases involving paid, profit-motivated speech about a constitutionally protected activity: reading books.[13] Finally, the *interests of the audience* in receiving the speech, and the question of whether those interests were purely economic or not, emerged as the decisive factor in three key cases.[14]

No precise definition or test for commercial speech has yet been formulated by the Supreme Court, despite the fact that it has fashioned in this area a significant departure in First Amendment theory, and made, in its name, a large number of very innovative and far-reaching decisions. The most significant element of the new commercial speech doctrine is that where decisions have resulted in a greater extension of First Amendment protection to commercial expression—and since *Bigelow* most have done so—the rationale has been the audience's right to receive it. Curiously, it has seldom been audiences, and more often advertisers and media firms, who have sought the protection of the audience's speech rights in this manner.

In the following sections of this chapter I argue that this discovery of new First Amendment rights for the audience was grounded in the Court's view of the connection between *markets* and *democracy*. The Court reasoned that

> if the free flow of commercial information is indispensable to the proper allocation of resources in a free-enterprise system, it is also indispensable to the formation of intelligent opinions as to how that system ought to be regulated or altered. Therefore, even if the First Amendment were thought to be primarily an instrument to enlighten public decision-making in a democracy, we could not say that the free flow of information does not serve that goal.[15]

There is no possibility of interpreting the now greatly increased latitude for commercial speech as a *right to advertise: that* notion was soundly laid to rest in the access caselaw as an unwarranted infringement of the expressive rights of media owners. There is no First Amendment

---

[12] *Metromedia Inc. v. City of San Diego*, 453 U.S. 490 [1981]; *Bolger v. Youngs Drugs Products Co.*, 463 U.S. 60 [1983].

[13] *Murdock v. Pennsylvania*, 319 U.S. 105 [1943], cited in *Dun & Bradstreet Inc.v. Greenmoss Builders Inc.*, 53 U.S.L.W. 4866 (June 26, 1985); *Breard v. City of Alexandria*, 341 U.S. 622 [1951].

[14] *Virginia Board of Pharmacy*; *Metromedia*; *Central Hudson Gas & Electric Corporation v. N.Y. Public Service Commission*, 447 U.S. 557 [1980].

[15] *Virginia Board of Pharmacy*, at 756.

right to advertise. The rights granted in the commercial speech decisions are the right of *audiences to receive* what media owners choose to offer—and the right of media firms and their clients to control those offerings with very little regard to the government's pursuit of *other* public interests.

Certainly governments have often used the licensing of speech opportunities as an occasion simply for the suppression of dissent; and, at least in principle, most citizens of liberal democracies agree that such prior restraint by government is inimical to the public interest. But regulation may have more positive goals than the suppression of dissent.[16] *Commercial free speech* is a justly controversial notion when advertising is targeted at 'vulnerable' groups (such as children), or represents parts of the population in ways they consider unfair (such as women), or promotes products which may endanger public health or safety (such as alcohol and tobacco), or undermines the protection of collective rights (such as language rights). When no right of reply to such advertising exists, it is hard to accept such commercial liberties at face value as an augmentation of the *audience*'s rights.

Considered in isolation, the *right to receive* does not endanger the public's interest in communication as an instrument of self-government; it is even a useful addition. But taken together with public exclusion from *speaking* roles in the media, and considering the private economic power and motives of media firms and their clients, the freedom from public regulation embodied in the new commercial speech rights doctrine can be understood as a further concentration of control over public discourse into private hands.

It is, however, interesting that in extending new commercial speech rights the Court has begun to use a model which analyzes the distribution of rights among actors and interests. In the instant case this has been characterized as a "hearer-centered" model of the First Amendment.[17] In the commercial speech case law the Court completes its codification of the rights of the various actors: to the 'speaking' rights of the media firm and its designated agents (editors and journalists) and contracted proxies (advertisers) are added the 'hearing' rights of the audience. This ultimately takes place as if the conflicts which reached the courts' adjudication were really conflicts between the audience—demanding the *right to receive* advertisements—and those tyrannical governments determined to deny this right.

The *right to receive* has its origins, prior to the 'new-look' commercial speech decisions, in the mass media case law of the 1960s. There was a

---

[16] And access regulations would seem to fall in this category—see *Red Lion* (Chapter 4).

[17] Neubourne (1987) (Chapter 1).

faint trace of it in the extension of editorial privilege in *Sullivan*;[18] and it was made explicit in *Red Lion*, where the function of compelled access was, not the speaker's interest in self-expression via the mass media, but the *audience's* right to receive her suppressed viewpoint. (This potential of the 'right to receive' to furnish a rationale for *access* rights is now apparently extinguished: the right extends only as far as the media firm's desire to accommodate it.) Here is how the Court in *Red Lion* saw it:

> It is the right of the viewers and listeners, not the right of the broadcasters, which is paramount. It is the purpose of the First Amendment to preserve an uninhibited marketplace of ideas in which truth will ultimately prevail, rather than to countenance monopolization of that market, whether it be by the Government itself, or by a private licensee. It is the right of the public to receive suitable access to social, political, aesthetic, moral, and other ideas and experiences which is crucial here.[19]

The development of the *right to receive* has important implications for our attempt to interpret the Court's representation of the audience's rights and interests, and to assess the political and economic value-premises and underlying theory of communication employed by the courts in mass media cases. The *right to receive* has become an 'obvious' and common-sense notion in the short period since its invention and routinely appears, without any explanation necessary, in the ordinary discourse of the mass media and the advertising industry themselves on speech rights topics, even in other jurisdictions.[20] A resolution passed at the 1985 General Assembly of the World Federation of Advertisers, for example, states quite baldly that

> the freedom to publicize and to receive information of a commercial nature is as necessary for the social and economic development of every individual human being and of society as a whole as the freedom to impart and receive information of a cultural and political nature.[21]

---

[18] 376 U.S. 254 [1964].

[19] 395 U.S. 367 [1969] (Chapter 4).

[20] For example, in the controversy surrounding the Canadian Government's recent passage of legislation to prohibit tobacco advertising, reference is routinely made to the right to receive as a common-sense formulation of citizens' speech rights in the mass media—see, e.g., "Newspapers defend tobacco ads," *Globe & Mail* July 10, 1987, p. A4; and the full-page ad from the Canadian Tobacco Manufacturer's Council on page *Globe & Mail*, July 17, 1987, p. A3. The same notion appears in reports on other consumer protection disputes. A judge of the Quebec Court of Appeal was quoted regarding the "right to send and receive commercial messages" in "Consumer groups promise to fight...,"*Globe & Mail* September 24, 1986.

[21] Quoted in "Flow of information," *Globe & Mail* June 12, 1985, p. B4.

The rest of this chapter describes the various case contexts in which commercial and corporate speech rights have been contested, and in which corporate assertion of the audience's *right to receive* has broadly prevailed over attempted public interest regulation. One instructive instance of its use in a context of *non*-commercial political speech is also reviewed. Here, in the context of a public lecture,[22] a curious reversal of the pattern in the access case law emerges. Whereas it was demonstrated in the last chapter that opportunities for expression denied in the mass media were generally upheld in the context of direct interaction, here the *right to receive*, *upheld* in the mass media context, is *denied* in the context of direct interpersonal communication.

CHALLENGES TO THE DOGMA

Chrestensen, Jones et al., and Breard

The Supreme Court first addressed the issue of constitutional protection for commercial speech in the 1942 *Chrestensen*[23] case. This unanimous decision, which firmly repudiated an advertiser's claim to First Amendment protection from government regulation, remained the controlling precedent until the mid-1970s.

In 1940 Mr. Chrestensen bought a surplus submarine from the U.S. Navy, piloted it from Florida, where he purchased it, to New York City, and moored it at a state-operated pier in the East River. Planning to profit from his investment by selling guided tours of the interior of his vessel to members of the public, he printed and began to distribute on the streets an advertising handbill. He was interrupted in this attempt to convert military equipment to peaceful use by the police, who informed him that his distribution of handbills violated Section 318 of the Sanitary Code of New York.

Mr. Chrestensen did some research and discovered that, while distribution of commercial and business advertising matter in the streets was prohibited, the distribution of handbills "devoted to information or public protest"[24] was exempt from this Section of the Sanitary Code. He thereupon went back to the printer with his handbills, which carried his advertisement on one side and were blank on the other, and had a protest against the wharfage rates of the City Dock Department printed on the blank side. He then resumed his leafleting activity.

---

[22] *Kleindienst v. Mandel*, 408 U.S. 396 [1974].

[23] 316 U.S. [1942].

[24] At 52.

The Court affirmed that "the streets are proper places for the exercise of the freedom of communicating information and disseminating opinion"; and it further acknowledged "the difficulty of apportioning... the contents of the communication as between what is of public interest and what is for private profit." But it nevertheless found that "the Constitution imposes no restraint on government as regards *purely commercial advertising*"[25]

> The affixing of the protest... to the advertising circular was with the intent, and for the purpose, of evading the prohibition of the ordinance. If that evasion were successful, every merchant who desires... need only append a civic appeal, or a moral platitude, to achieve immunity from the law's command.[26]

Although the Court had not previously had opportunity to articulate its view on this question, the position it took in *Chrestensen* was a traditional one, and by no means departed from then-current doctrine. The central function of freedom of speech was to safeguard democracy, and the strength of any claim to the protection of speech against government regulation was measured by its relation to that purpose. As an Ontario High Court Justice put it more recently:

> Pure commercial speech says nothing about how people are governed, or how they should govern themselves. Indeed, it stands outside of public discourse: it could be said in a tyranny or a democracy, a monarchy or a society without a government at all.[27]

The lower court decision in *Chrestensen* had focused on the *content* of the handbill, and had carefully avoided reliance on the motive of the speaker. On the basis of its content (the protest added to the reverse side) constitutional protection of the handbill was *affirmed*. Despite the apparent clarity and simplicity of the Supreme Court's reversal of the lower court judgment, it actually opened, by its reliance on *motive*, a complex and difficult question which ultimately had to be rethought many times over the next several decades. As two recent authors observe, the distinction between commercial and non-commercial speech asserted in this decision failed to distinguish usefully "the many different senses in which expression may be said to be commercial, the ways in which its commercial nature is totally irrelevant to its protected status, and the senses in which its commercial nature may possibly be of some constitutional relevance."

---

[25] At 55; emphasis added.

[26] At 56.

[27] *Re Klein and Law Society of Upper Canada*, 16 D.L.R. (4th) 489 [1985] at 534, Callaghan, J., for the Court.

> Speech may be 1) commercial in content and commercial in its motivation, or 2) commercial because of the nature of the speaker's motivation, but political or non-commercial in its content, e.g., critical of government action, but occasioned by government action that impinges on the private, economic interests of the speaker, or 3) non-commercial in its motivation and non-commercial in its content, e.g., classical political comment concerning abstract ideological issues, or 4) non-commercial in its motivation but commercial in its content, e.g., the handbill... giving notice of [a political meeting] but containing a schedule of admission charges.[28]

Within months of the *Chrestensen* decision the Supreme Court was obliged to begin its reconsideration of the commercial speech doctrine. A flurry of cases appeared as a result of conflicts which emerged at this time between the Jehovah's Witnesses and municipal governments all across the country.[29] These were, moreover, not ordinary civil disputes, but contests between the moral and justiciary authority of the Court's constitutional texts and the Divine Power of God's Word as revealed in Holy Scripture.

A central religious practice of the Jehovah's Witnesses, then as now, is the demonstration of their "conformity to the teachings of St. Matthew 10: 11-14 and 24: 14, by going from city to city, from village to village, and house to house, to proclaim them."[30] Perhaps recognizing the formal similarity between the Court's temporal discourse and the other spiritual one, Jehovah's Witnesses came before the Supreme Court in large numbers to argue that sanitary codes and ordinances governing door-to-door solicitation could not legitimately be applied to "the exercise of their beliefs concerning their duty to preach the gospel."[31]

The initial problem was that, while preaching the gospel, the Jehovah's Witnesses distributed printed learning aids in the form of handbills and magazines, and solicited donations for this material from respondents. The charitable, nonprofit organization, which printed the material and collected the receipts, used these donations solely to extend its activity in witnessing Jehovah's works; but it remained a fact, in the eyes of municipal and state authorities, that the Witnesses were engaged in commercial solicitation on the street and from door to door in contravention of the relevant bylaws and without obtaining and paying for the necessary licenses.

---

[28] Rome and Roberts (1985, pp. 18–19). Rome and Roberts also corroborate my analysis of the emergence of the right to receive.

[29] *Murdock v. Pennsylvania*, ibid; *Jones v. City of Opelika, Sanders v. City of Fort Smith, Bowden v. City of Fort Smith, Jobin v. Arizona*, all 316 U.S. 584 [1942], all vacated 319 U.S. 103 [1943]; *Jamison v. Texas*, 318 U.S. 413 [1943]; *Douglas et al. v. City of Jeannette*, 319 U.S. 157 [1943]; *Martin v. City of Struthers*, 319 U.S. 141 [1943].

[30] *Jones et al.*, at 606–7.

[31] At 589.

In its first decisions, in the immediate aftermath of *Chrestensen*, the Court denied the Witnesses the protection of the First Amendment (which of course also protects freedom of religion along with speech, press and association). The reasoning in *Jones*, *Bowden*, *Sanders* and *Jobin*,[32] while accepting the sincerity of the religious motive involved, found that the pecuniary element of the contested speech acts *did* strip them of their constitutional protection and make them subject to the commercial speech exception articulated a few months before. It was also stated, however, that these were simply "time, place and manner" restrictions.[33] The Court pointed out that the mixture of noncommercial with commercial content was not enough to exempt the commercial conduct from regulation: the fact that money was earned brought these cases within the ambit of *Chrestensen*.

The justices considered the possible similarity of this instance of government licensing of published material with other famous instances, such as the Star Chamber censorship that moved Milton to write the *Areopagitica* in 1640, or the contribution of King George's Stamp Tax to revolt in the Colonies. In this case, though, the Court equated the sought-after exemption from the license requirements with a government *subsidy* to the Witnesses, and found this wholly repugnant.[34]

The Supreme Court found against the Jehovah's Witnesses in the 1942 cases. But although a majority opinion was produced, the Court remained sharply divided on these cases and took the unusual step of vacating its own decision shortly after the judgement was handed down. The dissenting views in the original judgement focused on the overall intent or motive of the Witnesses, which was clearly noncommercial, and thus found their activity constitutionally protected because there was no *conspiracy* to shield illegal motives (i.e., the avoidance of legitimate license expenses) behind lawful acts. On rehearing the arguments the following year the Court reversed its judgment in all cases.

The new judgment in the Witnesses' favor in *Jones et al.*, as also the favourable judgments in *Murdock* and *Jamison* in 1943,[35] rested, in the last analysis, on the sincerity of their religious motive and the ancillary evidence thereof in the charitable character of the enterprise, the devotion of its revenues to expand its religiously motivated activities, and the willingness of the organization to distribute its publications without charge to those who could not pay and to enter cheerfully into the occasional financial losses thereby incurred. This meant, however, that in

---

[32] 316 U.S. 584 [1942].

[33] At 594.

[34] At 599.

[35] 319 U.S. 105 [1943]; 318 U.S. 413 [1943].

some important sense the reasoning in *Chrestensen* was either in sharp contradiction with, or was broadly augmented by the reasoning in these cases. *Jamison*[36] is a good example. Unlike all the cases decided in 1942, there was no issue in this case of refusal to pay a license fee for street solicitation: the violated ordinance quite simply prohibited the distribution of handbills. The handbill distributed by the offending Witness was, like Mr. Chrestensen's, printed on both sides, with an invitation to a religious gathering on one side and a solicitation for the purchase of two religious books on the other. On the basis of Jamison's religious motive his conviction was overturned and his First Amendment claim for exemption from the bylaw upheld. Thus *Chrestensen* and *Jamison*, taken together, illustrate that communication that is "commercial because of the nature of the speaker's motivation, but political or non-commercial in its content," must indeed be distinguished carefully from communication which is "non-commercial in its motivation but commercial in its content."

In *Martin*[37] another issue was raised. The contested by-law in this case (somewhat like that in *Jamison*) simply prohibited the disturbance of householders for the purpose of distributing handbills, whether by ringing the doorbell, knocking on the door, or other means. Neither the Witness herself nor her literature in this instance solicited funds: the purpose of the door-to-door visits was simply to invite the city's residents to a free religious service. The bylaw, and Ms. Martin's conviction, were overturned, but *not* simply on the basis that this was an instance of non-commercial speech. Canvassing door-to-door could not be prohibited outright, because the potential annoyance of commercial solicitation could not effectively be prevented without a greater harm to all varieties of political and religious expression that might rely on a direct canvass for their dissemination. The Court weighed "the conflicting interests of the appellant in the civil rights she claims, as well as the right of the individual householder to determine whether he is willing to receive her message, against the interest of the community which by this ordinance offers to protect the interests of all of its citizens, whether particular citizens want that protection or not."[38] The priority interests they chose to protect in this case were the interests of potential *receivers* of information who might wish to be exposed to it.

The last of these early commercial speech cases, the 1951 *Breard* case,[39] was quite similar to the others in that it involved municipal prohibition of direct (door-to-door) communication involving a commercial

[36] 318 U.S. [1943].

[37] 319 U.S. [1943].

[38] At 143.

[39] *Breard v. City of Alexandria*, 341 U.S. [1951].

element. The primary new inflection was the combination of press freedoms with the issue of public solicitation. The Louisiana municipality of Alexandria had an ordinance forbidding uninvited *sales* visits to residences, and the constitutionality of this ordinance was affirmed. But the convicted canvasser, who was soliciting magazine subscriptions as a business agent of the publisher, based his defense on the First Amendment's protection of the press. The Court was obliged to specify that it was the *profit motive* of the canvassing activity that exposed it to regulation. The decision affirmed the constitutional protection of publishers with respect to the content of their publications, but found their interest in disseminating those publications as they saw fit weaker than the privacy interests of residents. Three members of the Court dissented, asserting the necessity of protecting publishers' freedom to disseminate their communication. In this case (and in *Murdock*) the last two elements of the Supreme Court's definition struggle with 'commercial speech' make their first appearance: the *nature of the product* that is the subject of the communication, and the *method of diffusion* of the speech.

Another question that arises here is how the profit motive that made publishers' sales agents subject to government regulation of their verbal communication is to be distinguished for constitutional purposes from the profit motive of publishers themselves in printing and distributing their products. Would the sales agent have been protected by offering residents a free leaflet containing some noncommercial information of general public interest along with his sales pitch? How would this be different from the publisher's activity? What would be the essential defect of a theory that proposed that all of the communicative activity of a commercial media corporation and its agents, including journalists, is 'commercial speech,' and thus subject—*because of its commercial character*—to some degree of governmental regulation?

In *Chrestensen*, *Breard*, and the Jehovah's Witness cases the Supreme Court maintained a consistent position: commercial speech does *not* enjoy constitutional protection—*when it can be clearly identified* as such. It remained adamant that government may regulate purely commercial advertising, and that such regulation is in fact an *exception* from the First Amendment's protection against government restraint of speech. In a sense the core of this doctrine has *not* changed in recent years, even though a very significant degree of constitutional protection has been extended to commercial advertising. The distinct category of expression discovered in *Chrestensen*—'commercial speech'—is still a distinct category. Whether the Court finds that commercial speech is completely *un*protected, *partially* protected or even *fully* protected, it continues to "recognize a difference between commercial price and product advertising and ideological communication."[40] The lines may blur in some instances, but the assumption is that there remains a region of 'pure' market information disseminated for 'pure' motives of profit, and this content and this motive are by definition *nonideological.*

Sullivan, Pittsburgh Press, and Bigelow

Every journalist is familiar with the *New York Times Co. v. Sullivan* case;[41] it was a momentous decision, simultaneously establishing a new and very liberal standard for libel in the criticism of government officials, new powers of journalistic privilege and editorial discretion, a further interpretation of the commercial speech doctrine, and a ringing declaration of citizens' rights to receive controversial and governmentally proscribed opinion in the commercial mass media. As well, the persuasive force of this decision helped confer a constitutional mandate on the civil rights movement of the 1960s.

On March 29, 1960, the *New York Times* ran a full-page advertisement sponsored by the Committee to Defend Martin Luther King and the Struggle for Freedom in the South. The advertisement contained, under a large banner headline reading 'Heed Their Rising Voices,' a 1000-word description of King's student-based protest movement and its reception in several southern communities, about 100 prominent supporters' names, and a financial pledge coupon. One of the protest demonstrations was described in the ad as follows:

> In Montgomery, Alabama, after students sang "My Country, 'Tis of Thee" on the State Capitol steps, their leaders were expelled from school, and truckloads of police armed with shotguns and tear-gas ringed the Alabama State College campus. When the entire student body protested to state authorities by refusing to re-register, their dining hall was padlocked in an attempt to starve them into submission.

One of the three elected Commissioners of the City of Montgomery—the Commissioner responsible, among other things, for supervising the Police Department (Sullivan)—sued the N.Y. Times and four of the ad's sponsors for libel. He won, and was awarded damages of $500,000 in Montgomery County Court; and he won the subsequent appeal of this decision to the Supreme Court of Alabama. Ralph Abernathy and the *New*

---

[40] Claire Bernstein, "Courts to examine advertisers' free speech rights," *Toronto Globe & Mail*, December 2, 1985, p. B8.

[41] 376 U.S. 254 [1964].

York Times both appealed again to the U.S. Supreme Court, which overturned the lower courts' decision.

On the question of the existence of a libel, the Supreme Court found that the advertisement was factually erroneous—but that in the case of comment on public officials in the performance of their duties, the First Amendment protected newspapers from punitive libel damages on the basis of error alone. "Actual malice" had to be proven, because otherwise the vital public function of the press in eliciting uninhibited debate on matters of public interest and controversy would be impaired. "The constitutional protection does not turn upon the truth, popularity, or social utility of the ideas and beliefs which are offered," said the Court.[42]

> 'Some degree of abuse is inseparable from the proper use of every thing; and in no instance is this more true than in that of the press.'[43]

This new standard for establishing libel against government officials (written by Justice Brennan) was greeted with jubilation by journalists, for it meant that self-censorship and the specter of crippling costs arising from honest error or misleading sources had been exorcised from the coverage of government affairs, and their professional privilege significantly extended.

But there was another aspect to the decision. The plaintiff had argued in part, citing *Chrestensen*, that the First Amendment was inapplicable to this case because the libel was contained in a paid advertisement, and was therefore commercial speech, exempt from constitutional protection. Brennan distinguished *Chrestensen* by *motive* and thus found that the advertisement in *Sullivan* was *not* commercial speech (despite the fact that it was paid for, and also contained a solicitation for donations):

> Any other conclusion would discourage newspapers from carrying 'editorial advertisements' of this type, and so might shut off *an important outlet for the promulgation of information and ideas by persons who do not themselves have access to publishing facilities*—who wish to exercise their freedom of speech even though they are not members of the press... To avoid placing such a handicap upon the freedoms of expression, we hold that if the allegedly libellous statements would otherwise be constitutionally protected from the present judgement, they do not forfeit that protection because they were published in the form of a paid advertisement.[44]

---

[42] Sullivan, quoting *NAACP v. Button*, 371 U.S. 415, at 445.

[43] *Sullivan*, quoting James Madison, in *Elliot's Debates on the Federal Constitution* (1876), at 571.

[44] *Sullivan*, at 266; emphasis added.

This rationale for constitutional protection of "editorial advertisements" was based on the interests of citizens *as speakers* and the concomitant result that "government may be responsive to the will of the people and ... changes obtained by lawful means."[45] But a related rationale for protection, one which was prefigured in the context of direct interaction in *Martin* and emerges later as an important element *within* commercial speech doctrine, is also articulated in *Sullivan*: The advertisement became something other than unprotected commercial speech because of the audience's interest in *receiving* it:

> The interest of the public here outweighs the interest of appellant or any other individual. The protection of the public requires not merely discussion, but information.[46]

In early 1972 two additional commercial speech rulings were handed down by the Supreme Court. Both of these decisions retreated from the complete exclusion of commercial speech from First Amendment protection, and thus paved the way for the new doctrine which emerged soon after. The first of these, *Pittsburgh Press Co. v. Pittsburgh Commission on Human Relations*,[47] concerned a newspaper's practice of dividing its classified 'help wanted' columns by gender. Pursuant to an ordinance of the Pittsburgh Human Relations Commission the newspaper was issued with a cease and desist order, which withstood appeal to the Pennsylvania Commonwealth Court. The Supreme Court also upheld the order.

The newspaper, of course, claimed First Amendment immunity from this regulation, relying on the broad findings of editorial discretion throughout the press case law,[48] including *Sullivan*. The Human Relations Commission relied almost entirely on *Chrestensen*. The Court took its task to be deciding whether the advertisements in questions more closely resembled the submarine tour solicitation or the civil rights appeal, and found them to be "classic" instances of commercial speech, and thus subject to regulation. The Court did not, however, extend *Chrestensen* (or even defend it very vigorously), preferring to withhold press protection in this case mainly on the argument that the gender classification of employment advertising was part of a broader category of illegal activity: employment discrimination. This foray into the regulation of commercial speech in the mass media forum is significant for later decisions because it identified in advance a relation between commercial speech and unlawful

---

45 At 269, quoting *Stromberg* (Chapter 3).

46 At 271.

47 413 U.S. 376 [1973].

48 See Chapter 3.

conduct that triggers, far more sensitively than for political speech, the outer boundary of constitutional protection:

> Any First Amendment interest which might be served by advertising an ordinary commercial proposal and which might arguably outweigh the governmental interest supporting the regulation is altogether absent when the commercial activity itself is illegal.[49]

This principle was soon tested. *Bigelow v. Commonwealth of Virginia*[50] considered the conviction of the editor of the *Virginia Weekly* (an 'underground' newspaper circulated largely on and around a university campus) for publishing the advertisement of an abortion referral agency located in New York City. Although *Roe v. Wade* and *Doe v. Bolton*[51] had recently affirmed a constitutional right to seek an abortion, the performance of abortions was still illegal in Virginia, and a criminal statute was also on the books prohibiting the advertisement of abortion services. The decision in *Bigelow* overturned this statute, along with Jeffrey Bigelow's two convictions by the Virginia courts.

Bigelow also overturned the Supreme Court's own 33-year-old commercial speech doctrine. Justice Blackmun's opinion for the Court was that, while the advertisement "did more than simply propose a commercial transaction...it contained factual material of clear public interest,"[52] the State of Virginia had demonstrated no clear interest to weigh against its publication. (This was more than slightly disingenuous, given the recent constitutional side-taking by the same panel of the Supreme Court in the enormous conflict over abortion rights.) He stated that neither the possible pecuniary motive of the publisher in printing the ad nor the commercial transaction it proposed stripped it of First Amendment protection,[53] and found that it shared with the *Sullivan* ad "the exercise of the freedom of communicating information and disseminating opinion."[54] Blackmun even took the step of firmly distancing the Court from *Chrestensen* in a footnote,[55] although nothing else in this decision explicitly repudiated the earlier doctrine. But he did *not* attempt to say that this was anything other than commercial speech; its protection in this instance was grounded in its substantive *content*, and not in any finding that it was differently *motivated*:

---

[49] *Pittsburgh Press*, at 389.
[50] 421 U.S. 809 [1975].
[51] 410 U.S. 113 [1973]; 410 U.S. 179 [1973].
[52] *Bigelow*, at 822.
[53] At 818.
[54] At 822.
[55] At 314, Note 6.

> To the extent that commercial activity is subject to regulation, the relationship of speech to that activity may be one factor, among others, to be considered in weighing the First Amendment interest alleged. *Advertising is not thereby stripped of all First Amendment protection. The relationship of speech to the marketplace of products or of services does not make it valueless in the marketplace of ideas.*[56]

The Court found this an auspicious occasion to recognize the interests of publishers and editors, adverting at the end of its decision to the "proper functioning" of the press as defined in *Tornillo.*[57] It also referred to the *rights of the audience to receive* the advertisement:

> Viewed in its entirety, the advertisement conveyed information of potential interest and value to a diverse audience... Thus, in this case, appellant's First Amendment interests coincided with the constitutional interests of the general public.[58]

THE NEW TESTAMENT

Virginia Board of Pharmacy

Bigelow, if only by its silences, held out at least some reason to expect that purely commercial advertising would continue to be excluded from the protection of the First Amendment unless the private commercial interests it advanced coincided to some sufficient degree with public interests outside the sphere of the market. The very next session of the Supreme Court destroyed this expectation. In its landmark decision in *Virginia Board of Pharmacy v. Virginia Citizens' Consumer Council*[59] an explicit rationale for constitutional protection of pure commercial speech was finally recognized by the Court.

The facts of the case are straightforward: like most jurisdictions, Virginia regulates the licensing of professionals such as lawyers, engineers, optometrists, and pharmacists. The advertising of prescription drugs by pharmacists was defined under the relevant statute as 'unprofessional conduct'[60] and accordingly disallowed. The statute was challenged

---

[56] At 825–826, emphasis added.

[57] 418 U.S. 241 [1974], (Chapter 4), 829.

[58] *Bigelow*, at 822.

[59] 425 U.S. 748 [1976].

[60] Many subsequent commercial speech cases contested the constitutionality of such limitations on client solicitation by professionals. The usual rationale for such forms of governance is that since licensing and regulation of the professions restrict market entry in

on First Amendment grounds and invalidated by the decisions of both the District Court and the U.S. Supreme Court. It was not, however, pharmacists themselves who brought the challenge forward, but a consumer advocacy group. The Virginia Citizen's Consumer Council claimed that prescription drug consumers had a *right to receive* drug price information in order to locate the lowest priced suppliers, and the Supreme Court's decision in their favor was premised explicitly on this argument.

The Court squarely faced the question of the continuing validity of its commercial speech doctrine under *Chrestensen*, and concluded that even pure commercial speech commanded, after all, some protection from the First Amendment.

> Our question is whether speech which does no more than propose a commercial transaction is so removed from any exposition of ideas, and from truth, science, morality and arts... that it lacks all protection. Our answer is that it is not.[61]

Reviewing the history of the *Chrestensen* doctrine the justices admitted that it had not "survived reflection";[62] and therefore, having found that commercial speech *was* entitled to protection they attempted to formulate rules for determining *how much* constitutional protection it enjoyed. They were careful to identify four continuing grounds for state regulation: (a) 'time, place, and manner' regulations; (b) prohibition of 'false and misleading' advertising (as regulated by the FTC); (c) prohibition of advertising which proposes illegal transactions (as in *Pittsburgh Press*); and (d) regulation of advertising in the inherently exclusionary and publicly owned airwaves. (None of these grounds were found to save Virginia's statute.) In general the new approach laid down in this case was that, although commercial speech now enjoyed First Amendment protection,

> commercial speech may be more durable than other kinds. Since advertising is the sine qua non of commercial profits, there is little likelihood of its being chilled by proper regulation.[63]

---

pursuit of such public interests as health, safety and accountability, their accredited members are insulated from competition. They may therefore legitimately be required to compensate for this privileged position in the market by conforming to professional codes designed to maintain the integrity of their profession's service to the public. See, e.g., Freedman (1977, p. 67).

[61] 425 U.S., at 762 (citations omitted).

[62] 425 U.S., Note 16.

[63] 425 U.S., Note 24.

But the Court's recognition of a different and *less* protected status for commercial than political speech was still a profound reinterpretation of the First Amendment. Rather than focusing on the specific relation of free speech to self-government the Court was content to assume that, by protecting communication in the service of 'free enterprise,' it would also serve the ends of democracy:

> So long as we preserve a predominantly free enterprise economy, the allocation of our resources in large measure will be made through numerous private economic decisions. It is a matter of public interest that those decisions, in the aggregate, be intelligent and well-informed. To this end, the free flow of commercial information is indispensable. And if it is indispensable to the proper allocation of resources in a free enterprise system, it is also indispensable to the formation of intelligent opinions as to how that system ought to be regulated or altered. Therefore, even if the First Amendment were thought to be primarily an instrument to enlighten public decision-making in a democracy, we could not say that the free flow of information does not serve that goal.[64]

In the following year (1977) the new doctrine enunciated in *Virginia Board of Pharmacy* was reaffirmed in two cases: one concerning Arizona's prohibition on advertising by lawyers;[65] and the other considering a New Jersey municipality's regulation of real estate signage.[66] Both decisions, like *Virginia Board of Pharmacy*, asserted the priority of the audience's First Amendment right to receive the contested commercial communication over the regulatory interests of government, even though these latter interests were acknowledged by the Court as valid and substantial.

The *right to receive* undergoes further development as an element of First Amendment analysis in these cases. Whereas in *Bigelow*, in *Red Lion*, and in *Sullivan* the respective audience's *noncommercial* interest in receiving the information was a significant part of the Court's determination that the contested communications were *protected* categories of speech, in *Virginia Board of Pharmacy* and the many cases that follow it the audience's right to receive *commercial* information becomes the central rationale for extending constitutional protection to it. The right to receive thus moves from the outside to the inside of the commercial speech doctrine. By positing an overriding First Amendment right of *audiences* as their instrument for the protection of commercial communication, the

---

[64] At 765.

[65] *Bates v. State Bar of Arizona*, 433 U.S. 350 [1977].

[66] *Linmark Associates Inc. v. Township of Willingboro*, 431 U.S. 85 [1977].

Court shielded private corporate speakers against public interest regulation by government—in the name of "the people as a whole."

Bellotti revisited; Buckley v. Valeo

Two examples of the corporate utility of the right to receive were given in cases decided in this period. *Buckley v. Valeo*,[67] handed down the same year as *Virginia Board of Pharmacy*, arose as a corporate challenge to the amendments to the Federal Election Campaign Act (FECA), which Congress enacted in the aftermath of the Watergate scandals. These amendments were designed to curb electoral campaign financing irregularities and prevent wealthy interest groups from 'buying' electoral success for their preferred candidates or otherwise dominating political discourse during elections. The amendments to FECA limited individual and corporate contributions to candidates; placed ceilings on candidates' and parties' campaign expenditures; limited *independent* expenditures that attacked or supported particular candidates; established a system of public funding of some campaign activities; instituted public disclosure requirements for campaign funding; and set up a Federal Election Commission to administer these provisions. On the basis of the right of citizens to receive electoral information the Supreme Court overturned a key provision in the amended FECA.

The most significant constitutional defect discovered by the Court in *Buckley v. Valeo* concerned the Act's limits on *independent*, third-party campaign expenditures. Limits on direct individual contributions to candidates' campaign funds were found to be constitutionally permissable; but the First Amendment, in the Court's view, prevented the Government from controlling *independent* advertising expenditures by interest groups who sought to place their views about candidates and their records before the public.

Of course, there was no implication in this judgment that newspaper publishers, billboard companies or other advertising media were required to carry such campaign advertising: the government was enjoined from either preventing any election-related expenditures of private third parties, or (under *DNC*) from requiring private media firms to sell them advertising opportunities. Private interests could raise as much money as they pleased for election publicity, and the media could choose which electoral clients they wished to service. The effect on the political process of unequal access to economic and communicative resources was dismissed

[67] 424 U.S. 1 [1976].

as irrelevant by the Court. "Virtually every means of communicating ideas in today's society," reasoned the Court ,"requires the expenditure of money."

> The distribution of the humblest handbill or leaflet entails printing, paper and circulation costs. Speeches and rallies generally necessitate hiring a hall and publicizing the event. The electorate's increasing dependence on television, radio, and other mass media for news and information has made these expensive modes of communication indispensable instruments of effective political speech. The [third-party] expenditure limitations...would appear to exclude all citizens and groups except candidates, political parties and the institutional press from any significant use of the most effective modes of communication.[68]

The Court concluded that the FECA's restrictions on third-party expenditures, while content neutral, did not fulfill their aim of providing reasonable 'time, place, and manner' guidelines for equalizing the *volume* of the political utterances of third parties. Rather, in the Court's view, they illegitimately restricted the right of citizens to receive the range of viewpoints made available by other citizens through a lawful allocation of private economic resources.

The evidence is, however, that the range of viewpoints available to voters has been *reduced* by the effects of this decision on electoral and referendum processes. Candidates favored by national Political Action Committees (PACs), organized to raise third-party election funds, are able to 'drown out' the voices of candidates supported only by local constituencies (or who are on PAC 'hit-lists'), by outspending them. Voting patterns have clearly been altered by this distortion of public discussion:

> A number of studies show that, in state after state, in election after election, massive spending and sophisticated media campaigns by special interest groups have swamped referenda that were initially favoured by a majority of voters.[69]

As a result, according to many U.S. commentators,[70] ordinary citizens in the U.S. have little incentive to participate in the electoral process, and this shows up in their very low election turn-outs. Candidates and elected officeholders pay less and less attention to constituency associations or party policies. Instead and by necessity candidates must try to please these private, third-party publicity and advertising clubs, whose mass

[68] 424 U.S., at 19. See also Wright, (1976, 1982); Tushnet (1982, p. 253).

[69] Wright (1982, p. 623). See also Mastro, Costlow, and Sanchez (1980).

media expenditures increasingly shape opinion formation among a public who may not themselves *speak* in the mass media by right.

That candidates for U.S. political office must answer to those sponsors who can afford—and to whom the corporate media are willing to *grant*—political advertising opportunities, is surely necrotic for the voluntary institutions of democratic citizenship. How can the First Amendment, the central value of which is, arguably, its contribution to self-government, function as an impediment to that process?

The answer may lie in the Court's failure to employ a distinction it has itself made in other cases: that between abridgements of *speech*, and abridgements of *freedom of speech*. The wording of the First Amendment forbids the latter, not the former. The source of this subtle distinction is Alexander Meiklejohn's 1948 work, *Free Speech and Its Relation to Self-Government*, in which he points out that regulation of speech-situations, especially those connected with a community's self-government, is necessary to any process of collective deliberation. The First Amendment, in Meiklejohn's view, aids self-government by protecting the "collective thought-processes of the community."[71] Thus, rules of order and standing, such as those employed by the chair of a town meeting, actually further the capacity of the assembled citizens to hear a full range of views, to have their own views heard, and to arrive at reasoned conclusions. The *speech* of any individual (especially windbags and loudmouths) may well be abridged by these rules, but only in order that everyone's *freedom of speech* may be enhanced. The Court has employed this distinction in resolving conflicts both between First Amendment interests and other values,[72] and among competing First Amendment values.[73] It this decision, it did not.

In Chapter 3 the case of *First National Bank of Boston v. Bellotti*,[74] decided two years after *Buckley*, was discussed in the context of whether the First Amendment's separate reference to 'freedom of the press' conferred greater speech privileges on media firms than on other corporations. Another important aspect of this 1978 case is that it also turned upon the notion of the audience's right to receive corporate speech. In this case the Massachussetts Supreme Court had upheld a state statute preventing corporations from using the media to influence the vote on state tax referenda. The Massachussetts Court agreed with the legislature that corporations had only those rights granted to them by government,

---

[70] See, for example Epstein (1980); Wertheimer (1980); Stern (1988); Sussman (1988).

[71] Meiklejohn (1948, p. 26).

[72] *Kovacs v. Cooper*, (Chapter 3).

[73] *Red Lion v. FCC*, (Chapter 4).

[74] 435 U.S. 765 [1978].

and that their property and due process rights only protected their freedom of speech on matters directly affecting their business or assets.

The U.S. Supreme Court overturned this decision, finding the speech rights of nonmedia corporations to be equivalent to those of media corporations or of natural persons. Since the contested speech related directly to the actions of government, it was a category of speech protected fully by the First Amendment. The interest of the state in preserving the political process from the distorting influence of corporate expenditures was of lesser import, said the Court, than the interest of citizens in receiving the views of corporations on referendum issues.

Neither *Bellotti* nor *Buckley v. Valeo* were argued to be instances of commercial speech—their connection with political discourse was too salient for any such argument to prevail. But both cases arose in the same period as the reformulation of the commercial speech doctrine, were concerned with the closely related area of corporate speech, made frequent reference to the recent commercial speech caselaw, and were decided fundamentally on grounds of the audience's right to receive the corporate speech. In *Bellotti*, for example, the Supreme Court noted:

> Nor do our recent commercial speech cases lend support to [the Massachussetts legislature's] theory. They illustrate that the First Amendment goes beyond protection of the press and the self-expression of individuals to prohibit government from limiting the stock of information from which members of the public may draw. A commercial advertisement is constitutionally protected not so much because it pertains to the seller's business as because it furthers the societal interest in the free flow of commercial information.[75]

It is apparent, then, that, on the grounds of the audience's interest in receiving it, both the political and the commercial speech of corporations began to attract significantly more constitutional protection just at the time when citizen rights of access to the mass media had been most firmly ruled out. The commercial media, of course, wished to be free to sell access for both commercial and political speech to whomever they chose, but were prevented in some instances from doing so by government regulation. The Court quickly obliged by finding much of this regulation unconstitutional. The state's role as a regulator was significantly narrowed in this period: the full exercise of professional judgement by editors and journalists superceded the state's interest in requiring citizen opportunities for access to the media, and the audience's right to receive the communications of the media's chosen clients equally precluded the state

---

[75] 435 U.S., at 783.

from preventing their dissemination. The regulatory role exercised by the state was thus, in important measure, handed over by the Court to the media firm.

Consolidated Edison and Central Hudson

Three significant decisions concerning commercial and corporate speech—all of which grappled with the problem of distinguishing clearly between the commercial and political utterances of corporations—were handed down in 1980. Two of them—*Consolidated Edison Co. of New York v. Public Service Commission* and *Central Hudson Gas and Electric Corp. v. Public Service Commission*[76] —were companion cases, handed down on the same day.

In January 1976, the billing envelopes mailed by the Consolidated Edison Company of New York to its electrical utility subscribers contained a printed insert entitled "Independence Is Still a Goal, and Nuclear Power Is Needed To Win The Battle"; this material, authored by the company, focused on the safety, economy and cleanliness of nuclear plants, asserted that "the benefits of nuclear power...far outweigh any potential risk," and stressed especially the role of nuclear power in helping the U.S. become independent of "foreign energy sources."[77] A citizen group, the Natural Resources Defense Council (NRDC), responded by sending Con Ed a rebuttal to this insert, and a request that it be printed and collated into the utility's next billing. Con Ed refused this request.

The NRDC then asked the state utility regulator, the Public Service Commission of New York, to "open Consolidated Edison's billing envelopes to contrasting views on controversial issues of public importance." The Commission also refused the NRDC's request, but issued a Statement of Policy on Advertising and Promotion Practices of Public Utilities that barred utility companies entirely from distributing billing inserts that expressed their viewpoints on controversial issues. The Commission reasoned that "customers who receive bills containing inserts are a captive audience of diverse views who should not be subjected to the utility's beliefs."[78]

Con Ed appealed on First Amendment grounds and the New York Court of Appeals upheld the Public Service Commission's policy as a "valid time, place and manner regulation designed to protect the privacy" of customers. The U.S. Supreme Court reversed this finding. In *Bellotti*, said the Court (referring obliquely to the audience's right to receive the

[76] 447 U.S. 530; 447 U.S. 557.

[77] *Consolidated Edison.*

[78] *Consolidated Edison.*

insert) "we rejected the contention that a state may confine corporate speech to specified issues."

> The Commission has limited the means by which Consolidated Edison may participate in the public debate on this question and other controversial issues of national interest and importance. Thus, the Commission's prohibition of discussion of controversial issues strikes at the heart of the freedom to speak.[79]

On the question of permissable time, place and manner restrictions Justice Powell (who wrote the opinion) said that they must be *content neutral*:

> Time, place and manner regulations must be applicable to all speech regardless of content... The First Amendment's hostility to content-based regulation extends not only to restrictions on particular viewpoints, but also to prohibition of public discussion of an entire topic. To allow a government the choice of permissable subjects for public debate would be to allow that government control over the search for political truth.[80]

What is curious about this argument is its apparent contradiction with the reasoning by which the Court itself defined the contested insert as an instance of political rather than commercial speech. This is nothing if not content-based. The utility used commercial revenues to pay the expenses of advancing a viewpoint which accorded with its own commercial interests, included it in the envelopes containing its customers' statements of account, and declined to provide opportunity for rebuttal by opponents who clearly considered it a political comment. But the Court determined—on the basis of the insert's *content*—that this was *not* commercial speech: it did *not* propose a commercial transaction and it *did* address an issue which in the view of the Commission and the Court was 'political.' Is the question of whether a communication is commercial or political speech a commercial or political question?

What, we may also wonder, would the outcome have been if the New York Public Service Commission had complied with the NRDC's request and *required* the mailing of their insert rebuttal? We may speculate that, since *media* firms (e.g., broadcasters) are immune from just such demands for the provision of rebuttal opportunities in circumstances where they also are regulated by a government commission,[81] and since the Court had

---

[79] *Consolidated Edison.*

[80] *Consolidated Edison.*

[81] See the companion case to *DNC*: *CBS v. Business Executives' Move For Vietnam Peace*, 412 U.S. 94 [1973]; and review *Tornillo*, Chapter 4.

already asserted in *Bellotti* the equal speech rights of media and nonmedia corporations, it would have found that such a requirement was unconstitutional.[82] Government may not control "the search for political truth," but, apparently, corporations may.

Powell dealt quite summarily with the other major argument advanced by the Commission—the argument that the privacy interests of the utility's 'captive audience' of customers were "being invaded in an essentially intolerable manner":

> The First Amendment does not permit the government to prohibit speech as intrusive unless the "captive" audience cannot avoid objectionable speech...The customer of Consolidated Edison may escape exposure to objectionable material simply by transferring the bill insert from envelope to wastebasket.[83]

Consolidated Edison, as well as illustrating the development of the Court's view of corporate speech rights, is also a particularly clear exposition—precisely because it considers here a particularly tangled array of property interests—of the role of state and law in the determination of the latter. This was the burden of Justice Blackmun's dissent from the majority opinion (and note how this anticipates the lower Court's ruling 6 years later in *PGE*[84]):

> States might use their power to define property rights so that the billing envelope is the property of the ratepayers and not of the utility's shareholders. If, under state law, the envelope belongs to the customers, I do not see how restricting the utility from using it could possibly be held to deprive the utility of its rights.[85]

The 1980 *Central Hudson* case was also the product of a dispute between a regulated utility and the New York Public Service Commission, dating from the 'oil crisis' of 1973–1974. The Commission, distinguishing between the "promotional" and the "institutional and informational" advertising of utility companies, completely banned the former on the basis that "the interconnected utility system in New York State does not have sufficient fuel stocks or sources of supply to continue furnishing all customer demands for the 1973–1974 winter."[86] The Commission's rule explicitly permitted "informational" advertising with

---

[82] For a discussion of the implications of *Consolidated Edison* regarding the utility's monopoly power and consequent involvement with state action, see Emerson (1981, at 827–828).

[83] 447 U.S.

[84] 106 S. Ct. 903 [1986] (Chapter 3).

[85] 447 U.S.

the intent that utilities "encourage *shifts* of consumption from peak demand times to periods of low electricity demand."[87]

The Supreme Court struck down the restriction on what it agreed *was* purely commercial speech, despite the compelling public interests in regulation claimed by the Commission. In doing so, the Court gave its fullest statement on the rationales behind the protection of commercial speech, and articulated a four-part test which has remained the basis of its decisions in this area. Its rationales were given as follows:[88]

> 1) Commercial speech not only serves the economic interest of the speaker, but also assists consumers and furthers the societal interest in the fullest possible dissemination of information;
>
> 2) People will perceive their own best interests only if they are well-enough informed, and... the best means to that end is to open the channels of communication, rather than close them;
>
> 3) Even when advertising communicates only an incomplete version of the relevant facts, the First Amendment presumes that some accurate information is better than no information at all.

The Court also re-affirmed that commercial speech enjoys a *lesser* degree of constitutional protection than other kinds of expression:

> Two features of commercial speech permit regulation of its content. First, commercial speakers have extensive knowledge of both the market and their products. Thus, they are well-situated to evaluate the accuracy of their messages and the lawfulness of the underlying activity. In addition, commercial speech, the offspring of economic self-interest, is a hardy breed of expression that is not particularly susceptible to being crushed by overboard regulation.[89]

In striking down the Public Service Commission's rule the following standard of review for constitutionally permissable regulation of commercial speech was articulated.[90] "At the outset we must determine," wrote Justice Powell,

> 1) whether the expression is protected by the First Amendment. For commercial speech to come within that provision, it at least must... concern lawful activity and... not be misleading. Next, we ask

---

[86] 447 U.S., at 559.
[87] 447 U.S., at 550; emphasis in original.
[88] At 562.
[89] At 564, Note 6.
[90] At 566.

2) whether the asserted governmental interest is substantial. If both inquiries yield positive answers, we must determine

3) whether the regulation directly advances the governmental interest asserted, and

4) whether it is not more extensive than is necessary to serve that interest.

While the Court recognized the validity of the governmental interests asserted by the Commission, it failed the Commission's regulation on the basis of points 3) and 4) in its test. As Justice Blackmun wrote in his concurring opinion,

> Permissable restraints on commercial speech have been limited to measures designed to protect consumers from fraudulent, misleading, or coercive sales techniques. Those designed to deprive consumers of information about products or services that are legally offered for sale consistently have been invalidated...If the First Amendment means anything, it means that, absent clear and present danger, government has no power to restrict expression because of the effect a message is likely to have on the public.[91]

Justice Rehnquist dissented from the Court's opinion. Rehnquist asserted that the First Amendment embodied a principle of remedial counterspeech which was inapplicable to the realm of commercial advertising. Since the Court found regulation and lawsuits—*and not access opportunities*—to be the appropriate remedies for *fraudulent* commercial propositions, commercial speech was removed entirely, in his view, from the ambit of the First Amendment:

> In the world of political advocacy and its market place of ideas, there is no such thing as a 'fraudulent' idea... The free flow of information is important in this context not because it will lead to the discovery of any objective 'truth', but because it is essential to our system of self-government...Fraudulent commercial speech is...separated by a world of difference from the realm of politics and government... For in a democracy, the economic is subordinate to the political, a lesson that our ancestors learned long ago, and that our descendants will undoubtedly have to learn many years hence.[92]

WNCN; Mandel

In most of the cases considered so far in this chapter, the audience was curiously passive in arguing its own 'right to receive'; an exception is the

[91] At 574.
[92] At 598–599.

key case in which the Court chose to fully unveil its new commercial speech doctrine, *Virginia Pharmacy*, in which the appellee was a consumer group. This diffidence is perhaps better understood in light of the two last decisions which will be considered here.

In *WNCN*,[93] a 1981 case from Minnesota, a citizens' group took the FCC to the Supreme Court in an attempt to force it to regulate a local radio station in line with the expressed interests of its audience. The WNCN Listeners' Guild was formed when a local commercial station overhauled its format, replacing the classical music it had aired for numerous years with a new emphasis on 'soft rock.'

The Listeners' Guild argued that, by catering to its *advertisers'* interests in the content of the station's broadcasts, the station was evicting one audience from its established enjoyment of a public resource and replacing it with another which was already well served by other locally available frequencies. The Guild pointed out that the motive of the exercise was purely private and commercial, and not pursuant to the station's responsibilities as a public trustee of the airwaves. The Guild directly asserted that the original audience's First Amendment rights were being trampled: it specifically claimed that the audience had a *right to receive* the classical music programming that it had supported for so long. It claimed that no alternative broadcast source for enjoyment of this material was locally available; and indeed, that the change in the radio station's format would significantly diminish the general availability of and level of support for classical music in the community.

The story has a straightforward ending, and no long exegesis is needed. As Mark Freiman summarizes,

> the Court held that the public's ownership of the airwaves does not give the broadcasting audience any specific rights with regard to the material being broadcast—there is no right to hear any specific messages or class of messages.[94]

The other case, *Kleindienst v. Mandel*,[95] also can be quickly summarized. *Mandel* arises in the statutory and caselaw context of "alien exclusions" from the U.S. Under the 1952 *Immigration and Nationality Act*[96] the U.S. Government denied entry to hundreds of writers, academics, artists, and political figures. Visas could be denied under the Act because of insanity, drug addiction, polygamy, or evidence that they are "affiliated with any organization that advocates or teaches," or have

---

93 *WNCN Listeners' Guild v. Federal Communications Commission*, 450 U.S. 582 [1981].

94 Freiman (1984, p. 112).

95 408 U.S. 753 [1972].

96 Known as the Walter-McCarran Act until its repeal in 1989.

> possession for the purposes of circulation...or display, any written or printed matter advocating or teaching...opposition to organized government, or...the economic, international and governmental doctrines of world communism."[97]

Exclusion under the Walter-McCarran Act, drafted during the height of the Cold War, was of course a valuable status symbol in some political circles. Although the *Mandel* decision predates the current commercial speech doctrine, it set a deferential standard for judicial review of "security"-related speech-and-association law which has prevailed until very recently.[98] The significance of the case for this chapter is the further illumination it casts upon the audience's *right to receive*.

Ernest Mandel, a socialist journalist and academic from Belgium, was invited in 1969 to give a U.S. lecture tour on a number of university campuses including Stanford, Princeton, and Columbia. Mandel, who was not shown to be insane, addicted to drugs, or polygamous, was denied a visa under the Act, largely on the basis of evidence that he had given a speech at a fund-raising event for the legal defense of students involved in the 1968 mobilization in France.

Subsequently, a number of the faculty and student associations who were sponsoring the tour sued Attorney General Kleindienst on First Amendment grounds. Their specific claim was that their *right to receive* information and ideas were unconstitutionally violated by the visa denial. They also brought evidence of Fifth Amendment violation of equal protection and due process, in that right-wing advocates of the overthrow of government were not similarly excluded.

The lower court issued the injunction sought by the plaintiffs. The Supreme Court reversed this finding. Although it recognized that First Amendment rights were indeed implicated, it found no power of judicial review of state action in this area sufficient to allow it to

> look behind the exercise of [Executive] discretion, nor test it by balancing its justification against the First Amendment interests of those who seek personal communication with the applicant.[99]

In these communicative circumstances, *any* rationale offered by the state for constraint of political speech is, apparently, adequate. The audience's right to receive, domestically protected with such enormous vigilance from state action (but subordinated to the claims of property, as

---

[97] 8 U.S.C. Section 1182 (a) (28).

[98] For example, the *Mandel* precedent was upheld without judicial comment in *Abourezk v. Reagan*, 56 U.S.L.W. 4001 [1987].

[99] 408 U.S., at 770.

in *WNCN*), is selectively subject, in the sphere of international communication, to the clear and absolute prior restraint of the state.

Some three dozen additional commercial and corporate speech cases have been heard by the Supreme Court in the past 15 years. These have considered municipal regulation of publicity and signage of porn theaters, bus and billboard advertising, real estate and political campaign lawn signs, storefront drug paraphernalia signage, and, again, door-to-door solicitation;[100] state regulation of advertising by lawyers, optometrists, utilities, casinos, and cable retransmitters of out-of-state programming;[101] and federal regulation of union boycotts and publications, contraceptive manufacturers' mail solicitations, investment circulars, fund-raising drives, and credit agency reports.[102] The formula stated by the Court in Central Hudson has been quite serviceable in these decisions, which have in turn consolidated a broad momentum for deregulation of advertising at all three levels of government, and indeed, internationally as well.

Note that in the context of in-person solicitation the outcome has reversed the access caselaw.[103] Home visits (or in *Ohralik*, bedside visits by ambulance-chasing attorneys) for commercial purposes are considered so intrusive and difficult for the 'captive audience' to avoid that they lose their constitutional protection. As in the early commercial speech doctrine, in-person solicitation may be regulated quite stringently. This means, however, that the forum of communication requiring the least capital to enter is the one most hedged about with regulations. Urgent as

---

[100] *Coleman Young v. American Mini-Theatres Inc.*, 427 U.S. 50 [1976]; *Splawn v. State of California*, 431 U.S. 595 [1977]; *State of New York v. P.I. Ferber*, 458 U.S. 747 [1982]; *Metromedia Inc. v. City of San Diego*, 453 U.S. 490 [1981]; *Lehman v.City of Shaker Heights*, 418 U.S. 298 [1974]; *Linmark Associates Inc. v. Township of Willingboro*, 431 U.S. 85 [1977]; *Members of City Council of Los Angeles v. Taxpayersfor Vincent, et. al.*, 466 U.S. 789 [1984]; *Village of Hoffman Estates v. Flipside*, 455 U.S. 489 [1982]; *Village of Schaumberg v. Citizens for a Better Environment*, 444 U.S. 620 [1980].

[101] *Bates v. State Bar of Arizona*, 433 U.S. 350 [1977]; *Ohralik v. Ohio StateBar Association*, 436 U.S. 447 [1978]; *In Re R.M.J.*, 455 U.S. 191 [1982]; *Zauderer v. Office of District Counsel of Supreme Court of Ohio*, 85 U.S. 652 [1985]; *Texas Optometric Association v. Rogers*, 440 U.S. 1 [1979]; *Pacific Gas and Electric Co. v. Public Utilities Commission of California*, 106 S. Ct. 903 [1986]; *Posadas de PuertoRico Associates v. Tourism Co. of Puerto Rico*, 106 S. Ct. 2968 [1986]; *Capital Cities Cable Inc. v. Oklahoma Alcoholic Beverage Control Board*, 467 U.S. 691 [1984].

[102] *Eastex Inc. v. National Labour Relations Board*, 437 U.S. 556 [1978]; *NAACP v. Claiborne Hardware Co.*, 458 U.S. 886 [1982]; *Carey v. Population Services International*, 431 U.S. 678 [1977]; *Bolger v. Youngs Drug Products*, 463 U.S. 60 [1983]; *Lowe v. Securities and Exchange Commission*, 105 S. Ct. 2557 [1985]; *Dun & Bradstreet Inc. v. Greenmoss Builders Inc.*, 105 S. Ct. 2939 [1985]; *Cornelius v.NAACP Legal and Educational Defense Fund*, 105 S. Ct. 3439 [1985]; *Bose Corp. v. Consumers Union of U.S. Inc.*, 466 U.S. 485 [1984].

[103] See, e.g., *Ohralik*, 436 U.S.

the protection of privacy may be, it is curious that this rationale for regulation does not extend far enough, for example, to permit tighter control of telephone solicitation or the sale of mailing lists. These—especially computerized telephone marketing—are arguably just as intrusive and disruptive of privacy.

Note also that nothing in these decisions challenges the power of media owners themselves to restrict expression, whether "because of the effect a message is likely to have on the public"[104] (for example, sowing public doubt about the quality or safety of the products of their primary advertising clients), or for other reasons:

> In spite of First Amendment victories for commercial speech, the media have compromised none of their rights of control over access and display of advertising. They may refuse advertising and dictate the conditions of its sale.[105]

The 'less protected' status of commercial speech serves to contain potential conflicts between media and nonmedia corporations, thereby consolidating and stabilizing a tacit First Amendment hierarchy. Media corporations are at the top of this hierarchy, priveleged simultaneously by their role in the political process as "surrogates of the public" and their economic control of communicative resources. Media firms exercise a virtually unbounded power of selection and rejection which appears sometimes in the form of speech rights, sometimes in the form of property rights, depending on the angle of view.

Other 'corporate citizens'—their clients—occupy a preferred position in the hierarchy, slightly inferior to media corporations. Since media firms are seeking to sell their services at the highest prices, and their clients to purchase them at the lowest, their interests are not identical. It is also possible for sharper short-run conflicts to arise, since the media sector's direct pecuniary interest in legitimating the market system as a whole may lead them, from time to time, to criticize the practices of particular firms. But in general, the commercial media are happy to produce and sell their stock-in-trade, large and well-researched audiences, especially to long-term, high-volume buyers; and their clients are just as pleased to be able to purchase expressive opportunities unencumbered by the questions and counterclaims of public regulators and other hecklers. Acquiescence to the selection procedures of media firms—the standards of relevance and 'taste' of their editors—is the reasonable cost for this kind of quality control.

---

[104] *Central Hudson*, Blackmun concurring.

[105] Gillmor and Barron (1984, p. 610).

Other citizens, in the audience, stand at the bottom of the hierarchy. They have, of course, the same rights as 'corporate citizens' to submit their views to the media for selection or rejection as part of public discourse, or to withhold those views. But individual citizens do not have big advertising budgets, and if what they want to say to other citizens seems likely to reduce the value of the medium as an effective marketing resource for major commercial clients, it stands a poor chance of coming to prominence, regardless of its contribution to rational debate. Audiences *do* contribute value as listeners and viewers, though, and they therefore have the right to *receive* whatever media firms wish to offer them. The audience's right to receive also functions as a very effective shield against government regulation for media firms and their long-term clients.

By international extension of the doctrines explored in the last three chapters, the world's commercial media and advertising firms, and many of their national regulators, now claim to foresee an emerging *global* regime of free speech and press. The First Amendment discourse on the allocation of speech rights in the mass media is a pivotal reference point in ideological struggles on the international stage, invoked especially by free enterprise enthusiasts against the claims of sovereignty and independence advanced by the developing nations.[106] These are the decisions which make up the domestic policy platform in the United States for the proclaimed arrival of an 'international free flow of information.' The overt rationale for the 'free flow' doctrine is its contribution to democracy:

> In addition to its economic benefits, free flow of information in the 'marketplace of ideas' serves to promote cultural development and to strengthen political liberty and effective self-government.[107]

The 'free flow' doctrine was originally a U.S. foreign policy response to the 'New World Information and Communications Order' (NWICO) championed by the less developed countries in the U.N. system, beginning in the 1970s. NWICO attempted to address the effects on other cultures of massive inflows from the industrial countries, especially the U.S., of low-cost films, sound recordings, and television programming (and the mass marketing tied in with this supply), and to moderate perceived distortions in how less economically powerful cultures and societies are represented

---

[106] This is not in fact the first effort to 'export the First Amendment': an earlier episode with, in some respects, very similar overtones, is documented in Blanchard (1986).

[107] *Long Range Goals in International Telecommunications and Information: An Outline for United States Policy: Report of the U.S. National Telecommunications and Information Administration to the U.S. Senate Committee on Commerce, Science and Transporation.* Reprinted as "Appendix B" in Leeson (1984, p. 129).

to developed-world audiences by the large transnational newsgathering and entertainment corporations. Where NWICO proposed international rules for rights of access, correction, and reply, and for a strengthening of public control of communications systems consonant with an understanding of their role in education and development, the free flow doctrine called for unrestricted international movement of information and programming as dictated by market forces, and "an extension of the First Amendment prohibition against laws 'abridging the freedom of speech, or of the press.'"[108] 'Free flow' grew over time into a coordinated U.S. policy initiative across a broad range of communications and information industries:

> U.S. telecommunications and information policy...reflects efforts to: enhance the free flow of information across national borders...and promote an international environment for the provision of telecommunications and information facilities, services and equipment—and for the production and dissemination of information itself—in which maximum reliance is placed on free enterprise, open and competitive markets, and free trade and investment with minimum direct government involvement or regulation.[109]

These divergent international agenda led to sustained conflict between the U.S., and the Non-Aligned Movement of developing countries, especially within UNESCO:

> Throughout the international telecommunications and information arena, the United States has encountered resistance by other countries to the application of marketplace and free flow principles...In the area of mass media and information policy, UN organizations have drafted "codes of conduct" in support of restrictive policies. We believe these codes fail to strike a reasonable balance between legitimate concerns over sovereignty and the fundamental doctrine of free flow of information advocated by the United States.[110]

The major trading partners of the U.S., aware of the rapid growth and high profitability of trade in entertainment and information services, also desire to expand their exports in these sectors. In a number of cases they have positioned themselves to do so by protecting their own domestic cultural and information services industries behind tariff, subsidy, and quota barriers, often employing sovereignty rationales. This eventually brought this dispute within the purview of the General Agreement on

---

[108] P. 131.

[109] pp. 127–128.

[110] pp. 129–130.

Tarriffs and Trade (GATT), by which the world trading system is regulated. In recent GATT negotiations intended to extend GATT rules to cover trade in intellectual property and in services the free flow doctrine has enjoyed an enhanced status. Since it is designed precisely to subsume communications issues under the conceptual apparatus of 'free trade' (namely, the 'free marketplace of ideas'), the free flow doctrine is ideally suited to the justification of national policies of deregulation of the communications industries.

The implications of this policy initiative in fact go well beyond the mass media sector, which is the focus of this study. The contemporary global industrial restructuring made possible by rapid innovations in digital technology is not only an engineering accomplishment; in its policy dimensions it rests equally upon an internationalization of commodified information and communications practices, and this is the hidden political meaning of the ubiquitous 'information society' rhetoric. The point here is that the enormous—perhaps determinative—cultural, political, and economic power of a small number of very large transnational communications and information services corporations, and the renewed and accelerated transfer of wealth from the poor to the rich signalled in that rhetoric, has its historical roots, and finds its most persuasive legal and political justifications, in the mass media jurisprudence of the U.S. Supreme Court.

Conclusions: Communicative Power and Communicative Justice

The United States of America, which is the heartland and original home of the world's commercial communications media, understands itself as also the chief residence of all liberty, especially the liberty of expression. Its citizens tend to believe they enact, personally and collectively, the living presence-in-the-world of free speech; and the reach and power of their media—the very impenetrability of their media to the influence of other value systems—are their best warrant for that belief.

In the American polity, as in other highly developed market polities, commercial communications media play a central role in both the economic and the political spheres: they are leading sectors of profit and growth, linking production to consumption through marketing and advertising. They also set public agenda, influence political actors, inform citizens, and generally link electorate to government. In fact it requires a concerted effort to disaggregate these roles. The ways in which the liberal reconstructions in 17th- and 18th-century European political thought were applied to statecraft in America, though highly pragmatic, also idealized from the outset the liberatory potential of laissez-faire market relations to such an extent (in the absence of the European precapitalist traditions) that the political and economic inflections of 'freedom' were largely indistinguishable. The economic successes which followed in the next two centuries stamped America's claims of Liberty with an unimpeachable warrant.

The interlocking conceptions of the public sphere in classical liberalism—the Enlightenment faith in the corrective of reasoned debate, and the attainability of rational, consensual truth; the scientific perfectibility of human beings and human institutions, especially through democratic rule; the necessity of an informed and tolerant populace to the functioning of a democracy; the rise, with the Industrial Revolution, of the economic value of mass literacy—continue to resonate, whether as achievements or mourned failures, throughout the institutions of contemporary American culture. These are powerful value commitments, underlying and informing the design strategies of school curricula, the public objectives of civil organizations, the invocations that unite sportsfans and concertgoers. They remain staples of political rhetoric at all levels of government, from City Hall to the White House. Above all, they are the symbolic trump suit of commodity advertisers in the mass media, where representations of these other cultural practices, gathered under the sign of Liberty, inflect consumption itself with patriotic significance.

This conflation of private and public spheres, of commerce and communication—this occlusion of the possibility that the marketplace might fail to elicit virtuous citizenship—betrays the repressed Romantic tendency residing even in conservative American political thought. The overt committment of the libertarian patriot is to laissez-faire; to Adam Smith, not Jean-Jacques Rousseau. And if, as Smith argued, the material inequalities and narrow justice of a commercial society were preferable to the egalitarian virtues of a Rousseauian republicanism precisely because only the abundance of a commercial society could ensure the material needs of its *poorest* members were met, the United States has perhaps confirmed his thesis in that one important respect. But this tradition also rejects the restraint of self-interest as a route to the common good; celebrates the division of labor (including the professions of government and administration) and the allocation of social goods by the 'invisible hand' of the market. Civic virtue is, simply, dispensable in the laissez-faire model: personalities, along with their virtues and satisfactions, become intensively private, and citizenship, in any more than a passive sense, a contradictory and 'unprofitable' pursuit. If the Philadelphia Convention was indeed "the highest point ever reached by civic humanist theory in practise," it is also true, as Pocock also notes, that "what America might have been remains a standing instrument of criticism of what it is."[1]

The body of constitutional case law we have examined in the foregoing chapters is the main authority for U.S. citizens' fervent and patriotic claims to freedom of speech and, by logical extension of its doctrinal underpinnings, the foundation also of much of their faith in the legitimacy of their democratic institutions. In historical perspective it is clear that the significant developments in First Amendment doctrine correspond to periods of widespread political challenge by popular movements, and to

[1] Pocock (1983, pp. 23, 244).

the counter initiatives with which political and economic elites have responded. The popular challenges, and their judicial echoes, tend to mobilize the Romantic communitarian themes of civic humanism; the elite responses to those challenges elicit the negative justice of Smith, and the preoccupations of the civil jurisprudence tradition with the stability of property claims and transactions. The ideological tension between these two models of social thought, personified in struggles between different social strata, remains undifferentiated and unresolved within the judicial texts.

THE FIRST PERIOD OF CHALLENGE

The first period of challenge and response originated in the speech rights struggles of popular movements between the two World Wars. The results of these struggles, which were fairly successful, were encoded in decisions having, in retrospect, two common doctrinal characteristics: they were predominantly cases of controversial and explicit *political* speech; and they are usually cases of direct, face-to-face communication. The typical fact pattern of these cases involved a rally, meeting, picket line, or pamphleting drive. When we begin to consider the juridical history of *mediated* communication, largely determined in the post-World War II period, the picture is very different. In the mass media we find a striking *failure* in the efforts of popular movements to assert citizen rights to opportunities for expression. The successes of the speech- and association-rights struggles waged approximately from 1920 to 1940 sensitized socialists and labor activists to the possibility of using the bourgeois media to organize against the capitalist status quo. Their failure to acquire broader First Amendment rights in the mass media is not only a result of events inside courtrooms, of course. This could easily be the topic of another study; here I wish only to note a few of the historical factors influencing these outcomes.

In the first place the ascendancy of popular movements such as the socialist and labour movements, not only in the U.S. but also in Europe, coincided in the 1930s with an extremely severe contraction in the industrial economy. Retaining control over political institutions and keeping the general direction of policy in the hands of the capitalist class clearly required some level of accommodation of working class aspirations *within* the framework of industrial capitalism. Despite their high-flown rhetoric of 'natural rights,' Holmes, certainly, and perhaps his colleagues too, were sharply aware of the practical role of the courts in organizing and carrying out these accommodations. This is clear from, for example, published papers of Holmes after his retirement.[2] The higher courts' liberal judgements in this period must be seen in relation to this changing balance of social forces in other spheres of U.S. society.

Secondly, progressive organizations had a well-founded distrust of the private press, and had also a lively, thriving network of newspapers of their own. Before World War II the left was winning a good many of its political battles; its energies were focused on immediate, street-level struggles, and the future dominant role of the mass media in the political process was not then so apparent. As the level of popular literacy, the advertising-supported mode of media financing, and the scale of media audiences developed and grew, the partisan labor and left press was left with a very small relative share of readership, and virtually no institutional presence in the radio spectrum. The need for legal protection for organizing efforts conducted through the media only became apparent after World War II, and by this time social conditions were no longer conducive to victory in the courts.

Thirdly, by the end of the 1950s there *were* no broad-based progressive movements in the U.S. Labor's strategy of entering partnership with capital and sharing the burgeoning industrial wealth of the post-World War II U.S. was paying off handsomely in its members' pay packets, and thus in their support of an accommodationist leadership. The price of success for labor was renunciation of its radical goals and expulsion of its radical members. Although these elements numbered in the millions (900,000 members were expelled from the CIO in 1949 alone) the anticommunist hysteria of the Cold War period quite effectively silenced them. Ties with the civil rights movement were broken. This rift has never been fully healed: Even in the late 1960s and early 1970s labor was still divorced from radical constituencies, and its support of the Vietnam War was a telling sign of this. Only very recently, and only in face of its own serious decline, has the labor movement in the U.S. made any motions towards re-entering progressive coalitions.

In the heyday of U.S. industrial dominance in the 1950s and 1960s the present situation would have been very difficult to imagine. Just as a symptomatic indicator, at the end of World War II the U.S. produced 40% of the world's industrial output; by 1984 this had declined to 8%. A global economic 'restructuring' in pursuit of the higher profits needed for effective international sectoral competition has resulted in huge U.S. trade deficits in the older and more marginal 'smokestack' industrial sectors. This has eviscerated the blue-collar ranks of the labor constitu-

[2] See Hodder-Williams (1980).

ency, probably forever. The restructuring has also been accompanied by a determined attack on social spending, with accompanying degradation and exploitation of (and political resistance from) women, the elderly, the disabled, youth and minorities. But organizing the five-sixths of the work-force who are now nonunion, mobilizing those who are 'structurally' or otherwise excluded from the work force, or mounting any kinds of new progressive political initiatives depend as never before on effective communication in the mass media.[3] In my view, initiatives to establish the necessary speech rights in that setting would have been far more likely to succeed 40 or 50 years ago.

This is especially so because the industrial strategy of the U.S. in the coming decades appears to rely on the extension into other economies of its established model of mass communication. One of the primary means the U.S. has to reverse the trend of declining productive investment and to balance its trade flows is its export of cultural commodities and information services and technology. In these sectors it still maintains a distinct competitive edge in the global economy, largely due to explosive growth in and aggressive protection of its information and cultural sectors. This strategy is evident in U.S. policies in international political fora such as the UN, GATT, and the ITU in regards to the so-called 'free flow' of information (as noted at the end of Chapter 5); in its open hostility to public forms of media ownership, domestically and abroad; and in its arm-twisting representations to other countries against defensive policies in such trade-related areas as copyright law, access to information services markets, subsidies to domestic publishers and filmmakers, and national broadcast advertising substitutions and content quotas.

This strategy is simultaneously an economic and a political strategy. The same measures that insure favorable terms of trade for U.S. communications industries also maximize the reach of its political ideology. Transformation of the structure of social communication in developing countries to give pride of place to private media owners and their corporate clients and to recast the electoral process as a specialized branch of marketing (as in the U.S. and, to a lesser extent, the other industrialized polities) marginalizes the formal and informal political campaigns of popular movements in other countries as reliably as it has done so at home. The close association of the notion of 'free speech rights' with the concepts of representative democracy and an unfettered market economy makes it a key conceptual apparatus for the extension of political and economic hegemony.

---

[3] Sara Douglas's (1986) study of the U.S. labour movement's current and historical public relations initiatives is highly informative on these questions.

THE SECOND PERIOD OF CHALLENGE

These foregoing remarks bring us to the second period of challenge and response, from the early 1960s to the early 1980s, in which the specific conditions of communicative interaction in the commercial mass media have been tested and codified. The mature development of commercial mass communications institutions has occasioned large-scale change in the structure of public discourse. The pluralist notion of a multiplicity of organized interests competing on more or less equal terms in an open and accessible 'marketplace of ideas' was perhaps most nearly realized in the 1930s, when interpersonal speech rights were broadly affirmed and before the communicative marketplace had yet been so fully rationalized in economic terms as it is today. But the organization of mass audiences as a tool for reducing the unit cost of message distribution and the high degree of control of message context which commercial firms were able to offer preferred clients radically changed the relative communicative power of competing interests.

In addition, the distributive efficiency of the burgeoning communications sector subtly altered the popular conceptual apparatus of liberal democracy. The concept of a 'citizen' for whom "public discussion is a political duty"[4] no longer matched the actual structure of public discourse, with its new emphasis on the passive role of the audience. The new conception was that the majority of citizens entered the 'marketplace of ideas' only as 'buyers' and not as 'sellers.' Since the media performed a dual role in distributing both economic and political utilities it was intellectually satisfying to the pragmatic liberal theorists on the bench to consider the citizen in the mass media forum as a political as well as an economic *consumer*.

The challenge, when it came, was in the form of a demand for citizen access to the mediated forum of public discourse, just as the earlier speech rights struggles were demands for access to the unmediated forum. The rights deliberated in *Tornillo*, *Pruneyard* and *DNC* demonstrate the range of possible forms of access to speech opportunities (in both fora), and also say something about the imperatives that shape their allocation. At one end of the spectrum lies the very narrowly constructed *right of reply* for candidates attacked by newspapers during elections; in *Tornillo* even this constricted form of access was denied. At the other end are the rights affirmed in *Pruneyard*: the wide-open rights of members of the public to initiate communication in privately owned public places, without cost or

---

[4] "...and this should be a fundamental principle of the American government", *Whitney v. California*, 274 U.S. 357 [1927], Justice Louis Brandeis for the Court.

license requirements, in their own words, and on virtually any subject. Between these two forms is the right to buy broadcast advertising, upheld in *Retail Store Employees* as a logical extension of *Red Lion*—but denied in *DNC*. This form of communication right would grant the speaker the choice of subject and format, but would impose high financial barriers and leave the broadcast-property owner in possession of final editorial power over that speech and the context of its reception.

We can distinguish two kinds of communications access rights here: the *right to reply*, and the *right to initiate:* both are denied in the mass media by a great deal of Supreme Court First Amendment jurisprudence.[5] We should also distinguish paid and unpaid access as different forms. With the FCC's recent abdication of the Fairness Doctrine, constitutional rights of either reply or initiation for audience members of the mass media in the U.S. (paid or unpaid) have become vestigial. In an era of technology and policy 'convergence,' and in face of the FCC's clear hostility, *Red Lion* seems unlikely to be reaffirmed by the Court (even if Congress ever does pass the Fairness Doctrine into statutory law). It's also unclear whether any state-enacted right-of-reply provisions would hold up after *Tornillo* and *PGE*.

In situations of direct interaction like *Pruneyard*, on the other hand, citizens retain very broad rights to take up both 'speaking' and 'listening' roles, and both in reply to, and for initiation of, discussion of chosen issues. Even highly structured contexts of direct interaction, such as 'town hall' meetings run under elaborate procedural rules, or public addresses with prearranged speakers, contain opportunities for questions from the floor and are conducted with important degrees of interaction between speakers and audiences, and these features pose no normative problems. As a matter of formal right, dissenting voices may generally mount information pickets at the site of public meetings. It is hard to avoid the conclusion that the denial of equivalent opportunities in mass-mediated public discourse is most of all a consequence of the pecuniary interests of media owners, rather than a disinterested application of already accepted norms of communicative justice. The burden of proof that this ranking of priorities is in the public interest has not been met.

The interactional structure of the commercial mass media is characterized by privately controlled choice of speakers, topics, and formats, and by a rigid separation of roles in which the vast bulk of the public is

---

[5] The *right to reply* could be even more narrowly drawn than in *Tornillo*, as, for example, a right to reply to defamatory falsehoods, and not to matters of opinion; but even this form of access as a remedy for a tort has been denied by the Court in favour of libel litigation: *Sullivan*, (Chapter 5); also *Gertz v. Robert Welch Inc.*, 418 U.S. 323 [1974]; but see also *Rosenbloom v. Metromedia*, 403 U.S. 29 [1971].

permitted to participate in public discourse only to the extent of regularly indicating whether they are still attending (i.e., through audience surveys). There are many models for organizing a more balanced and 'dialogic' structure of communication in the mass media that would form a better analog of the structure of speech rights in direct interaction: local and state initiatives such as Florida's rejected statute; more generous interpretation of the Fairness Doctrine, including *DNC*'s proposed right to buy advertising; or even the democratic editorial decision structure of some community-licensed radio and TV stations are all known measures that hold a degree of this potential. Existing access fora now controlled by media owners, such as letters columns or open-line radio shows, could also be extended and formalized as opportunities for the exercise of community speech rights; these might be able to make fruitful use of voluntary regulatory structures such as community press and media councils. And of course the priorities of the broadcast licensing process itself could be reshaped in favor of citizen access. It seems apparent from these cases that the 'monologic' structure of the commercial media is *not* a necessary or intrinsic characteristic of large-scale communications facilities. This is, rather, a failure in law and policy to balance the new speech rights claims that have emerged in the newly dominant contexts of commercial mass communication.

The radical difference between the structure of speech rights found in *Pruneyard* or in the early landmark cases, and that found in *Tornillo* and *DNC*, illustrates this imbalance. Despite the accompanying rhetoric of 'free flows of information' and 'free markets of ideas,' the economic development of the mass communications industries has been accompanied by *reduced* opportunities for expression in relation to the means available. As long as communication is not itself the basis of profitable exchange (as it was not in *Pruneyard*), the citizen's speech rights are interpreted in a generous manner. As soon as a price and a profit are attached to the communicative activity, however, those rights quite dramatically shrink (to the dimensions of *Tornillo* and *DNC*).

The new communications technologies (CATV, pay-TV, pay-per-view, VCR, videotext, electronic messaging and conferencing, direct mail database/publishing) are widely touted as remedies for this situation, and in conjunction with the continuing phenomenon of audience fragmentation, seem, at first glance, to hold out the promise of vastly increased citizen access opportunities and diversity of media content. I believe, however, that such speculations are naive, considering how little is yet known about the eventual *market* structure of these developments. They may for the moment offer lower entry barriers at the *production* end of the communications process, but they do nothing to alleviate the continuing high entry barriers to effective *distribution*. In fact, the role of such new technologies in producing media *competition*, and thus driving advertising costs *down*, may be just as likely in the long term to help larger firms consolidate market share and thus generate even higher levels of concentration and conglomeration in media and media-dependent sectors. For one example, although most of the regulation of the CATV industry in the U.S. is performed at the municipal level—and is therefore the occasion of frequent grassroots campaigns for community access and content standards—ownership of the U.S. CATV industry itself is rapidly concentrating into a small number of large corporate portfolios. For another example, technical innovation in the 'enhanced services' segment of telecommunications markets appears to be leading towards rapid merger and acquisition activity between telecommunications and financial services organizations. In any case the structure of rights examined here applies both at the innovative margin and the maturing center of the communications sector. Although legal doctrine governing these new media is still evolving rapidly, it is, predictably, evolving in precisely the commercially driven direction indicated by this study.

The most frequent rationale for the above-mentioned distortion in the balance of rights in mass media contexts is the presence of responsible editors and journalists, and especially *their* First Amendment rights to be free from prior restraint. But the rights they deploy are proxy rights: in legal terms the extraordinary speech privileges of editors and journalists are derived from their actions as the agents of media firms and their owners, because it is those firms, as corporate legal persons, who actually *own* the rights of selection, rejection, interpretation, and definition that are invoked by the courts to preclude audiences' rights to *speak*. Editors and journalists have no *rights* to publish what the owners of the communicative apparatuses they employ say shall *not* be published.[6] But there is no reason to believe that the editorial function is intrinsically incapable of being organized to facilitate citizen speech. We have to look elsewhere than the purely literary function of editors to understand the deployment of editorial discretion in this way by the courts.

The editor (or broadcast producer) has also an economic role, shaping and managing the production of a product that is competitively priced, attractively packaged, and effective as a factory tool. The product they

[6] An example illustrating this assertion is conveniently at hand from the last Canadian federal election campaign. According to the *Vancouver Sun*, Clark Davey, publisher (for Southam) of the *Montreal Gazette*, "caused a rift with the paper's editorial board and uproar in the newsroom" because he directed the paper to run an editorial favoring free trade "although his editorial board has for weeks been denouncing the treaty. Davey said he doesn't usually interfere with editorial-board decisions, 'but in this case my opinion is going to be the official position of the paper.'" *Vancouver Sun*, November 19, 1988, p. A17).

produce is the newspaper or program, and the 'buyer' is the broadcast or print media firm which produces it as a 'producer's commodity,' and consumes it itself (for the price of its production).[7] The media firm produces its media content as a factor in the production of the commodity it sells to its clients, mainly governments and other large firms. The function of the editorial content of the newspaper or programme is to attract an audience which can be sold to these advertiser clients.

Even closely limited protection of the public's use of mass media speech forums in the U.S. has yielded to commercial firms' desire to buy and sell access to audiences of consumers. Editors direct this work of producing audiences as the salaried staff of internal departments of the media firm, rather than as subcontractors of the finished product; journalists may produce their subcomponents as wage laborers or as 'freelance' contractors. The particular concern of both is the establishment of a compelling relationship between themselves and the audience: It is they who *speak* to the audience. If they have done their research on the intended audience and spoken effectively to it, the audience, and the advertiser, will both 'stay tuned.'

Were systematic access opportunities to be upheld by the courts as a matter of citizen rights, this could have a serious effect on the value of the commodity offered to advertisers. If citizens had access rights editors might have great difficulty in shaping noncontradictory contexts for advertising materials which maximize their persuasive force. How valuable would an automobile manufacturer's TV spot during a major sports event be if a labor organization or well-financed third-world solidarity group had the *right* to buy an opportunity in the same context to criticize the company's labor practices in developing countries?

In the courts the notion that communication is an interactional exchange is substituted by the metaphor of communication as economic exchange—the 'free marketplace of ideas.' This has been politically justified by an idealized account of the expressive activities of journalists and editors in their self-styled role as the 'watchdogs' of the public interest. Certainly the perceived autonomy of the media is vital to its ability to mobilize consent to market relations in general, and certainly this requires vigorous attack on the 'excesses' and normative deviations of both corporate and government actors (especially as defined by law). But however autonomous they may be with respect to the other institutions of a market polity, the commercial media are directly reliant on the continued growth of the market per se, and this confers an identifiable structure on the public discourse they are willing to permit.

---

[7] See the discussion of the 'Blindspot' debate, Chapter 2.

THE BUSINESS RESPONSE: THE CONSUMER'S RIGHT TO RECEIVE

For a time—in the late 1960s and early 1970s—the media challenges mounted by the civil rights and antiwar movements began to succeed in their constitutional initiatives. Already, however, their partial successes (for example, *Sullivan* and *Red Lion*) were being recast in that case law in the language of consumerism rather than of citizenship—the audience's right to receive rather than the citizen's duty of public discussion. The media and their clients, accustomed to control and management of the 'marketplace of ideas,' mounted a sharp and focused response from the mid-1970s onward. This response was successful, leading first to the reversal of the citizen access gains in broadcasting, and then to the appropriation of the audience's right to receive as a very effective shield against most kinds of government activity in their marketplace. The core of this successful initiative is the modern commercial speech doctrine of the Supreme Court.

It is difficult to see in what sense commercial advertising in the mass media really shares the interactive characteristics or public interest objectives of the speech liberties championed by Mill (and some jurists). In Mill and derivative arguments it is the opportunity for the clash of views—for debate, disagreement, and interested advocacy—which leads to the discovery of truth, to a democratic political culture, and to peaceful social change. The structure of the communicative event in commercial advertising is not freely interactive in this way. Rather, it is rigid, formalized, and hierarchical:

- speaking and listening are rigidly divided roles. Listeners remain in the audience role and seldom (virtually never by right) alternate into the speaking role;
- all communicative activity of parties occupying the speaking role is multiple and public; all communicative activity of listeners is singular and private;
- control of the topic rests with the party occupying the speaking role, and listeners have no opportunity for reply or redefinition of the topic or any of its constituent elements;
- the goals and outcomes of the communicative event are set by the speaker and oriented to the speaker's interests.

A structure of expression that could be characterized as *free*, in the Meiklejohn sense,[8] would arguably require opportunities to alternate between both roles (speaker and listener) and both conditions (public and

[8] See Chapter Five, text at notes 71–3.

private) and include a degree of symmetry for all participants with regard to agenda setting, rules of standing and evidence, and opportunities for rebuttal and reply. 'Free' speech would have multiple goals and potential outcomes reflective of the different interests of participants. It is questionable, then, whether commercial advertising is predominantly an instance of other-regarding speech at all: Given its pecuniary motives and objectives, it might more usefully be categorized as self-regarding conduct and thus exempt from constitutional protection, as indeed the early commercial speech case law held.[9] Certainly the audience's *receipt* of advertising messages is a self-regarding activity, and *not* an other-regarding one, and should therefore find its constitutional protection somewhere other than the First Amendment.

The extension of constitutional protection to commercial speech of course simply ratified the already existing structure of the mass media speech forum. But this is only to say that advertising itself had already transformed the structure of public discourse in such a way that *other* communicative events in the same forum acquired a similar hierarchical and monologic division of communicative roles. Part of the burden of the argument in these pages has been to show that, while this interactional structure serves well the communicative purposes of commercial advertisers, it is damaging—and should be subordinated—to the political interests of citizens if we wish to take our own democratic political values seriously.

The very definition of *commercial speech* within the public discourse of a capitalist social formation is problematic. Is all communication in the commercial media *commercial speech?* What distinguishes political speech from commercial speech in this forum? Consider the example of *Retail Store Clerks* (Chapter 4). In that case, from the perspective of the commercial radio station, a department store's paid broadcasts urging the audience to buy its merchandise were *not* political speech, were uncontroversial, and were acceptable for airing without other comment needed. Paid broadcasts from the store's employees' union in the same time period urging the audience *not* to buy the store's merchandise until it had concluded a labor contract *were* instances of controversial political speech and were *not* acceptable; only the broadcasting firm's journalists were allowed to speak on *this* issue. What made the difference?

In the mass media context the property rights of owners are paramount over the citizen's communicative rights. The corporate initiative in the First Amendment field in the 1970s and 1980s has resulted in a cumulative denial of citizen rights to access or reply to the commercial press,

---

[9] Mishan (1977, p. 59) makes more or less this point, from the economist's perspective. Legal reasoning supporting this interpretation is offered by Farber (1979) "Commercial Speech" and by Jackson and Jeffries (1979).

including paid access, that is nearly absolute. The public's interest in the use of the broadcasting spectrum fared marginally better under the FCC's Fairness Doctrine, but this was eventually blocked in the courts, and has now been repudiated by the FCC. In the mass media—the central public forum of contemporary political culture—*freedom of speech* is, for citizens, *only* the freedom to *receive* messages.

The protection of commercial speech has been a partial protection: Full constitutional protection would have been unconducive to a mutual accommodation of the interests of media corporations and their clients. If corporations had a right of access, so would citizens, and the value of citizen exclusion from speaking roles would have been lost to media and nonmedia corporations alike. But the denial of citizen access left the field open to the media to operationalize their accommodation with corporate clients *in the name of the audience.* In reality the audience's interests have in all respects been subordinated to the property rights of the media firm and of its private clients in the 'marketplace of ideas.' The combined effect of the Court's prohibition of government regulation in regards either to compulsion or restraint of private media firms has been to confirm these utterly undemocratic institutions as the legitimate regulators of public discourse.

SPEECH, PROPERTY, AND THE STATE REVISITED

I believe my analysis has shown that the Supreme Court's representation of the constitutional speech interests of citizens, legislatures, media firms, and other corporations has systematically and erroneously conflated the processes of social communication with those of commodity production and market exchange, especially through the metaphor of the 'free marketplace of ideas.' This representation of fundamental social relationships in the discourse of constitutional law has generated a corresponding allocation of legitimating rights and effective power that represses the communicative interests of citizens and 'overdetermines' their communicative domination by large-scale property interests. As Christian Bay notes in discussing the concept of the 'free marketplace of ideas':

> Equality in any marketplace perishes quickly. Each victory tends to strengthen one competitor and weaken others for future contests; growing trends towards lopsidedness and unfair advantage are inescapable, and monopoly or oligopoly is the normal end state as decades and generations go by, for ideas as well as commodities.[10]

[10] Bay (1977, p. 31).

Where we may be willing to countenance great inequalities of material wealth and power if a paretian calculation convinces us that the interests of the *least* advantaged parties will be better served by this arrangement than by any alternative (and this is a large 'if'), monopolies of information and communication are a different category of inequality entirely. They not only increase the cost of acquiring useful knowledge or participating in the life of the community, but they thereby diminish the potential for self-realization of the affected parties themselves. Any pretense at generating a pareto optimum in these conditions is mere intellectual prestidigitation.

Smythe's arresting notion of the audience as a form of commodity expresses this diminished human potential inherent in the commodification of communication. There is nothing sinister about the Court's affirmation of an audience right to receive corporate and commercial speech—until this is placed in perspective beside the Court's prior *rejection* of the audience's right to *reply* to what it hears. It is this conjunction of citizen access denial and corporate access protection which seems to me to buttress Smythe's analysis. I do not claim that the Court has *explicitly* recognized the audience as a commodity produced, owned, and exchanged by media firms, but I believe it has been shown that the First Amendment discourse is carefully structured to permit this outcome. We might better say that what media produce (by means of a set of legally sanctioned property and exchange relations) is a surplus, not of audiences per se, nor of "audience power," nor of "audience time," but a surplus, simply, of *speech rights*. Logically and morally, perhaps, these rights ought to belong to the audience; just as, logically and morally, the surplus products of labor ought arguably to belong to their producers. But in point of legal fact, both kinds of surplus—surpluses of labor power and surpluses of communicative power—belong to the owners of firms in these respective sectors. And in the media sector, it is precisely this surplus of communicative right and that which media firms sell to their clients in the form of advertising opportunities.

It is apparent from the analysis that this body of law disguises a distinct prejudice in favor of property owners by clothing it in the ideological form of rights bestowed equally on all citizens (e.g., the *right to receive* commercial advertising). Here we have, as Pashukanis would describe it,[11] the production of forms of legal right that *correspond* to the forms of commodity production: in this case the production of communicative rights in law that correspond to the production, by media firms, of expressive opportunities for sale to advertisers. This correspondence illustrates the function of law as an ideological condition of development of

[11] See Chapter 2.

the capitalist economy. Legal discourse does not simply articulate the coercive intentions of a ruling class. It is not only because it "sustains relations of domination," but because it invests these relations with different and reverse meanings—such as justice, equality, obligation, and consent—that legal discourse must be described as ideological, and yet understood also as functionally integral to the *productive* relations of a capitalist mode of production.

Another example of the correspondence of legal and commodity form in the area of speech rights is present in William Meckling's argument for the creation of radio spectrum *property* rights. Meckling's discussion[12] of the frequency allocation regime in the U.S. notes, to begin with, that it has the dual objectives of maximizing frequency utilization, and minimizing frequency interference. This is *contradictory*, to Meckling, because

> The way to minimize interference is to prohibit all but one individual from radiating. The way to maximize utilization is to let everyone radiate.[13]

To advance his laissez-faire argument for spectrum property rights he describes and critiques the FCC's actual method of regulation:

> The FCC now generally specifies the rights of individual users in terms of production inputs, like the size and shape of the antenna, power level at the transmitter, etc. This... has two disadvantages: first, it makes it difficult for the user to make input substitutions, e.g., of transmitter power for antenna size; secondly, it results in different levels of interference as a function of time of day, day of the year, sun spot cycle, etc.[14]

The solution to these and many other inefficiencies attendant on public ownership of the resource, according to Meckling, is spectrum *property rights*:

> Instead of specifying the physical inputs users can employ... it would be desirable to specify energy levels they are permitted to impose at various geographic points. From an interference standpoint there is no reason why we should be concerned about how those energy levels are created.[15]

Meckling concludes from this that government should create a new form of property right, consisting of the *right to be received* at a given

---

[12] Meckling [1968].
[13] p. 28.
[14] p. 30.
[15] p. 30.

frequency, location, and radiated power. He indicates that he wants government to allocate this form of property by selling permanent, privately transferable licenses in the open market.

The problem here is the precisely matching inverse of that in the commercial speech doctrine. The right to *be* received is defined (by Meckling) as a form of self-regarding *property* right, properly available to those possessing the necessary financial qualifications—when it is really a strongly other-regarding *speech* right. The right to *receive* is defined (by the Court) as a fundamental speech right, available freely to all, when it is *not really a speech right at all.*

COMMUNICATIVE POWER AND COMMUNICATIVE JUSTICE

The critique of speech rights in the mass media is an illuminating case for the broader critique of bourgeois law and legal institutions and the study of political power in general. To Canadian constitutional scholar Allan Hutchinson, the entry point for the critique of liberal rights is the legal system's enforcement of a distinction between public and private spheres of action:

> The liberal theory of rights and political justice is premised on the belief that individuals possess a pre-political sphere of pure autonomy and freedom that does not depend for its existence upon the state: individuals are independent and complete entities who interact with others out of a grudging necessity to better satisfy their self-regarding wants and preferences. Accordingly, the major function of a liberal charter is to police the boundary that separates the political and the collective from the pre-political and the individual—to contain the state so as to prevent it from intruding, in its utilitarian zeal, upon the 'natural' realm of individual liberty. The major difficulty confronting adherents of liberalism lies in identifying the line that separates the domain of individual liberty from the domain of state action.[16]

Hutchinson distinguishes between natural law theorists—the "line finders," who seek to show that "the boundary is a product of the natural order of social life"—and legal positivists—the "line drawers," who, recognizing the arbitrariness of the distinction, depend on the identification of a prevailing social consensus. But both schools of liberal jurisprudence "assume that the bounds of private action [are] drawn by the

[16] Hutchinson and Petter (1988).

invisible hand of the market" and therefore tend to draw (or find) the line between public and private just where the market encounters the state. The root ideological premise of liberal law is this pretense that the market can and does function independently of state power:

> The state is implicated in the market in the same way that it is implicated in any other political choice made within its territorial jurisdiction. Its claim to sovereignty implies that a decision not to intervene and regulate, or mere inaction, is as much a governmental responsibility as a decision to do so. Thus the attempt to limit state activity [and its constitutional oversight - MAR] to efforts directed at changing the status quo is misconceived; the state is equally implicated in the retention of the status quo... The entitlements of private property-owners exist only insofar as the state is prepared to recognize and lend support to those entitlements in the face of competing claims. What is referred to as 'private power' is in reality public power that has been delegated to certain individuals and that can be wielded in a largely unchecked and democratically unaccountable way.[17]

In the speech rights case law, then, we can discern the operation of all three forms of political power described by Lukes.[18] The power to cause an event to take place is illustrated, for example, by *Pruneyard*, in which a property owner was compelled by the Court to make its premises available to public speakers without charge. The power to prevent an action taking place is illustrated throughout the case law in the disposition of the 'state action' question. For example, the decision in *Tornillo* prevented the State of Florida from compelling a political candidate's access to a newspaper, and most of the modern commercial speech caselaw likewise enforces government inaction with respect to advertising. The contemporary result of the enforced inaction of the state is of course simply a further imbalanced weighting of the already vastly inequitable relation between the political power of property owners and other citizens:

> Property is the foundation upon which [constitutional] rights are conferred, protected and enhanced. The less property one has, the less one can exercise and enjoy one's rights. There is a strong correlation between finance and franchise. In our technological society, wealth is a pre- condition of being able to speak broadly and effectively. Although anyone can stand on the street corner, only the rich can have direct access to our homes through the costly channels of the media. When the rights of property owners and speakers collide, speakers stand dumb before the claims of property.[19]

---

[17] Hutchinson and Petter (1985, pp. 12–13); see also Horowitz (1982); Kronman (1980).

[18] See Introduction.

[19] Hutchinson and Petter (1985, p. 25).

Freedom of expression is conceived in the liberal tradition as a purely individual right, pertaining only to the sphere of private action. And yet if what the First Amendment protects—as liberal political philosophy so eloquently asserts—is the 'other-regarding' character of communication, then communication itself is in a fundamental sense an ineluctably *public* activity. *Speech*, in constitutional discourse, refers to an activity which is protected from regulation because it provides such a basic service to the public interest: It constitutes the public sphere.

The Court's treatment of this public, interactive character of speech illustrates the workings of Lukes's third form of power, the power to *define* the issue. The subject is complicated by the fact that the media themselves clearly employ their constitutional privileges to exercise 'definitional' power in respect to the full range of social and political issues, including issues before the courts. But these privileges are at least partly rooted in the form in which communication is *defined* in the Court's discourse on justice and communication. Legal norms in any area ought to be applied to the most plausible extant facts, if the vitally important decisions of jurists are to be considered valid, accepted as just by the plurality of citizens, and have something like their intended results. But in examining the case law, it becomes evident that jurists and lawyers pay little attention to the findings of social scientists who study communication. How, in general terms, is human communication theorized, implicitly or explicitly, in First Amendment case law? What are the significant features of the models of social communication jurists prefer in mass media cases? What, in *communicational* terms, are the objectives of the relevant constitutional guarantees? What judicial notice is taken of the *structure* of a given communicative situation? What communicative roles and relationships are sanctioned by the courts?

This is the area which calls most clearly, I believe, for further attention; I have only noted in passing in the study some of the evidence that a 'transmission' model of social communication, largely counter indicated in the social science literatures, is a predominant theme in the Supreme Court's own utterances.

Here is a legal definition of communication, as drawn from an eminent communication lawyer's submission to a U.S. Congressional committee concerning a bill to ban tobacco advertising. Typical in substance of how the problem of defining communication is settled in decision law, the entire question of what communication *is* was resolved in a single sentence:

> Speech, as a process, involves three participants—a speaker, one or more hearers and, increasingly in modern society, a conduit acting as a go-

> between, delivering and amplifying the speaker's message to ever larger audiences.[20]

Now, communication, as it is understood by social scientists of varying disciplines and persuasions, is *not* in any simple sense the 'sending and receiving of messages,' or not if we mean that a 'message' is a discrete object or event encoding a 'correct' meaning, or that failure to take the intended meaning necessarily constitutes misinterpretation of a message. Up to the late 1950s this *was* the dominant paradigm in the sociology of communications. Known now as the 'transmission' or 'bullet' theory, it assumed that the 'reception' of a message was essentially passive and that a speaker more or less 'fires' a self-evidently meaningful message into the listener's awareness. The communicative power of the message was a function of its objective content. The only variables in this model were "*Who* says *what*, through what *channels* of communication, to *whom*, [with] what *results*."[21]

Modelling communication in this naively empiricist manner excited many sociologists of the period, because if it held any reasonably precise predictive power, such a research program would have highly interesting applications in the area of opinion management. Perhaps it even fed dreams, for some, of equal status and funding with the physical sciences. But researchers in this tradition, attempting to isolate the effects of various message contents and channels, soon found that new variables "emerged in such a cataract that we almost drowned."[22] Writing on the efforts up to 1960 to apply the 'bullet' theory to mass communications, Klapper enumerated these previously disregarded variables:

> Audience predispositions, self-selection, and selective perception;... various aspects of contextual organization; the audiences' image of the sources; the simple passage of time; the group orientation of the audience member and the degree to which he values group membership; the activity of opinion leaders; the social aspects of the situation during and after exposure [to the message] and the degree to which the audience member is forced to play a role; the personality pattern of the audience member, his social class, and the level of his frustrations; the nature of the media in a free enterprise system; and the availability of social mechanisms for implementing action drives...

---

[20] Neuborne (1987, p. 2).
[21] Smith, Laswell, & Casey (1946, p. 121).
[22] Klapper (1960, p. 3).

"Almost every aspect of the life of the audience member and the culture in which the communication occurs," Klapper wrote, "seems susceptible of relation to the process of communication effect."[23] This expanded view of the process of social communication contained a tacit political challenge. Its emphasis on the importance of familial, ethnic, class and subcultural influence was highly corrosive of prevailing assumptions about the 'naturalness' of the beliefs and values of economically (and communicatively) dominant groups in society.

Klapper and his colleagues concluded that the most they could claim about message 'effects' was that "some kinds of communication on some kinds of issues, brought to the attention of some kinds of people under some kinds of conditions" might *reinforce* some existing values and opinions,[24] but that programmatically *altering* values and opinions in preferred directions was at best unlikely. "Seeking simple and direct effects of which mass communication is the sole and sufficient cause"[25] was a fruitless venture.

Social scientists, then—even those in the positivist tradition—recognized some decades ago that the 'receivers' of communications are engaged in complex and purposive activities, and that those activities, as well as innumerable features of the context in which they take place, are important factors in the construction of the meanings of 'messages.' They accordingly abandoned the 'transmission' or 'bullet' theory. It continues, however, to lead a vigorous life in the policy arena, and especially in the First Amendment case law.

The conservative, laissez-faire contribution to First Amendment interpretation, in which the transmission model is most commonly advanced, has been a literal and absolutist reading, a kind of constitutional bible thumping in which the mass media themselves have been the most eager, proselytizing part of the congregation. This judicial fundamentalism posits a prescient elect—the 'framers of the Constitution'—whose text is transparent and fixed in meaning. "Congress shall make no law abridging freedom of speech, or of the press" is what it says, and, as Justice Black liked to repeat, "no law means *no law*!"[26]

The competing tradition—the civic humanist inheritance --advances what Justice Brennan has called a 'structural' model of the First Amendment.[27] Several Supreme Court justices—notably Brennan and Frank-

[23] p. 3.

[24] Berelson (1948, p. 172).

[25] Klapper (1960, p. 257).

[26] Woodward and Armstrong (1979, p. 148).

[27] This is of course the tradition in which Alexander Meiklejohn should be included (cited in Chapter 5); Thomas Emerson's 'affirmative' model, while stressing different core values, is compatible in some respects (cited in Chapter 3).

furter—have called for a focus on the *structure* of rights allocated among the interests in mass communication. This more 'interactional' interpretation of the First Amendment accords far better with the evidence from the social sciences, and forms an immanent judicial challenge to the dominance of the 'transmission' model. The jurists of this tradition expect, perhaps naively, that their decisions should result in a considered balance of speech rights among the various interests at play in the mass media, such that effective democratic processes may evolve in that context side by side with the obvious commercial opportunities. Supreme Court Justice Brennan has championed this model in a number of dissenting opinions and academic papers:

> The First Amendment fosters the values of democratic self-government. Another way of saying this is that the First Amendment protects the structure of communications necessary for the existence of our democracy. This insight suggests the second model to describe the role of the press in our society. This second model is structural in nature. It focuses on the relationship of the press to the communicative functions required by our democratic beliefs.[28]

This structural model may be a more suitable apparatus for normative analysis of the *interactive* dimensions of communication. A transmission model of communication, on the other hand, is a highly effective tool for defining and controlling claims of authorial property and contractual obligation. The thematization of communication as the transmission of information—and its conceptual inventory of self-evident 'messages,' 'codes,' 'channels,' and 'sending' and 'receiving' functions—permits the institutions of law to transform ineluctably interpretive relations between persons, into the kinds of instrumental relations it is far better equipped to regulate: those associated with the possession, transference, and administration of property. It must therefore be recognized that even the latent definitions of social processes imbedded in legal discourse have vast entailments with respect to the allocation of material resources and social power.

The rambling edifice of liberal political philosophy, scene of centuries of family argument (never quite resolved) among such distant cousins as republicanism and utilitarianism (and where Thomist grandparents can usually be found muttering in the background), is also the birthplace of that most refractory of philosophical offspring, historical materialism. Some modern philosophical reconstructions of the Marxist project exhibit

---

[28] Justice William J. Brennan, quoted in Gillmor and Barron (1984, p. 149). See also Brennan (1965, 1979).

a striking turn towards problems of normative justification. The 'discourse ethics' developed by Karl-Otto Apel and Jurgen Habermas seems particularly relevant here, as a starting point for future research into the definitional conundrums that beset liberal theories of communicative justice.[29] This approach—refuting relativist, skepticist, and contractarian ethical positions—draws on a broad range of materials from the philosophy of language, social and cognitive psychology, systems theory, hermeneutics, and critical and Weberian action theory to provide a thorough reformulation of neo-Kantian theories of justice along procedural lines. Briefly stated, discourse ethics, in Habermas's version a 'formal-pragmatic' theory, attempts to

> articulate those rules and communicative presuppositions that make it possible for participants in a practical discourse to arrive at a valid, rational consensus on social norms... and serve[s] as the standard for distinguishing between legitimate and illegitimate norms.[30]

The distinction in this perspective between substantive and procedural norms exempts its claims from the cross-cultural and communitarian critiques levelled against other neo-Kantian positions (such as Rawls's). Discourse ethics recommends no particular normative *content*, defending instead a universalistic conception of the *structure* of normative argumentation, derived from analysis of the empirical features of normative justifications as a specific class of utterances (with inescapable cognitive entailments). This strongly differentiates it from the ahistorical and idealist contructions of all versions of contractarianism, as well as from ethically skeptical 'realisms' (which can be shown to violate their own premises merely by engaging in political argumentation). And its ontological distinction between communicative action—involving speakers in an interpretive distanciation from their own interests—and strategic action—oriented to prediction and control—allows discourse ethics to show the connections between the linguistic structures of normative justification and larger scale institutional structures of social interaction.

Because of these features it occupies a unique position within argumentation concerning the normative regulation of communication itself. In other normative conflicts, discourse ethics has the status merely of a

---

[29] See Habermas (1984, 1987, 1990); Boston: Apel (1980); Wren (1990); McCarthy (1978, pp. 272–357). Two special issues on contemporary debates in ethics and social theory in recent periodical literature are also quite useful: XXI/1–2 (Fall–Winter) *Philosophical Forum* (1989–1990); and 14/3–4 *Philosophy and Social Criticism* (1988).

[30] Cohen (1988, p. 316).

distinct (though compelling) philosophical position on the conditions of rational debate, and has no presumptive entailments for their substance. But with respect to explicit argumentation about the normative regulation of *communication* practises, it has also the status of a *methodology* for evaluating the adequacy—more precisely, the "communicative rationality"—of all substantive philosophical positions within such debates.

For questions of communicative justice, narrowly conceived (and for these questions alone), discourse ethics is both substantively and procedurally prescriptive. Therefore, while its substantive prescriptions may nominally require justification on the same plane of abstraction as competing positions (e.g., utilitarianism, communitarianism, contractarianism), the derivation of those prescriptions from, and their identity with, the higher level *procedural* requirements of discourse ethics renders such a justification redundant. The actual case is the reverse of this, for to succeed as an adequate theory of communicative justice, any competing position will have to accomplish one of two tasks: it must either invalidate the procedural claims of discourse ethics (e.g., the dialogical character of justification processes), triggering conditions of cognitive uncertainty towards *any* ethical norms in the process; or it must provide an alternative metaethics with equivalent or greater explanatory power *for the case of communications regulation.* The latter in turn requires of competing positions that they be able to explain the premises and account for the evidence upon which the claims of discourse ethics rest, showing how these premises or evidence, or the process of reasoning from them, are flawed.

I wish to conclude, then, by pointing beyond the critique of liberal rights to a cautiously hopeful historical vista. In the sense expressed in the 'formal pragmatic' model of discourse ethics, the notion of freedom of expression has not only the repressive meanings we have explored but also a transformative potential, transcending liberal ideology. Market allocation of resources is an outcome of public policy choices, not the 'natural' order of society. The conduct of citizens is ontologically distinguishable from the conduct of consumers, and the interests of corporations are not the primary interests at play in the public forum. The very centrality and force of 'free speech rights' as an ideological condition of development of contemporary market forces may in the end contribute to breaking down the counterassumptions, and stimulating once again in a more comprehensive form popular challenge to the prevailing models of communicative justice.

The Supreme Court of the United States has on several occasions avowed that the purpose of the constitutional guarantee of free speech was to ensure the "unfettered interchange of ideas for the bringing about of political and social changes desired by the people."[31] The prospective achievement anywhere of effective means for popular discussion and implementation of political change is highly threatening to important sectors of capital. On the other hand the failure to achieve it may imply an even more threatening attenuation of our capacity for reasoned popular response to the many looming threats of social, economic, geopolitical, and environmental immiseration. I believe that 'free speech' *is* a necessary element of effective practical reason, authentic democracy, and consensual justice, even though these may be incompatible with the stability and growth of the capitalist market system. Collective self-determination—perhaps even collective survival—now requires the *audience's* appropriation of the media. We have urgent need of their fuller and freer public use so that we may reason together and respond to the perilous state we are in.

[31] Justice Felix Frankfurter for the Court, *Roth v. United States*, 354 U.S. 476 [1957].

References

I. TABLE OF CASES

(Numbers in parentheses show citations in the text.)

Abourezk v. Reagan, 56 U.S.L.W. 4001 [1987] (134).
Abrams v. United States, 250 U.S. 616 [1919] (62, 63).
Amalgamated Food Employees Union Local 590 v. Logan Valley Plaza, 391 U.S. 308 [1968] (87).
Approved Personnel Inc. v. Tribune Co., 177 So. 2d 704 [Fla. 1965] (68).
Associated Press v. United States, 326 U.S. 1 at 20 [1945] (69, 70, 71, 74).
Banzhaf, 8 FCC 2d 381 [1967].
Bates v. State Bar of Arizona, 433 U.S. 350 [1977] (107, 123).
Bigelow v. Virginia, 421 U.S. 809 [1975].
Bolger v. Youngs Drugs Products Co., 463 U.S. 60 [1983] (108, 135).
Bose Corp. v. Consumers Union of U.S. Inc., 466 U.S. 485 [1984].
Breard v. City of Alexandria, 341 U.S. 622 [1951] (108, 115–116).
Buckley v. Valeo, 424 U.S. 1 [1976] (124, 126, 127).
Capital Cities Cable Inc. v. Oklahoma Alcoholic Beverage Control Board, 467 U.S. 691 [1984] (135).
Carey v. Population Services International, 431 U.S. 678 [1977] (135).
CBS v. Business Executives' Move For Vietnam Peace, 412 U.S. 94 [1973] (22, 79, 84, 95–96, 97, 98, 129).
Central Hudson Gas & Electric Corp. v. Public Service Commission of New York, 447 U.S. 557 [1980] (128, 130, 135, 136).
Chicago Joint Board, Amalgamated Clothing Workers of America, AFL-CIO v. Chicago Tribune, 435 F.2d [17th Cir. 1970].
Citizen Publishing Co. v. United States, 394 U.S. 131 [1968].
Chrestensen v. Valentine, 316 U.S. 52 [1942] (107, 111–116, 118, 119, 122).
Coleman Young v. American Mini-Theatres Inc., 427 U.S. 50 [1976].
Columbia Broadcasting System v. Democratic National Committee, 412 U.S. 94 [1973] (22, 79).
Commonwealth of Massachusetts v. Davis, 162 Mass. 510 [1895] (61).

Consolidated Edison Co. of New York v. Public Service Commission of New York, 447 U.S. 530 [1980] (128–129, 130).

Cornelius v. NAACP Legal and Educational Defense Fund, 105 S. Ct. 3439 [1985] (135).

Cox v. Louisiana, 379 U.S. 536 [1965] (99).

Davis v. Massachussetts, 167 U.S. 43 [1897] (61).

Dennis v. United States, 341 U.S. 494 [1951] (55).

Doe v. Bolton, 410 U.S. 179 [1973] (120).

Dorsey v. Stuyvesant Town Corp., 299 N.Y. 512; certiorari denied, 339 U.S. 981.

Douglas et al. v. City of Jeannette, 319 U.S. 157 [1943] (113).

Dun & Bradstreet Inc. v. Greenmoss Builders Inc., 105 S. Ct. 2939 [1985] (108, 135).

Eastex Inc. v. National Labour Relations Board, 437 U.S. 556 [1978] (135).

Evans v. Newton, 382 U.S. 296 [1966] (72–73, 74).

Fairness Report, 48 FCC 2d 1 [1974].

FCC v. Allentown Broadcasting Corporation, 349 U.S. 358 [1954] (72).

FCC v. Sanders Bros. Radio Station, 309 U.S. 470 [1939] (71, 72).

First National Bank of Boston v. Bellotti, 435 U.S. 765 [1978] (65, 76, 84–85, 98, 99, 127, 130).

Fitzgerald v. National Rifle Association, 383 F. Supp. 162 [D.N.J. 1974] (70–71, 72).

Fowler v. Rhode Island, 345 U.S. 67 [1953] (99).

Friedenberg v. Times Publishing Co., 127 So. 345 [La.1930] (88).

Gertz v. Robert Welch Inc., 418 U.S. 323 [1974] (147).

Gitlow v. New York, 268 U.S. 652 [1925].

Hague v. CIO, 307 U.S. 496 [1939] (62).

Herbert v. Lando, 441 U.S. 153 [1979].

Home Placement Service v. Providence Journal, 682 F. 2d 274 [1st Cir. 1982] (70, 71).

Hudgens v. NLRB, 424 U.S. 507 [1976].

In Re Louis Wohl, Inc., 50 F2d 254 [E.D.Mich.1931].

In Re Primus, 436 U.S. 412 [1978].

In Re R.M.J., 455 U.S. 191 [1982].

J.J. Gordon Inc. v. Worcester Telegram Publishing Co., 177 N.E.2d 586 [Mass. 1961] (68).

Jamison v. Texas, 318 U.S. 413 [1943] (113–115).

Jobin v. Arizona, Jones v. City of Opelika, Sanders v. City of Fort Smith, Bowden v. City of Fort Smith, all 316 U.S. 584 [1942], all vacated 319 U.S. 103 [1943] (113–114).

Joseph Burstyn Inc. v. Wilson, 343 U.S. 495 [1952] (64).

Kleindienst v. Mandel, 408 U.S. 396 [1974] (111, 133, 134).

Kovacs v. Cooper, 336 U.S. 77 [1949] (64, 92, 126).

Lehman v. City of Shaker Heights, 418 U.S. 298 [1974] (135).

Linmark Associates Inc. v. Township of Willingboro, 431 U.S. 85 [1977] (123, 135).

Lloyd v. Tanner, 407 U.S. 551 [1972] (86, 87).

Lorain Journal Co. v. United States, 342 U.S. 143 [1951] (70, 71).

Lowe v. Securities and Exchange Commission, 105 S. Ct. 2557 [1985].

Mack v. Costello, 143 N.W. 950 [S.D.1913] (88).

Marsh v. Alabama, 326 U.S. 501 [1946].

Martin v. City of Struthers, 319 U.S. 141 [1943] (113, 119).

Members of City Council of Los Angeles v. Taxpayers for Vincent, et. al., 466 U.S. 789 [1984] (135).

Metromedia Inc. v. City of San Diego, 453 U.S. 490 [1981] (108).

Miami Herald Publishing Co. v. Tornillo, 418 U.S. 241 [1974] (65, 76, 82, 86).

Mink, 59 FCC 2d 987 [1976].

Murdock v. Pennsylvania, 319 U.S. 105 [1943] (108, 113–114, 116).

NAACP v. Claiborne Hardware Co., 458 U.S. 886 [1982] (135).

Near v. Minnesota, 283 U.S. 697 [1931] (62).

New York Times v. Sullivan, 376 U.S. 254 [1964] (65, 107, 117).

Niemotko v. Maryland, 340 U.S. 268 [1951] (99).

Ohralik v. Ohio State Bar Association, 436 U.S. 447 [1978] (107, 135).

Pacific Gas and Electric Co. v. Public Utilities Commission of California, 106 S. Ct. 903 [1986] (75–77, 80, 85–86, 135, 147).

Pennekamp v. Florida, 328 U.S. 331 [1946] (64).

Pittsburgh Press Co. v. Pittsburgh Commission on Human Relations, 413 U.S. 376 [1973] (119, 120).

Posadas de Puerto Rico Associates v. Tourism Co. of Puerto Rico, 106 S. Ct. 2968 [1986] (135).

Poughkeepsie Buying Service Inc. v. Poughkeepsie Newspapers, Inc., 131 N.Y.S.2d 515 [1954] (68).

Pruneyard Shopping Center v. Robbins, 447 U.S. 74 [1980] (85–89, 95, 146, 147–148, 157).

Re Klein and Law Society of Upper Canada, 16 D.L.R. (4th) 489 [1985].

Red Lion Broadcasting v. Federal Communications Commission, 395 U.S. 367 [1969] (64, 91, 93, 94, 95, 97, 102, 103, 104, 110, 123, 126, 147, 151).

Retail Store Employees Union, Local 880, Retail Clerks International Association, AFL-CIO v. FCC, 43b F. 2d 248 [D.C. Circuit 1970].

Robbins v. Pruneyard Shopping Center, 23 Cal. 3d 899, [1979].

Roe v. Wade, 410 U.S. 113 [1973] (120).

Rosenbloom v. Metromedia, 403 U.S. 29 [1971] (147).

Roth v. United States, 354 U.S. 476 [1957].

Shuck v. Carroll Daily Herald, 247 N.W. 813 [Iowa 1933] (68).

Splawn v. State of California, 431 U.S. 595 [1977] (135).

State of New York v. P.I. Ferber, 458 U.S. 747 [1982].

Stromberg v. California, 283 U.S. 359 [1931].

Texas Optometric Association v. Rogers, 440 U.S. 1 [1979] (135).

Uhlman v. Sherman, 22 Ohio N.P., N.S., 225, 31 (Ohio Dec. 54) [1919] (8, 71).

United States v. Greater Buffalo Press, Inc., 402 U.S. 549 [1971].

United States v. Radio Corporation of America, 358 U.S. 334 [1959].

Village of Hoffman Estates v. Flipside, 455 U.S. 489 [1982] (135).

Village of Schaumberg v. Citizens for a Better Environment, 444 U.S. 620 [1980] (135).

Virginia State Board of Pharmacy v. Virginia Citizens Consumer Council, Inc., 425 U.S. 748 [1976] (19, 107, 108, 123, 124, 133).

Wall v. World Publishing Co., 263 P. 2d 1010 [Okl. 1953] (88).
Watchtower Bible and Tract Society v. Metropolitan Life Insurance Co., 297 N.Y. 339; certiorari denied, 335 U.S. 886 (73).
West Virginia Board of Education v. Barnette, 319 U.S. 624 [1943] (76)
Whitney v. California, 274 U.S. 357 [1927].
Wisconsin Association of Nursing Homes, Inc. v. The Journal Co., 285 N.W. 2d 891 [WISC. 1979].
WNCN Listeners' Guild v. Federal Communications Commission, 450 U.S. 582 [1981]. (133–34)
Wooley v. Maynard, 430 U.S. 705 [1977] (76, 87–88).
Zauderer v. Office of District Counsel of Supreme Court of Ohio, 85 U.S. 652 [1985].

OTHER WORKS CITED

Altheide, D.L. (1976). *Creating reality: How TV news distorts events.* London: Sage.
Althusser, L. (1977). Ideology and ideological state apparatuses. *Lenin and philosophy and other essays.* London: New Left Books.
Apel, K-O. (1980). *Towards the transformation of philosophy.* London: Routledge and Kegan Paul.
Aristotle. (1962). *Nichomachean ethics* (M. Ostwald, Trans.) New York: Library of Liberal Arts.
Baker, C.E. (1989). *Human liberty and freedom of speech.* New York: Oxford University Press.
Balbus, I.D. (1977). Commodity form and legal form. *Law and Society Review, 11*, 571.
Barron, J.A. (1984). Access to the press—A new First Amendment Right. In D.M. Gillmor & J.A. Barron, *Mass communication law.* St. Paul: West Publishing.
Barron, J.A. (1986). Public access to the media under the charter: An American appraisal. In P. Anisman & A.M. Linden (Eds.), *The media, the courts, and the charter.* Toronto: Carswell.
Bay, C. (1977). Access to political knowledge as a human right. In I. Galnoor (Ed).*Government secrecy in democracies.* New York: Harper.
Berelson, B. (1948). Communications and public opinion. In W. Schramm (Ed.), *Communications in modern society.* Urbana, IL: University of Illinois Press.
Berlin, I. (1970). John Stuart Mill and the ends of life. In *Four essays on liberty.* New York: Oxford University Press.
Berman, H. (1978). The background of the Western legal tradition in the folklaw of the peoples of Europe. *University of Chicago Law Review, 45*, 553.
Bernays, E.L. (1928). *Propaganda.* New York: Horace Liverwright.
Blanchard, M.A. (1986). *Exporting the First Amendment: The press-government crusade of 1945–1952.* New York: Longman.
Blasi, V. (1977). The checking value in first amendment theory. *American Bar Foundation Research Journal, 523*, 561.

Bollinger, L.C., Jr. (1976). Freedom of the press and public access: Towards a theory of partial regulation of the mass media. *Michigan Law Review, 75*, 1.

Boyd-Barrett, J.O. (1984). Cultural dependency and the mass media. In M. Gurevitch, T. Bernett, J. Curran, & Woolcott (Eds.), *Culture, society and the media*. London: Methuen.

Braverman, H. (1974). *Labour and monopoly capital*. New York: Monthly Review Press.

Brennan, W.J. (1979). Freedom of the press. *Rutgers Law Review, 32*, 173.

Brennan, W.J. (1965). The Supreme Court and the Meiklejohn Interpretation of the First Amendment. *Harvard Law Review, 79*, 1.

Brown, D., & Harrison, M.J. (1978). *A sociology of industrialization*. London: MacMillan.

Burke, P. (1986–1978). Comment: Pacific Gas & Electric v. Public Utilities Commission of California: Negative First Amendment rights for corporations. *Review of Law and Social Change, xv*, 371.

Carter, S. (1984). *Yale Law Journal, 93*, 581.

Canada, House of Commons. *Royal Commission on Newspapers*. Ministry of Supply and Services.

Chevigny, P. (1988). *More speech: Dialogue rights and modern liberty*, Philadelphia: Temple University Press.

Chomsky, N., & Herman, E.S. (1979). *The Washington connection and third world fascism*. Boston: South End Press.

Clarke, D. (1982). Second-hand news: Production and reproduction at a major Ontario television studio. L. Salter, (Ed.), in *Communication studies in Canada*, Toronto: MacMillan.

Coase, R.H. (1977). Advertising and free speech. In A. Hyman & M.B. Johnson (Eds.), *Advertising and free speech*. Lexington, MA: Lexington Books.

Cohen, G.A. (1978). *Karl Marx's theory of history: A defense*. Princeton, NJ: Princeton University Press.

Cohen, J. (1988). Discourse Ethics and Civil Society. *Philosophy and Social Criticism, 14*(3–4), 315 [1988].

Collins, H. (1984). *Marxism and law*. Oxford: Oxford University Press.

Cotterell, R. (1976). Commodity form and legal form. *Ideology and Consciousness, 6*, 111.

Curran, J., Ecclestone, J., Oakley, G., & Richardson, A. (Eds.). (1986).*Bending reality: The state of the media*, London: Pluto.

Davies, W., & Fouracre, P. (Eds.). *The settlement of disputes in early medieval Europe*. Cambridge, UK: Cambridge University Press.

Douglas, S. (1986). *Labor's new voice: Unions and the mass media*, Norwood, NJ: Ablex Publishing Corp.

Downing, J. (1984). *Radical media: The political experience of alternative communication*. Chicago: South End Press.

Dreier, P. (1982). Capitalists v. the media: An analysis of an ideological mobilization among business leaders. *Media, Culture and Society, 4*.

Dworkin, R. (1977). *Taking rights seriously*. London: Duckworth.

Dyer, G. (1982). *Advertising as communication*. London: Methuen.

Edelman, B. (1979). *Ownership of the image*. London: Routledge & Kegan Paul.

Ehrlich, E. (1975). *Fundamental principles of the sociology of law*. (W.L. Moll, Trans.). New York: Arno Press. (Original work published 1936)

Emerson, T. The affirmative side of the First Amendment. *Georgia Law Review, 15*, 795.

Emerson. (1970). *The System of Freedom of Expression.*

Epstein. The PAC phenomenon: An overview. *Arizona Law Review, 22*, 355.

Ewen, S. (1976). *Captains of consciousness: Advertising and the social roots of the consumer culture*. New York: McGraw-Hill.

Farber, D.A. (1979). Commercial speech and first amendment theory. *Northwestern University Law Review, 74*, 372.

Fejes, F. (1981). Media imperialism: An assessment. *Media, Culture and Society, 3.*

Fox, J.J. (1973). Our ancestors spoke in pairs: Rotinese views of language, dialect and code. In R. Bauman & J. Sherzer (Eds.), *Explorations in the Ethnography of Speaking*. New York: Cambridge University Press.

Freedman, M. (1977). Advertising and solicitation by lawyers: Legal ethics, 'commercial' speech, and free speech. In A. Hyman & M.B. Johnson (Eds.), *Advertising and free speech*. Lexington, MA.: Lexington Books.

Freiman, M.J. (1984). Consumer sovereignty and national sovereignty in domestic and international broadcasting regulation. In *Cultures in collision: A Canadian–U.S. conference on communications policy*. New York: Praeger.

Freire, P. (1970). *Pedagogy of the oppressed*. New York: Herder and Herder.

Freire, P. (1982), *Education for critical consciousness*. New York: Continuum.

Freud, S. (1953–1974). *The Interpretation of Dreams* (Vol. 4, standard edition of the complete psychological works of Sigmund Freud). London: Hogarth Press.

Galbraith, J.K. (1967). *The new industrial state*. Boston: Houghton Mifflin.

Gans, H.J. (1980). *Deciding what's news*. New York: Vintage.

Geertz, C. (1983). Local knowledge: Fact and law in comparative perspective. In C. Geertz (Ed.), *Local knowledge: Further essays in interpretive anthropology*. New York: Basic Books.

Gillmor, D.M., & Barron, J.A. (1984). *Mass communication law*. St. Paul, MN: West Publishing.

Ginsburg, D.H. (1979). *Regulation of Broadcasting*. St. Paul, MN: West Publishing Co.

Gitlin, T. (1980). *The whole world is watching*. Berkeley, CA: University of California Press.

Goffman, E. (1974). *Frame analysis*. New York: Harper Colophon.

Gramsci, A. (1971). *Prison notebooks*. (Q. Hoare & G.N. Smith, Trans.). New York: International.

Habermas, J. (1989). *The structural transformation of the public sphere: An inquiry into a category of bourgeois society* (T. Burger, Trans.), Cambridge, MA: MIT Press. (Original work published 1962)

Habermas, J. (1986–1987). *The theory of communicative action. Volume 1: Reason and the rationalization of society; Volume 2: Lifeworld and system: A critique of functionalist reason*. Boston: Beacon Press.

Habermas, J. (1990). *Moral consciousness and communicative action.* Cambridge, MA: MIT Press.

Hackett, R.A. (1986). For a socialist perspective on the news media. *Studies in Political Economy, 19.*

Hart, H.L.A. (1961). *The concept of law.* Oxford: Clarendon Press.

Hartley, J. (1982). *Understanding news.* London: Methuen.

Hegel, G.W.F. (1967). *The philosophy of right.* (T.M. Knox Ed. & Trans.). London: Oxford University Press. (Original work published 1820)

Hirst, P. (1979). *On law and ideology.* Atlantic Highlands, NJ: Humanities Press.

Hodder-Williams, R. (1980). *The politics of the U.S. Supreme Court.* London: George Allen and Unwin.

Hont, I., & Ignatieff, M. (Eds.). (1983). *Wealth and virtue: The shaping of political economy in the Scottish enlightenment.* Cambridge, UK: Cambridge University Press.

Horning. (1969). The First Amendment right to a public forum. *Duke Law Journal, 31.*

Horowitz, M. (1982). The history of the public/private distinction. *University of Pennsylvania Law Review, 130,* 1423.

Hutchinson, A.C., & Petter, A. (1985). *Private rights/public wrongs.* Unpublished paper, Osgoode Hall Law School/ University of Victoria.

Immigration and Nationality Act, 8 U.S.C. Section 1182 (a) (28). U.S. 530.

Jackson, T.H., & Jeffries, J.C., Jr. (1979). Commercial speech: Economic due process and the First Amendment. *Virginia Law Review, 65,* 1.

Jhally, S. (1982). Probing the blindspot. *Canadian Journal of Political and Social Theory, 6* (1–2).

Jhally, S. (1984). *The codes of advertising: Fetishism and the context of meaning in modern society.* Unpublished doctoral dissertation, Simon Fraser University.

Jhally, S., & Livant, B. (1986 Fall). Watching as working: The valorization of audience consciousness. *Journal of Communications.*

Kairys, D. (1965). Freedom of speech. In D. Kairys (Ed.), *The Politics of Law.* New York: Pantheon.

Kalven. (1965). The concept of the public forum: Cox v. Louisiana. *Supreme Court Review, 1,* 1415.

Kemp, T. (1969).*Industrialization in nineteenth-century Europe.* London: Longman.

Klapper, J.T. (1960). *The effects of mass communication.* New York: MacMillan.

Kronman, A.T. (1980). Contract law and distributive justice. *Yale Law Journal, 89,* 472.

Lebowitz, M.A. (1986 Autumn). Too many blindspots on the media. *Studies in Political Economy* p. 21.

Leeson, K.W. (1984). *International communications: Blueprint for policy,* Amsterdam: Elsevier Science Publishers.

Levitt, T. (1960). Marketing myopia. *Harvard Business Review, 38.*

Livant, B. (1979). The audience-commodity: On the blindspot debate. *Canadian Journal of Political and Social Theory, 3* (1).

Livant, B. (1982). Working at watching: A reply to Sut Jhally. *Canadian Journal of Political and Social Theory, 6* (1–2).

Locke, J. *Second Treatise of government.* (C.B. Macpherson, Ed.). Cambridge, UK: Hackett Publishing. (Original work published 1690)

Lukes, S. (1974). *Power: A radical view.* London: MacMillan.

Macpherson, C.B.(1962). *The political theory of possessive individualism.* London: Oxford University Press.

Macpherson, C.B. (1966). The social bearings of Locke's political theory. In J.N. Shklar (Ed.), *Political theory and ideology*, London: MacMillan.

Macpherson, C.B. (1977). *The life and times of liberal democracy.* Oxford: Oxford University Press.

Marshall, T.H. (1977). Citizenship and social class. In Marshall, *Class, citizenship and social development.* (1949). Chicago: University of Chicago Press.

Mastro, Costlow, & Sanchez. (1980). Taking the initiative: Corporate control of the referendum process through media spending and what to do about it. *Federal Communications Law Journal, 32*, 315.

Mathias, P. (1969). *The first industrial nation: An economic history of Britain 1700–1914.* London: Methuen.

Mattelart, A. (1983). For a class and group analysis of popular communication practises. In A. Mattelart & S. Siegelaub (Eds.), *Communication and class struggle*, (Vol. 2). New York: International General.

Mattelart, A., & Siegelaub, S. (Eds.). (1983). *Communication and class struggle* (Vol. 2). New York: International General.

MacDonald, J.G. & Parker, H. (1963). Creating a strategy for international growth. In Clifton, *Marketing insights.* New York: Appleton-Century-Crofts.

Marx, K. (1972). *Grundrisse*, (Martin Nicolaus, Trans.) Harmondsworth, UK: Penguin. (Original work published 1858)

Marx, K. (1971). *A contribution to the critique of political economy.* London: Lawrence and Wishart.

Marx, K., & Engels, F. (1975). *The German ideology, Marx and Engels collected works* (Vol. 5). London: Lawrence and Wishart

Mauser, G.A. (1983). *Political marketing.* New York: Praeger.

McCarthy, T. (1978). *The critical theory of Jurgen Habermas.* Cambridge, MA: MIT Press.

McGarry, E.D. (1958). The propaganda function in marketing. *Journal of Marketing, 23*, 139.

McWhinney, E. (1986). *Supreme courts and judicial law-making: Constitutional tribunals and constitutional review.* Dordrecht: Martinus Nijhoff.

Meckling, (1968). Management of the frequency spectrum. *Washington University Law Review, 1*, 26.

Meiklejohn, A. (1948). *Free speech and its relation to self-government.* New York: Harper & Row.

Meiklejohn, A. (1952). What does the First Amendment mean? *University of Chicago Law Review, 20*, 461.

Meiklejohn, A. (1961). The First Amendment is an absolute. *Supreme Court Review*, p. 245.

Meiklejohn, A. (1965). *Political freedom: The constitutional powers of the people.* New York: Oxford University Press.

Meltzer, B.N., & Petras, W.J. (1970). The Chicago and Iowa schools of symbolic interactionism. In T. Shibutani (Ed.), *Human nature and collective behavior.* Englewood Cliffs, NJ: Prentice-Hall.

Merrill, T.W. (1970). (1976). First Amendment protection for commercial speech. *University of Chicago Law Review, 44*, 205.

Miliband, R. (1973). *The state in capitalist society.* London: Quartet Books.

Mill, J.S. (1971). Of the liberty of thought and discussion. *On Liberty.* London: Oxford University Press. (Original work published 1859)

Mills, C.W. (1956). *The power elite.* New York: Oxford University Press.

Mishan, E. (1977). Commercial advertising: A skeptical view. In A. Hyman & M.B. Johnson (Eds.), *Advertising and free speech*, Lexington, MA: Lexington Books.

Morley, D. (1980). *The nationwide audience: Structure and decoding.* London: British Film Institute.

Murdock, G. (1978). Blindspots about Western Marxism: A reply to Dallas Smythe. *Canadian Journal of Political and Social Theory, 2* (2).

Murdock, G. (1982). Large corporations and the control of the communications industries. In M. Gurevitch, T. Bennett, J. Curran, & J. Woollacott (Eds.), *Culture, society and the media.* London: Methuen.

Murdock, G., & Golding P. (1977). Capitalism, communication and class relations. In J. Curran, M. Gurevitch, & J. Woollacott (Eds.), *Mass communication and society.* London: Edward Arnold.

Nadel, M.S. *Fordham Urban Law Journal, 12*, 183.

Nader, L., & Todd, H.F. Jr., (Eds.) (1978). *The disputing process: Law in ten societies*, New York: Columbia University Press.

Neubourne, B. (1987). *Free speech–free markets–free choice: An essay on commercial speech.* New York: Association of National Advertisers.

Pashukanis, E.B. (1978). *Law and Marxism.* (C.J. Arthur, Ed. & Trans.). London: Ink Links.

Phillips, P. (1980). *Marx and Engels on law and laws.* Oxford, Martin Robertson.

Plamenatz, J. (1963). *Man and society* (Vol. 2.) London: Longman.

Pocock, J.G.A. (1983). Cambridge paradigms and Scotch philosophers. In Hont & M. Ignatieff (Eds.), *Wealth and virtue: The shaping of political economy in the Scottish enlightenment*, Cambridge, UK: Cambridge University Press.

Posner, R. (1986). *The Economic analysis of law* (3rd ed.). Boston, MA: Little, Brown.

Rabban, D. (1981). The First Amendment in its forgotten years. *Yale Law Journal, 90*, 514.

Raboy, M. (1984). *Movements and messages: Media and radical politics in Quebec* (D. Homel, Trans.). Toronto: Between-the-Lines Press.

Rome, E.P., & Roberts, W.H. (1985). *Corporate and commercial free speech.* Westport, CT: Quorum Books.

Rowbotham, S. (1989). *The past is before us: Feminism in action since the 1960's.* London: Pandora Press.

Schauer, F. (1982). *Free speech: A philosophical enquiry.* Cambridge, UK: Cambridge University Press.

Schiller, H. (1980). Whose new international economic and information order? *Communication 5.*

Schiller, H. (1981). *Who knows: Information in the age of the fortune 500.* Norwood, NJ: Ablex.

Schiller, H. (1986). *Information and the crisis economy.* New York: Oxford University Press.

Sharpe, R.J. (1987) Commercial expression and the charter. *University of Toronto Law Journal, 37*, 229.

Smith, B.L., Laswell, H.D., & Casey, R.D. (1946). *Propaganda, communication and public opinion.* Princeton, NJ: Princeton University Press.

Smythe, D.W. (1977). Communications: Blindspot of Western Marxism. *Canadian Journal of Political and Social Theory, 1* (3).

Smythe, D.W. (1981). *Dependency road: Communications, capitalism, consciousness and Canada.* Norwood, NJ: Ablex Publishing Corp.

Smythe, D.W. (1982, Winter). Radio: Deregulation and the relation of the private and public sectors. *Journal of Communications.*

Soper, P. (1984). *A theory of law.* Cambridge, MA: Harvard University Press.

Stern, P.M. (1988). *The best Congress money can buy.* New York: Pantheon.

Stewart, P. (1975). Or of the press. *Hastings Law Journal, 23*,631.

Sussman, B. (1988). *What Americans really think.* New York: Panteon.

Thompson, J.B. (1984). *Studies in the theory of ideology.* Berkeley, CA: University of California Press.

Tuchman, G. (1978). *Making news: A study in the construction of reality.* New York: The Free Press.

Tuck, R. (1979). *Natural rights theories: Their origin and development.* Cambridge, UK: Cambridge University Press.

Tully, J. (1980). *A discourse on property: John Locke and his adversaries.* Cambridge, UK: Cambridge University Press.

Tushnet, M. (1982). Corporations and free speech. In D. Kaivys (Ed.), *The politics of law.* New York: Pantheon.

United States Senate. (1983). *Long range goals in international telecommunications and information: An outline for United States policy.* Report of the U.S. National Telecommunications and Information Administration to the U.S. Senate Committee on Commerce, Science and Transporation.

Watzlawick, P., Bavela, J., & Jackson, D. (1967). *Pragmatics of human communication.* New York: W.W. Norton.

Wertheimer, F. (1980). The PAC phenomenon in American politics. *Arizona Law Review, 22*, 603.

Williams, R. (1975). *Television, technology and cultural form.* New York: Schocken Books.

Woodward, B., & Armstrong, S. (1979). *The Brethren: Inside the Supreme Court.* New York: Avon.

Wren, T. E. (Ed.). *The moral domain.* Cambridge, MA: MIT Press.

Wright, J. S. (1982). Money and the pollution of politics. *Columbia Law Review, 82*, 609.

Wright, J. S. (1976). Politics and the Constitution: Is money speech? *Yale Law Journal, 85*, 1001.

Yudof, (1979). Access to state-owned communications media—The public forum doctrine. *U.C.L.A. Law Review, 26*, 1410.

Author Index

S

T

W

Y

Subject Index